The Essential Role of Language in Survey Research

Edited by
Mandy Sha and Tim Gabel

RTI Press

RTI INTERNATIONAL

Library of Congress Control Number: 2020935779

ISBN 978-1-934831-23-6
(refers to print version)

RTI Press publication No. BK-0023-2004
https://doi.org/10.3768/rtipress.bk.0023.2004
www.rti.org/rtipress

Cover design: Dayle Johnson

The RTI Press mission is to disseminate information about RTI research, analytic tools, and technical expertise to a national and international audience. RTI Press publications are peer-reviewed by at least two independent substantive experts and one or more Press editors.

RTI International is an independent, nonprofit research institute dedicated to improving the human condition. We combine scientific rigor and technical expertise in social and laboratory sciences, engineering, and international development to deliver solutions to the critical needs of clients worldwide.

This publication is part of the RTI Press Book series.

RTI International
3040 East Cornwallis Road, PO Box 12194
Research Triangle Park, NC 27709-2194, USA
rtipress@rti.org
www.rti.org

To the power of collaboration.

Contents

List of Figures and Tables

Figures

Tables

Acknowledgments

One year is an ambitious timeline to publish any book. Thanks to the power of collaboration among our 28 contributors, we were propelled to complete this book project within that time frame.

We would like to acknowledge the American Association for Public Opinion Research (AAPOR) for providing a platform in the form of an annual conference where we cultivate ideas, foster collaborations, and champion each other's efforts. The AAPOR conference short course by Daphna Oyserman and Norbert Schwarz ignited our passion for writing this book to share with a broad audience survey research theories, practices, and outlook in cross-cultural contexts. The incredible support from the leadership at RTI International's Social, Statistical and Environmental Sciences (SSES) Group made the publishing idea viable.

We owe RTI Press a deep debt of gratitude for the thoughtful and rigorous editing, guidance, and trust during the past year and for making the book open access. We thank Editor-in-Chief Jenny Wiley, Senior Manager Anna Wetterberg, and Publishing Editor Annie Gering. We thank the anonymous reviewers for their review of the manuscript. We also thank Senior Editors Sharon Barrell, Merrie Aiken, and Marceline Murawski at RTI's Multimedia Communication Services. Melinda Welch facilitated many aspects of the process and we appreciate her help. We acknowledge Lisa Thalji, Douglas Currivan, Murrey Olmsted, Marjorie Hinsdale-Shouse, Rachel Caspar, and Craig Hill.

Last but not least, we are grateful of the Foreword penned by Daphna and Norbert and the Afterword by Comparative Survey Design and Implementation consortium's Julie de Jong, Kristin Cibelli Hibben, Jennifer Kelley, and Dorothée Behr. Our special thanks go to Peter Mohler for his helpful review comments. It is the vision and role-modeling from these pioneers and many others that gave, and continue to give, many of us the courage to create our own path.

Foreword

Daphna Oyserman and Norbert Schwarz

University of Southern California

Asking and answering questions are the core elements of survey research. Nevertheless, the field has long been characterized by a science of sampling on the one hand and an "art of asking questions" on the other hand. Aiming to turn that art into a science, psychologists and survey methodologists brought theories of language comprehension, communication, memory, and judgment to bear on the survey response process, resulting in an interdisciplinary research area that became known as CASM—cognitive aspects of survey measurement. This work illuminated the interplay between semantic and pragmatic aspects of asking and answering questions and showed that even apparently "clear" and "simple" questions can dramatically change in meaning depending on who asks whom and in which context. These complexities at the interface of semantics, pragmatics, and social context are compounded when researchers and respondents do not share the same cultural background, use different languages, or both.

If the researcher is lucky, pretest respondents will complain about "bad" questions or provide answers that are sufficiently odd to indicate a problem. But such lucky discoveries of complications related to culture and language are not necessarily the norm. More likely, participants will construe a meaning that is subjectively plausible in their own cultural and language context and provide answers that do not raise any flags. Unfortunately, those answers may be answers to questions that the researchers did not intend to ask or did not intend to ask in that form. Failing to notice this, researchers are likely to interpret all answers as responses to the same substantive question and may interpret differences between groups as differences in opinion and behavior rather than differences in question interpretation. As cognitive research showed, all of these problems can arise in surveys within a single country, conducted in the same language. However, they are compounded in cross-national and cross-cultural research, where researchers may translate questions from another culture without full awareness of culture-specific connotations and differences in pragmatic meaning or complications arising from administering the survey in the temporary context of culturally significant holidays or commemorations of sacred events. Such differences are particularly difficult to notice when research teams collect data within their own culture without being exposed to the issues arising during data collection in other cultures.

This book provides ample illustrations of these and related complexities and identifies ways to address them. The contributions range from integrative reviews to reports of novel findings and solutions. They highlight the importance of language issues for data quality, provide frameworks for conceptualizing the underlying processes, present diverse methods for identifying problems at an early stage, and illustrate and evaluate potential solutions in the form of improved translation and pretesting procedures. We congratulate the editors and authors on this stimulating volume and are delighted that their collaboration emerged from a workshop we taught at the 74th Conference of the American Association for Public Opinion Research in Toronto, Canada. We look forward to the new wave of research emerging from the stimulating ideas presented in this volume.

Co-editors' Preface

Mandy Sha and Tim Gabel

This book discusses the role of language in survey research when comparisons across groups, cultures, and countries are of interest. Language use in surveys is dynamic, including words, symbols (e.g., arrows), and even emojis. Language users, such as survey respondents and interviewers, must speak the same language literally and figuratively to interact with each other. As diversity grows in the United States and globally, interviewers and respondents may speak a different language or speak the same language differently in a way that reflects their own cultural norms of communication.

The entire survey life cycle is carried out through language. Researchers write or translate questions and instructions that will address research questions and then pretest them using various techniques, including qualitative inquiry that focuses on context beyond just "the numbers." Human or virtual data collectors use persuasive messages to communicate with survey respondents and encourage their survey participation. Respondents must comprehend and interpret survey questions and instructions to provide a response. All of these survey processes and products contribute to data quality, and the role of language is essential.

Organization of the Book

We have divided the book into two parts. The first six chapters in Part I focus on language influences on survey responses and data quality, and the next six chapters in Part II discuss sociolinguistic factors that inform survey design and implementation, including qualitative and innovative methods. We organized the book this way to acknowledge that language functions within social and cultural contexts. To reach the target populations, we must understand the underlying theories and current practices surrounding language influences on survey responses and data quality (Part I) before advancing existing or innovative methods to design and implement surveys (Part II). The book is structured to help the reader develop this understanding, consider the relevant quantitative and qualitative methods, and come away with forward-looking perspectives. At the end of the book, the afterword relates each chapter to the survey life cycle through the multinational, multiregional, and multicultural (3MC) framework.

We begin each of the two parts with a chapter focused on theory and/or prior published literature. The remainder of the chapters demonstrate a comparative perspective or challenge, as well as the strategies that were undertaken to address them. Some of the literature is reviewed in more than one chapter to establish a connection between the theories and the specific topic under study.

Part I. Language Influences on Survey Responses and Data Quality

In Chapter 1, Emilia Peytcheva applies the existing response formation model to a cross-cultural and multilingual context. Her chapter combines theories from psycholinguistics and survey methodology and can serve as a primer for readers who are new to cross-cultural surveys or survey research in general. In Chapter 2, Evgenia Kapousouz, Tim Johnson, and Allyson Holbrook examine behavior coded survey interviews conducted in English, Spanish, and Korean to see whether characteristics of the interviewer (e.g., same sex as respondent) and factors related to the respondent (e.g., demographics, acculturation, language of the interview) predict whether respondents request clarifications regarding deliberately problematic questions. Overall, only language was predictive, such that respondents who were interviewed in Korean or Spanish were more likely to ask for clarifications. But few respondents in any language asked for clarifications of problematic survey questions. Thus, they encourage researchers to carefully design questionnaires and pretest them with each of the cultural groups that will be surveyed.

In Chapter 3, Heather Kitada Smalley investigates the effects of household language on data quality in the American Community Survey (ACS). Using publicly available microdata from 2006 through 2017, Heather provides a longitudinal, quantitative perspective. The sequential aspect of ACS survey mode phases and translation aids across modes led to significant differences in mode distribution across five major language groups: English, Spanish, Other Indo-European, Asian and Pacific Island, and a final group that encompasses other languages. Heather also provides data science education by sharing the R code she developed for the weighting scheme and the data visualization techniques.

Chapters 4, 5, and 6 examine interview language from different perspectives. In Chapter 4, Sunghee Lee and colleagues illustrate an assessment of measurement equivalence between English and Spanish response scale translation by randomizing interview language with bilingual English- and Spanish-speaking Latino American respondents. They conclude that overall there was a language effect when bilingual Latinos were interviewed in English as opposed to in Spanish. Chapter 5, by Charles Q. Lau, Stephanie Eckman, Luis Sevilla-Kreysa, and Benjamin Piper, also examines issues surrounding interview language in Africa. Many Africans are multilingual. This means respondents and interviewers may not share the same home (native) language. Although the respondent and interviewer may speak a common language for the interview, that language may not be the native language for either of them. By describing patterns of survey language use in 36 African countries that participated in Afrobarometer Round 6, Charles and his coauthors have deepened our knowledge about language choice in African survey research and methodological considerations on data quality. Chapter 6 is a research brief by Nicholas Heck-Grossek and Sonila Dardha, who study interview language from the angle of language barriers. In large-scale comparative surveys in Europe, one of the criteria to be an eligible household is the ability to speak the official language(s) of the country. Nicholas and Sonila find that migrant communities with language barriers are "hidden segments" in the three largest European countries. For example, in Germany, France, and the United Kingdom, sampling units with a language barrier tend to have poor living conditions. These migrants might differ significantly from the general population on demographic, attitudinal, or behavioral traits, but inferences cannot be reliably made until the "void of the voiceless" is addressed in study design.

Part II. Survey Questionnaire Development and Implementation

Pretesting is crucial to the questionnaire design process in any language prior to survey implementation. In the second part of the book, Eva Aizpurua provides an extensive literature review (Chapter 7) on the current state of pretesting methods in cross-cultural surveys, including a section on combining multiple methods. Many of these methods produce qualitative information, and there is an existing gap in the literature about evaluating focus groups and translation expert reviews as comparative research methods.

Chapters 8, 9, and 10 fill this gap. In Chapter 8, Mandy Sha, Hyunjoo Park, Yuling Pan, and Jennifer Kim demonstrate that focus groups can be used as a credible research method, despite notable cross-cultural differences in focus group interactions they have identified. Using a coding scheme based on sociolinguistic theory, they analyze the linguistic behavior of speakers of five languages (English, Chinese, Korean, Spanish, and Vietnamese) and those speakers' participatory patterns in a focus group discussion about survey data collection materials. Chapters 9 and 10 introduce the reader to translation evaluations prior to data collection and advocate for the expert review model. Chapter 9 is a collaboration between scholars in the United States and China. Led by Maichou Lor, the authors explore the assumptions and implications of using "back translation," a common procedure of translating a document *from* the source language (e.g., English) into the target language (e.g., Hmong) and *back* to the source language. The purpose of back translation is to identify discrepancies between the source and the back translation to assess the translation quality in the target language. However, using examples from Hmong and Chinese, they find that back translation is inappropriate as a quality assessment tool. Instead, they recommend that the international research community follow modern survey translation methodology that inherently includes translation expert review. Chapter 10 is a collaboration between scholars from Spain and the United States. Led by Nereida Congost-Maestre, the authors question the applicability of a previously developed Spanish translation in the United States to other Spanish-speaking countries in which it is now used. Specifically, evaluation of the Spanish translation of the internationally recognized Quality of Well-Being Scale–Self-Administered (QWB-SA) through an expert review demonstrates that the QWB-SA cannot be readily adopted for use in Spain. The chapter provides many poignant examples, from the perspective of the reviewer in Spain, showing translation issues at both linguistic and sociocultural levels in the QWB-SA.

Chapters 11 and 12 provide a glimpse into what the future holds for language and its users in designing and implementing survey research. In Chapter 11, Arundati Dandapani presents a research brief about emerging uses and the best practices for designing chatbot surveys. Arundati describes a chatbot as a computer program that uses artificial intelligence (AI) "to communicate via text or audio, simulating the conversation of humans through messaging apps, websites, mobile apps, smart devices, or even through the telephone." The innovative use of AI-powered chatbots opens up new possibilities to survey specific populations and to collect qualitative insights. The final chapter is a research brief written by a team of UX researchers and designers led by Aaron Sedley. Instead of presenting a satisfaction scale that uses translated labels or is numerical, Aaron and his colleagues at Google use smiley faces (emojis) and examine their performance across six cultural and language settings: United States (English), Germany (German), Spain (Spanish), Brazil (Portuguese), India (English), and Japan (Japanese).

In these 12 chapters, we show the essential role of language in survey responses, data quality, and questionnaire development and implementation across national, linguistic, and social boundaries and among multicultural populations within one nation. By disseminating survey theories and methods in accessible content and format, this book addresses a pressing need among researchers and practitioners to reach the increasingly diverse target populations with clearer survey questions, greater sensitivity, and more effective data collection methods.

PART I

Language Influences on Survey Responses and Data Quality

CHAPTER 1

The Effect of Language of Survey Administration on the Response Formation Process

Emilia Peytcheva

Introduction

With the increasing number of people of multiple cultural backgrounds in modern societies, surveys of ethnic minorities and immigrants are becoming more common. One obvious source of measurement differences is the necessary use of different languages when intending to measure the same phenomena in multiple ethnocultural groups. Typically, surveys allow respondents to answer in the language of their choice, possibly introducing self-selection bias to the extent to which those who choose their mother tongue differ in background characteristics (e.g., level of acculturation, education), substantive answers, and response patterns (e.g., "don't know" responses) from those who choose the mainstream language. However, although self-selection certainly plays a role in differences observed across the different language versions of a survey, it is premature to consider it the sole source of all observed differences.

There is a known link between language and cognition (e.g., Whorf, 1956). To study language influences on the response formation process in surveys, we need to assert that the various language versions of a survey are free of translation problems and convey the same constructs. Thus, any observed differences between responses provided by the same respondent in different languages can be attributed to language priming a particular mind frame and influencing the thought processes.

To examine the potential effects of language on survey responses, we focus on the response formation model (Sudman, Bradburn, & Schwarz, 1996; Tourangeau, Rips, & Rasinski, 2000). The right-hand side of Figure 1-1 presents the tasks that respondents perform to answer a survey question: attending to the question and response options (comprehension), retrieving the necessary information (retrieval and judgment), assessing the

Figure 1-1. Effect of language on the survey response formation process

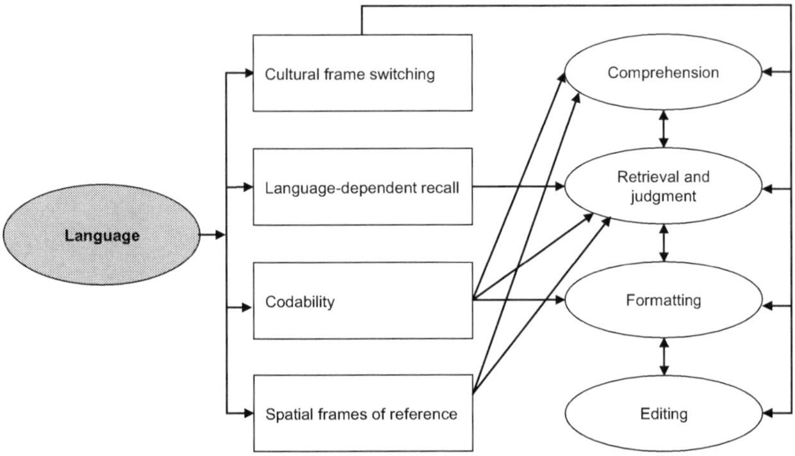

completeness and relevance of the memories (formatting), and editing the response before mapping to the provided response categories (editing). These tasks are not necessarily sequential or independent but are presented as such for simplicity. The left-hand side of Figure 1-1 represents the mechanisms related to language influences that are most likely to be present at each stage of the response formation process. We limit our discussion only to mechanisms well known to yield reporting differences, namely, cultural frame switching, language-dependent recall, language codability, and spatial frames of reference inherent in each language. We acknowledge that other language influences might be at play, but as of now, they remain undiscovered.

The language influences presented in the model can only be apparent among bilingual respondents, so we discuss them within the context of more than one language being available to communicate with respondents. We describe each of these mechanisms and examine their possible effects at each step of the response formation model by reviewing the existing literature from relevant fields and deriving conclusions about consequences for surveys.

Comprehension

Survey data are meaningless if respondents do not understand the survey questions as intended by the researchers. Question comprehension involves processing the syntactic structure and understanding the semantic (literal) and pragmatic (intended) meaning. In cross-cultural surveys, in addition to the direct impact of translation, comprehension problems may occur as a result of differences related to cognition. Because language is a tool for information exchange among people of the same culture, it reflects the meaning system of the culture. Thus, word meaning and sentence meaning in language comprehension depend on preexisting background knowledge about not only the grammatical norms associated with the language, but also the cultural norms and practices related to it. Furthermore, lexical ambiguity is inherent in languages, and recall of the lexical meaning of words is often context dependent. Languages differ in their contextual dependency, and this difference is reflected in the conversational norms across cultures. For example, many words in Chinese acquire meaning only in the conversational context and cannot be translated word for word; this is related to the practice of East Asian cultures to read between the lines (for an overview, see Nisbett [2003]). Thus, the same question presented in Chinese or English to a bilingual respondent may convey a different meaning depending on how much contextual information is incorporated from previous questions.

Cultural Frame Switching

Differential context dependency can have consequences for question interpretation when partially redundant information is presented (e.g., Haberstroh, Oyserman, Schwarz, & Kühnen , 2002). In bilingual respondents, such context sensitivity is likely to depend on which cultural frame is primed by the survey question. Research on acculturation has demonstrated that individuals can possess more than one cultural identity (e.g., Berry & Sam, 1996; Hong, Morris, Chiu, & Benet-Martinez, 2000) and move between different cultural meaning systems, depending on situational cues and requirements. This phenomenon, known as "cultural frame switching" (Briley, Morris, & Simonson, 2005; Hong et al., 2000), is likely to have a strong effect on survey responding because each cultural meaning system serves as an interpretive frame that affects an individual's cognition, emotion, and behavior (Geertz, 1993; Hong, Chiu, & Kung, 1997; Kashima, 2000; Mendoza-Denton, Shoda, Ayduk, & Mischel, 2000).

Language can serve as a situational cue for the cultural system associated with it; thus, it may prompt bilingual respondents to differential question interpretation based on the cultural frame induced by it. Indeed, studies that have experimentally manipulated language assignment among bilinguals report responses consistent with the cultural system associated with the assigned language (e.g., Peytcheva, 2019; Ross, Xun, & Wilson, 2002; Trafimow, Silverman, Fan, & Law, 1997). Such studies provide evidence that language is a powerful cue for the interpretive frame bilingual respondents adopt when answering survey questions.

Codability

Language codability is the ease with which a concept can be expressed in a language. Not surprisingly, the most highly codable concepts are presented by the most frequently used words, which are short and easy to write and pronounce (see Whitney, 1998). Codability affects cognitive processes such as retrieval (Lucy, 1992; Lucy & Shweder, 1979; Lucy & Wertsch, 1987) and comparative judgment (Kay & Kempton, 1984). However, codability may also influence question comprehension in surveys; the question target may be very different depending on whether a specific word exists in the language for a given attitude or behavior or whether several less specific terms are used to describe it. For example, in Chinese, there are separate terms for family members that have only one English equivalent—different words describe whether your "uncle" is your mother's brother or father's brother and whether he is a younger or older brother. Thus, it can be hypothesized that when asked in Chinese about two or more related people who can be labeled differently, respondents may think of them differently relative to when questions are asked in English when a common label is used. This difference may lead to inclusion errors when respondents are asked in English because of the failure to draw a lexical distinction across referents. Such interpretational differences across two languages may affect various respondent tasks in surveys (for example, household roster construction).

Spatial Frames of Reference

Languages have inherent frames of reference for describing relationships among objects. Psycholinguists distinguish between relative and absolute languages (also known as egocentric and allocentric). Relative languages, such as most Western languages, use a viewer-centered perspective, giving rise to descriptions such as "in front of me" and "to the left." Absolute languages use external reference frames, such as cardinal directions or an up–down axis; for example, speakers of Arrernte (Australia) will say "the fork is to the north of the spoon" (Majid, Bowerman, Kita, Haun, & Levinson, 2004).

Such intrinsic language differences may potentially affect comprehension in bilingual speakers of languages with different dominant spatial frames of reference because these reference frames have been found to determine many aspects of cognition (see Levinson [2003]). Experiments by Pederson et al. (1998) demonstrate that the domination of a linguistic frame of reference in a language reliably correlates with the way its users conceptualize in nonlinguistic domains. For example, speakers of Mopan (Mayan) and Kilivila (Austronesian) cannot distinguish between two photographs of a man facing a tree when the position of the man and the tree are left–right mirror images of one another because such a relationship between the objects in both photographs is described as "tree at man's chest."

For survey practitioners, such findings suggest that speakers of languages that use different frames of reference may interpret survey visual images and response scales differently. For example, the orientation of a scale (vertical or horizontal) may influence how similar or distinct response categories are perceived, depending on the language used and its inherent frame of reference. However, such effects are likely to occur only in cases where the dominant frames of reference used in two languages are not functional equivalents of one another (as in the example with Mopan speakers where there were no functional equivalents of "left" and "right" in the described mirror-image photographs); thus, their impact on the survey response processes may be very limited. However, the relationship between dominant frames of reference and cultural orientation (individualistic vs. collectivistic; for reviews on documented social and cognitive differences, see Oyserman, Coon, and Kemmelmeier (2002) and Oyserman and Lee (2007)) remains unknown. To the extent to which ego-centered frames of reference are related to individualistic identities across cultures that use such languages and vice versa, the language of administration will be an important factor influencing survey responses. Similar to cultural frame switching, a speaker of languages that use different frames of reference would endorse more individualistic or collectivistic responses depending on the cultural identity evoked by the egocentric or allocentric frame of reference inherent to the language of survey administration. Such possibility deserves further investigation.

Retrieval and Judgment in Behavioral Reports

The information requested in a survey question is rarely readily available, and often respondents need to retrieve memories and assess their relevance on the spot. Because this process is somewhat different for behaviors and attitudes, we discuss each separately, starting with behavioral reports.

Behavioral questions often ask about past events that took place in a respondent's life. When such events have low frequency of occurrence or are of particular importance to the respondent, they may be directly accessible in memory (for reviews of issues related to asking behavioral questions, see Bradburn, Rips, and Shevell, 1987; Schwarz, 1990; and Strube, 1987). However, respondents often need to recall relevant information and count instances of occurrence (enumeration) or compute a judgment (rate-based estimation). The success of retrieving the information and its accuracy depend on time on task (e.g., Williams & Hollan, 1981), the elapsed time since event (Cannell, Miller, & Oksenberg, 1981; Loftus, Smith, Klinger, & Fiedler, 1992; Means, Nigam, Zarrow, Loftus, & Donaldson, 1989; Smith & Jobe, 1994), the availability and adequacy of retrieval cues (for a review, see Strube, 1987), and the match between the encoding and recall contexts (Tulving & Thompson, 1973). The context may vary from physical context (Godden & Baddeley, 1975; Smith, 1988) to mental and emotional states (Bower, 1981; Bower, Monteiro, & Gilligan, 1978; Eich, Weingartner, Stillman, & Gillin, 1975). Several studies have demonstrated that the language in which mental activity is carried out during information encoding creates an internal context analogous to a mental state and can serve as a retrieval cue during information recall; similarly, the language spoken aloud during an event creates an external context analogous to a physical context and can serve as a situational cue during event recall (Marian & Neisser, 2000; Schrauf & Rubin, 1998, 2000). Thus, a match between language of encoding and language of recall in surveys should yield more accurate responses among bilingual respondents.

Language-Dependent Recall

Language-dependent recall is the notion that the language may influence retrospective reports. This phenomenon has been demonstrated in several bilingual groups in terms of number of recalled memories (e.g., Bugelski, 1977) and time in life when the recalled events took place (e.g., Schrauf & Rubin, 1998). Going beyond earlier findings of language-congruity effects, Marian and Neisser (2000) investigated whether a match between language of encoding and recall facilitated retrieval because the language matched words used during the original event or because the language at the time of recall induced a more general mindset, resembling the processes assumed to underlie state-dependent memory. The results showed that the effect of ambient language was significantly stronger than the effect of word-prompt language, further "strengthening the analogy between language-dependent recall and other forms of context dependency" (Marian & Neisser, 2000, p. 366).

The implication of such findings for surveys that involve immigrant and ethnic minority populations is that the choice of language of survey administration affects both the quality and quantity of recall. Specifically, first-language cues tap into first-culture memories, while second-language cues likely activate more recent memories. This suggests that language of survey administration in bilingual respondents may be switched throughout the survey, depending on life periods for which researchers are interested in collecting data. Additionally, bilingual immigrants or ethnic minorities are likely to use different languages in different life domains, for example, at work and at home. We can expect that the match between language spoken at home and language of survey administration will yield the most accurate information regarding home events, the highest number of such reported events, and the lowest response latencies for home-related questions, and vice versa. Such hypotheses, if supported, would further argue for a language switch across domains in surveys of bilinguals.

Codability

Often, there is no direct correspondence across languages with respect to terms that describe the same phenomenon; thus, using phrases or multiple words to describe the concept of interest is necessary during translation. Research related to language codability would predict difficulty in recall with difficult-to-code words because easily coded words (and, therefore, events associated with them) are remembered more easily (Lucy, 1992; Lucy & Wertsch, 1987). However, analogous to question decomposition, multiple words may provide more contextual cues that can ease recall and eventually improve report accuracy. To date, it remains unknown how such processes operate for users of two languages with different levels of specificity for the same concept.

Spatial Frames of Reference

A different aspect of language-dependent recall is demonstrated in studies of spatial cognition; the frames of reference used in a language to describe specific situations are likely to induce the same frame of reference in the nonlinguistic coding of the same situations (Levinson, 2003). Various experiments (Levinson, 2003; Pederson et al., 1998; Wassmann & Dasen, 1998) have shown that when speakers of languages with different dominant frames of reference are given various memory and spatial reasoning tasks, the nonlinguistic frames of reference used to carry out these tasks match the dominant frames of reference of the languages (see Levinson, 2003; Pederson et al., 1998; Wassmann & Dasen, 1998). Specifically, speakers of languages that use absolute frames of reference (e.g., Balinese, Indonesia; Belhare, Nepal; Arrernte, Australia) preserved the absolute coordinates of objects when performing tasks such as memorizing order and direction of objects within an array, while speakers of relative languages, such as Dutch, Japanese, and Yukatek (Mexico), preserved the relative coordinates of objects (Levinson, 1996; Pederson et al., 1998).

The cognitive consequences of being bilingual in languages that use different frames of reference remain unclear. One possibility is differential perceptual tuning due to the use of different frames of reference because languages have been found to affect perception such that individuals become more or less attuned to certain features of the environment (Goldstone, 1998; Sloutsky, 2003). For survey practitioners, this may mean that what is reported during recall tasks may be related to what language is used during initial information encoding and later, during the survey interview. In an extreme example, certain information may not be encoded *because* of the language spoken during an event that predetermines on what speakers focus their attention. Furthermore, similar to language-dependent recall, it can be expected that a match between language frames of reference during encoding and retrieval could facilitate remembering.

Retrieval and Judgment in Attitudes

Attitude questions often require respondents to form an opinion on the spot in the specific context of a survey (Sudman et al., 1996). To do so, they need to form a mental representation of the question target based on the most accessible relevant information. Preceding questions, visual aids, and interviewer characteristics can make certain information more accessible; language of survey administration can also determine what information is accessible at any given time by activating the cognitive–affective cultural framework associated with it. By using a particular language, a "language-specific self" is activated, who acts like a filter through which information is both encoded and retrieved (Schrauf, 2000).

Cultural Frame Switching

Language can affect what information is temporarily accessible by evoking a particular mindset related to the cultural meaning system associated with it. For example, a study of Greek students attending an American school in

Greece showed that the correlation between the same attitudinal questions administered in English and in Greek was low for domains in which the Greek and American norms differed in what was considered socially desirable and high for domains in which the cultural values converged (Triandis, Davis, Vassiliou, & Nassiakou, 1965). Similar results were reported for English–Spanish bilinguals by Marín, Triandis, Kashima, and Betancourt (1983).

Another aspect of cultural frame switching relates to differences in how Westerners and East Asians organize the world: Westerners show preference for grouping objects based on taxonomy or common category membership, while East Asians prefer groupings based on relationships (Chiu, 1972; Ji, Schwarz, & Nisbett, 2000). Such grouping preferences can be manipulated by the language used during the cognitive task; for example, Ji, Zhang and Nisbett (2004) found that relationship-based grouping shifted to categorical when Chinese speakers from Mainland China and Taiwan were asked questions in English. Recent studies in psycholinguistics have also demonstrated that language can affect comparisons (Bowerman & Choi, 2003; Gentner, 2003), and to the extent to which languages classify according to different criteria, the extracted similarities also differ (Boroditsky, 2001; Boroditsky, Schmidt, & Phillips, 2003; Lucy & Gaskins, 2001).

These findings have several implications for surveys of bilingual respondents. First, the information that is accessible to form an opinion will vary depending on the language of survey administration. Hence, to achieve maximum equivalence of different language versions, open-ended questions should be avoided. Second, the same question can be perceived to have different affective characteristics depending on the language and cultural norms it activates; thus, more or less socially desirable opinions will be expressed, depending on language. Knowing in advance how cultures differ in terms of a question's affective characteristics may better inform questionnaire design, and various techniques can be used to reduce social desirability or sensitivity across language versions. Third, judgments can be language dependent because comparisons are based on culture-approved practices and how language systems are organized. Such hypotheses necessitate systematic investigation of language effects and the underlying dynamics across question types.

Codability

Studies in psycholinguistics have demonstrated that codability affects judgment. Kay and Kempton (1984), for example, showed that color-naming practices affect judgments of colors: speakers of Tarahumara (a Mexican

Indian language that does not have separate words for blue and green) differentiated among color chips on the blue–green color continuum based on their physical characteristics—namely, wavelength of reflected light. In contrast, English speakers differentiated among the same color chips based on labels, such as "shade of green" and "shade of blue." Thus, English speakers evaluated colors in terms of categories in which they were easily coded, while Tarahumara speakers, lacking such codability of colors, based their evaluations on physical characteristics. Similarly, Hoffman, Lau, and Johnson (1986) examined the extent to which the codability of personality description (existence of stereotypes) in a language influenced the impression about a person. The study found that terms that were readily available in the language led to stereotyped impressions, and participants were more likely to elaborate on the described person's characteristics using terms consistent with the stereotype than when a verbal label was not available.

Such findings may have implications for the use of scales in surveys of bilingual respondents. For example, scales may be judged differently depending on whether scale labels are easily codable in both languages. If label equivalents are not easily codable in one language, respondents may be more likely to consider solely the numeric values of the scale when making judgments, resulting in response differences across language versions.

Response Formatting

The ability to differentiate among response options may be influenced by language codability, and the stimuli used to anchor the points of a rating scale may be affected by the cultural meaning system primed by language.

Cultural Frame Switching

Cultural frame switching can further complicate the investigation of language effects at the formatting stage because scale anchoring may be affected by the reference frame primed by a language. Such differences in scale anchoring may be reflected in the observed differential response styles across cultures. For example, several studies have reported that East Asians avoid extreme responses (Chen, Lee, & Stevenson, 1995; Chun & Campbell, 1974; Hayashi, 1992; Stening & Everett, 1984; Zax & Takahashi, 1967). Although such differences are often attributed to differential emphasis on conflict avoidance and humbleness, it is unclear whether these differences are an artifact of self-presentation as a result of language priming culture or true differences in perception, independent of language. Moreover, the extent to which respondents use the range of a presented frequency scale as a frame of reference when answering survey questions is also culture dependent. A study by Ji, Schwarz, and Nisbett (2000) demonstrated that Chinese students were influenced by the range of frequency scales only when asked to report private, unobservable behaviors (e.g., having nightmares, borrowing books from the library). However, no scale effects were found for public behaviors (e.g., being late for class), possibly reflecting the importance of "fitting in" in Asian cultures related to monitoring (and thus having better memory representation of) one's and others' public behaviors. In contrast, consistent with previous research on scale effects (for a review, see Schwarz [1996]), American students relied on the presented response scale frequency range to estimate both private and public behaviors. For surveys of bilingual respondents, such findings suggest that, depending on the cultural identity primed by the language of interview, different estimation strategies may be employed.

Codability

Similar to the effect of language codability on retrieval and judgement, response formatting may also be affected by the availability of a label for a given concept. For example, scales may be used differently by speakers of different languages as a result of different scale label codability; thus, the meaning of the same number on a labeled scale may be affected by what language is used. Taken to an extreme, there are cultures whose languages have terms only for one, two and many (Greenberg, 1978), which further limits the ability of their speakers to make comparisons (Hunt and Agnoli, 1991). At this point, little is known how this may affect the cognitive processes in bilinguals whose other language allows for utilization of the whole numeric scale. It can be speculated, that the ability to make comparisons may remain language dependent.

Response Editing

Respondents sometimes edit their responses before reporting them, reflecting social desirability and self-presentation concerns (Sudman et al., 1996). Gender, age, socioeconomic status, and various survey design characteristics have been found to be correlates of socially desirable responding (for a review, see DeMaio, 1984). Recent work in cross-cultural research suggests that culture influences social desirability through interpretation based on cultural experiences, and response editing depends on the need to conform with particular social norms (Fu, Lee, Cameron, & Xu, 2001; Lee, Xu, Fu, Cameron & Chen, 2001).

Cultural Frame Switching

The same survey question may be perceived to have different levels of socially desirable content depending on the respondent's cultural identity. For example, maintaining harmony and face-saving are more socially desirable traits in Asian cultures than in the Western world (Triandis, 1995). Similarly, mental health is stigmatized in Arab and Hispanic societies (Bazzoui & Al-Issa, 1966; Chaleby, 1987; Okasha & Lotalif, 1979; Silva de Crane & Spielberger, 1981) to a greater extent than in the United States. For bilingual respondents, this means that, depending on the language of the survey interview and the cultural frame primed by it, such questions might be perceived to have different affective characteristics, and respondents would be likely to edit their answers to match the values of the culture associated with the language. The studies by Triandis et al. (1965) and Marín et al. (1983) presented earlier illustrate this effect. For survey practitioners, such language effects would require thorough advance knowledge of where cultural differences related to questions' affective characteristics are to be expected to determine the language assignment of bilingual respondents or to employ questionnaire design techniques that reduce differentially perceived social desirability or sensitivity across language versions.

Summary

A substantial body of literature in psycholinguistics and cross-cultural psychology suggests that language used in survey interviews can affect every stage of the response formation process, and different mechanisms may simultaneously play a role at each step. As our discussion indicates, depending on language, respondents may answer the same question differently as a result of different question interpretation, different mental representations of the question target, a mismatch between the language of encoding and language of recall, different accessible information at the time of the survey request, differential anchoring of response scales, and differential self-presentation concerns.

Two shortcomings of the presented theoretical framework relate to its application. It is desirable to directly connect the outlined model to published survey research and possibly reinterpret puzzling results in light of the proposed language influences, but the existing cross-cultural survey data do not offer such an opportunity. Thus, the proposed framework remains largely speculative. Next, some of the presented mechanisms are demonstrated through research in settings, tasks, and languages that are very different from common survey tasks and languages in which surveys are typically conducted. At this stage, it is unclear to what extent the outlined mechanisms would be detectable in survey responses collected in mainstream (rather than indigenous) languages or whether they are task and language specific. We believe the merits of this theoretical model are to present possibilities for language influences and to stimulate further discussion and action related to these issues.

References

Bazzoui, W., & Al-Issa, I. (1966). Psychiatry in Iraq. *The British Journal of Psychiatry, 112*, 827–832.

Berry, J., & Sam, D. (1996). Acculturation and adaptation. In J. Berry, M. Segall, & C. Kagitcibasi (Eds.), *Handbook of cross-cultural psychology, volume 3: Social behavior and applications* (pp. 291–325). Boston, MA: Allyn & Bacon.

Boroditsky, L. (2001). Does language shape thought?: Mandarin and English speakers' conception of time. *Cognitive Psychology, 43*, 1–22.

Boroditsky, L., Schmidt, L., & Phillips, W. (2003). Sex, syntax and semantics. In D. Gentner & S. Goldin-Meadow (Eds.), *Language in mind* (pp. 61–79). Cambridge, MA: MIT Press.

Bower, G. H. (1981). Mood and memory. *The American Psychologist, 36*, 129–148.

Bower, G. H., Monteiro, K. P., & Gilligan, S. G. (1978). Emotional mood as a context for learning and recall. *Journal of Verbal Learning and Verbal Behavior, 17*, 573–585.

Bowerman, M., & Choi, S. (2003). Space under construction: Language-specific spatial categorization in first language acquisition. In D. Gentner & S. Goldin-Meadow (Eds.), *Language in mind: Advances in studies of language and thought* (pp. 387–427). Cambridge, MA: MIT Press.

Bradburn, N. M., Rips, L. J., & Shevell, S. K. (1987). Answering autobiographical questions: The impact of memory and inference on surveys. *Science, 236*, 157–161.

Briley, D., Morris, M., & Simonson, I. (2005). Cultural chameleons: Biculturals, conformity motives, and decision making. *Journal of Consumer Psychology, 15*(4), 351–62.

Bugelski, B. R. (1977). Imagery and verbal behavior. *Journal of Mental Imagery, 1*, 39–52.

Cannell, C., Miller, P., & Oksenberg, L. (1981). Research on interviewing techniques. *Sociological Methodology, 12*, 389–437.

Chaleby, K. (1987). Women in polygamous marriages in out-patient psychiatric services in Kuwait. *International Journal of Family Psychiatry, 8*(1), 25–34.

Chen, C., Lee, S., & Stevenson, H. W. (1995). Response style and cross-cultural comparisons of rating scales among East Asian and North American students. *Psychological Science, 6*, 170–175.

Chiu, L. H. (1972). A cross-cultural comparison of cognitive styles in Chinese and American children. *International Journal of Psychology, 7*, 235–242.

Chun, K. T., & Campbell, J. B. (1974). Extreme response styles in cross-cultural research: A reminder. *Journal of Cross-Cultural Psychology, 5*, 465–480.

DeMaio, T. J. (1984). Social desirability and survey measurement: A review. In C. F. Turner & E. Martin (Eds.), *Surveying subjective phenomena* (p. 2). New York, NY: Russell Sage Foundation.

Eich, J. E., Weingartner, H., Stillman, R. C., & Gillin, J. C. (1975). State-dependent accessibility of retrieval cues in the retention of a categorized list. *Journal of Verbal Learning and Verbal Behavior, 14*, 408–417.

Fu, G., Lee, K., Cameron, C. A., & Xu, F. (2001). Chinese and Canadian adults' categorization and evaluation of lie and truthtelling about prosocial and antisocial behaviors. *Journal of Cross-Cultural Psychology, 32*, 720–727.

Geertz, C. (1993). *The interpretation of cultures.* New York, NY: Basic Books.

Gentner, D. (2003). Why we're so smart. In D. Gentner & S. Goldin-Meadow (Eds.), *Language in mind* (pp. 195–235). Cambridge, MA: MIT Press.

Godden, D. R., & Baddeley, A. D. (1975). Context-dependent memory in two natural environments: On land and under water. *British Journal of Psychology, 66*, 325–331.

Goldstone, R. L. (1998). Perceptual learning. *Annual Review of Psychology, 49*, 585–612.

Greenberg, J. H. (1978). *Generalization about numeral systems. Universals of human language. Word structure.* Stanford, CA: Academic Press.

Haberstroh, S., Oyserman, D., Schwarz, N., & Kühnen, U. (2002). Is the interdependent self more sensitive to question context than the independent self? Self-construal and the observation of conversational norms. *Journal of Experimental Social Psychology, 38*, 323–329.

Hayashi, E. (1992). Belief systems, the way of thinking, and sentiments of five nations. *Behaviormetrika, 19*, 127–170.

Hoffman, C., Lau, I., & Johnson, D. R. (1986). The linguistic relativity of person cognition: An English–Chinese comparison. *Journal of Personality and Social Psychology, 51*, 1097–1105.

Hong, Y. Y., Chiu, C. Y., & Kung, T. M. (1997). Bringing culture out in front: Effects of cultural meaning system activation on social cognition. In K. Leung, Y. Kashima, U. Kim, & S. Yamaguchi (Eds.), *Progress in Asian social psychology* (pp. 135–146). Singapore: Wiley.

Hong, Y., Morris, M., Chiu, C. Y., & Benet-Martinez, V. (2000). Multicultural minds: A dynamic constructivist approach to culture and cognition. *American Psychologist, 55*(7), 709–720.

Hunt, E., & Agnoli, F. (1991). The Whorfian hypothesis: A cognitive psychology perspective. *Psychological Review, 98*, 377–389.

Ji, L., Schwarz, N., & Nisbett, R. E. (2000). Culture, autobiographical memory, and behavioral frequency reports: Measurement issues in cross-cultural studies. *Personality and Social Psychology Bulletin, 26*, 586–594.

Ji, L., Zhang, Z., & Nisbett, R. E. (2004). Is it culture or is it language? Examination of language effects in cross-cultural research on categorization. *Journal of Personality and Social Psychology, 87*(1), 57–65.

Kashima, Y. (2000). Conceptions of culture and person for psychology. *Journal of Cross-Cultural Psychology, 31*, 14–32.

Kay, P., & Kempton, W. (1984). What is the Sapir-Whorf hypothesis? *American Anthropologist, 86*, 65–79.

Lee, K., Xu, F., Fu, G., Cameron, C. C., & Chen, S. (2001). Taiwan and Mainland Chinese and Canadian children's categorization and evaluation of lie- and truth-telling: A modesty effect. *British Journal of Developmental Psychology, 19*, 525–542.

Levinson, S. (1996). Frames of reference and Molyneux's question: Cross-linguistic evidence. In P. Bloom, M. Peterson, L. Nadel, & M. Garrett (Eds.), *Language and space*. Cambridge, MA: MIT Press.

Levinson, S. (2003). *Space in language and cognition: Explorations of cognitive diversity.* Cambridge, UK: Cambridge University Press.

Loftus, E. F., Smith, K. D., Klinger, M. R., & Fiedler, J. (1992). Memory and mismemory for health events. In J. M. Tanur (Ed.). *Questions about questions: Inquiries into the cognitive basis of surveys* (pp. 102–137). New York, NY: Russell Sage Foundation.

Lucy, J. A. (1992). *Language diversity and thought: A reformulation of the linguistic relativity hypothesis.* Cambridge, UK: Cambridge University Press.

Lucy, J. A., & Gaskins, S. (2001). Grammatical categories and the development of classification preferences: A comparative approach. In M. Bowerman & S. Levinson (Eds.), *Language acquisition and conceptual development* (pp. 257–283). Cambridge, UK: Cambridge University Press.

Lucy, J. A., & Shweder, R. A. (1979). Whorf and his critics: Linguistic and nonlinguistic influences on color memory. *American Anthropologist, 81*, 581–615.

Lucy, J. A., & Wertsch, J. V. (Eds.), (1987). *Vygotsky and Whorf: A comparative analysis. Social and functional approaches to language and thought.* Orlando, FL: Academic Press.

Majid, A., Bowerman, M., Kita, S., Haun, D. B. M., & Levinson, S. C. (2004). Can language restructure cognition? The case for space. *Trends in Cognitive Sciences, 8*(3), 108–114.

Marian, V., & Neisser, U. (2000). Language-dependent recall of autobiographical memories. *Journal of Experimental Psychology General, 129*(3), 361–368.

Marín, G., Triandis, H. C., Kashima, Y., & Betancourt, H. (1983). Ethnic affirmation versus social desirability: Explaining discrepancies in bilinguals' responses to a questionnaire. *Journal of Cross-Cultural Psychology, 14*(2), 173–186.

Means, B., Nigam, A., Zarrow, M., Loftus, E. F., & Donaldson, M. S. (1989). Autobiographical memory for health-related events. *Vital and health statistics*. Washington, DC: National Center for Health Statistics.

Mendoza-Denton, R., Shoda, Y., Ayduk, O. N., & Mischel, W. (2000). Applying cognitive-affective processing system (CAPS) theory to cultural differences in social behavior. In D. L. Dinne, D. K. Forgays, S. A. Hayes, & W. J. Lonner (Eds.), *Merging past, present, and future in cross-cultural psychology* (pp. 205–217). Lisse, Netherlands: Swetz and Zeitlinger.

Nisbett, R. (2003). *The geography of thought. How Asians and Westerners think differently… and why*. New York, NY: Free Press.

Okasha, A., & Lotalif, F. (1979). Attempted suicide: An Egyptian investigation. *Acta Psychiatrica Scandinavica, 60*, 69–75.

Oyserman, D., Coon, H., & Kemmelmeier, M. (2002). Rethinking individualism and collectivism: Evaluation of theoretical assumptions and meta-analyses. *Psychological Bulletin, 128*(1), 3–72.

Oyserman, D., & Lee, S. W. (2007). Priming "culture": Culture as a situated cognition. In S. Kitayama & D. Cohen (Eds.), *Handbook of cultural psychology*. New York, NY: Guilford Press.

Pederson, E., E. Danziger, Wilkins, D., Levinson, S., Kita, S., & Senft, G. (1998). Semantic typology and spatial conceptualization. *Language in Society, 74*, 557–589.

Peytcheva, E. (2019). Can the language of a survey interview influence respondent answers? In T. P. Johnson, B.-E. Pennell, I. A. L. Stoop, & B. Dorer (Eds.), *Advances in comparative survey methods: Multinational, multiregional, and multicultural contexts (3MC)* (pp. 325–337). Hoboken, NJ: John Wiley & Sons.

Ross, M., Xun, W. Q. E., & Wilson, A. E. (2002). Language and the bicultural self. *Personality and Social Psychology Bulletin, 28*(8), 1040–1050.

Schrauf, R. W. (2000). Bilingual autobiographical memory: Experimental studies and clinical cases. *Culture and Psychology, 6*(4), 387–417.

Schrauf, R. W., & Rubin, D. C. (1998). Bilingual autobiographical memory in older adult immigrants: A test of cognitive explanations of the reminiscence bump and the linguistic encoding of memories. *Journal of Memory and Language, 39*, 437–457.

Schrauf, R. W., & Rubin, D. C. (2000). Internal languages of retrieval: The bilingual encoding of memories for the personal past. *Memory & Cognition, 28*, 616–623.

Schwarz, N. (1990). Assessing frequency reports of mundane behaviors: Contributions of cognitive psychology to questionnaire construction. In C. Hendrick & M. S. Clark (Eds.), *Research methods in personality and social psychology* (pp. 98–119). Newbury Park, CA: Sage.

Schwarz, N. (1996). *Cognition and communication: Judgmental biases, research methods, and the logic of conversation*. Hillsdale, NJ: Erlbaum.

Silva de Crane, R., & Spielberger, C. D. (1981). Attitudes of Hispanic, Black, and Caucasian university students toward mental illness. *Hispanic Journal of Behavioral Sciences, 3*, 241–255.

Sloutsky, V. M. (2003). The role of similarity in the development of categorization. *Trends in Cognitive Sciences, 7*, 246–251.

Smith, A. F., & Jobe, J. B. (1994). Validity of reports of long-term dietary memories: Data and a model. In N. Schwarz & S. Sudman (Eds.), *Autobiographical memory and the validity of retrospective reports* (pp. 121–140). Berlin: Springer-Verlag.

Smith, S. M. (1988). Environmental context-dependent memory. In G. M. Davies & D. M. Thomson (Eds.), *Memory in context: Context in memory* (pp. 13–34). Chichester, England: Wiley.

Stening, B. W., & Everett, J. E. (1984). Response styles in cross-cultural managerial study. *The Journal of Social Psychology, 122*, 151–156.

Strube, G. (1987). Answering survey questions: The role of memory. In H. J. Hippler, N. Schwarz, & S. Sudman (Eds.), *Social information processing and survey methodology* (pp. 86–101). New York, NY: Springer-Verlag.

Sudman, S., Bradburn, N., & Schwarz, N. (1996). *Thinking about answers: The application of cognitive processes to survey methodology*. San Francisco, CA: Jossey-Bass.

Tourangeau, R., Rips, L. J., & Rasinski, K. (2000). *The psychology of survey response.* Cambridge, UK: Cambridge University Press.

Trafimow, D., Silverman, E. S., Fan, R. M.-T., & Law, J. S. F. (1997). The effect of language and priming on the relative accessibility of the private self and the collective self. *Journal of Cross-Cultural Psychology, 28,* 107–123.

Triandis, H. C. (1995). *Individualism and collectivism.* Boulder, CO: Westview Press.

Triandis, H. C., Davis, E. E., Vassiliou, V., & Nassiakou, M. (1965). *Some methodological problems concerning research on negotiations between monolinguals.* Urbana, IL: University of Illinois Urbana Group Effectiveness Research Lab.

Tulving, E., & Thompson, D. (1973). Encoding specificity and retrieval processes in episodic memory. *Psychological Review, 80,* 352–373.

Wassmann, J., & Dasen, P. R. (1998). Balinese spatial orientation: Some empirical evidence of moderate linguistic relativity. *Journal of the Royal Anthropological Institute, 4,* 689–711.

Whitney, P. (1998). *The psychology of language.* Boston, MA: Houghton Mifflin.

Whorf, B. L. (1956). *Language, thought, and reality: Selected writings of Benjamin Lee Whorf.* New York, NY: Wiley.

Williams, M. D., & Hollan, J. D. (1981). The process of retrieval from very long-term memory. *Cognitive Science, 5,* 87–119.

Zax, M., & Takahashi, S. (1967). Cultural influences on response style: Comparison of Japanese and American college students. *The Journal of Social Psychology, 71,* 3–10.

Seeking Clarifications for Problematic Questions: Effects of Interview Language and Respondent Acculturation

Evgenia Kapousouz, Timothy P. Johnson, and Allyson L. Holbrook

Introduction

For scholars in various fields of inquiry, surveys are a critical and widely used tool for the systematic collection of information from respondents, using standardized instruments. The cognitive process by which respondents answer survey questions is generally believed to be a four-stage process. A question is administered to a respondent, and the respondent has to (1) comprehend the question and understand what it is asking him or her to do, (2) retrieve relevant information from memory, (3) form a judgment based on the information retrieved, and then (4) provide an answer using the response format provided (Tourangeau, Rips, & Rasinski, 2009). Error can be introduced into survey estimates through various mechanisms at each stage of this process. Ongena and Dijkstra (2006) suggested that the interview, its structure, and administration may represent underlying determinants of both good and poor survey responses. Consequently, errors associated with survey design, survey questions, interviewers, and respondents must all be considered when evaluating and addressing the quality of survey data. In the following, we review how error can be introduced by each of these sources and examine how survey respondents behave when error is introduced by asking deliberately bad survey questions.

Survey Design as a Source of Error

Face-to-face interviews collect information through direct communication between an interviewer and a respondent. Although face-to-face interviews are costlier compared with self-administered surveys, they continue to have a vital role in data collection in the United States (Garbarski, Schaeffer, & Dykema, 2016). The interview is intended to be an interpersonal event, where the interviewer and respondent in effect participate in scripted ways

(Fowler & Cannell, 1996; Lepkowski, Siu, & Fisher, 2000). However, because they involve people, survey interviews also operate as social and conversational interactions (Tourangeau et al., 2009). The form and quality of the interaction between respondent and interviewer can significantly affect the quality of answers provided by respondents during the interview process. In particular, the relationship of interviewers and respondents must be established very quickly and in an environment that is welcoming and nonthreatening for respondents to feel at ease. Interviewers also need to inspire respondent trust, especially when the interview includes sensitive questions (Fowler & Mangione, 1990).

Standardized interviewing is considered one of the keys to minimizing the measurement error that may be attributed to interviewers (Fowler & Mangione, 1990; Groves, 2004). All respondents should have as similar an experience as possible during an interview to ensure that any differences in the data collected are not due to the interview process, but rather to true differences in survey responses (Fowler & Mangione, 1990). Standardized interviews are expected to follow an established script. Accordingly, when respondents are unsure of the meaning of a question, interviewers can only provide standardized, nondirectional information, such as "Please, answer according to your understanding of the term" (Bell, Fahmy, & Gordon, 2016). Although standardization is preferred, it may at times limit the interaction between the interviewer and respondent in ways that can actually damage data quality (Bell et al., 2016; Fowler & Mangione, 1990).

Supporters of conversational interviewing underscore the belief that unscripted conversation during the interview process may significantly improve data quality. Specifically, Conrad and Schober (1999) reported that conversational interviewing—in which interviewers are trained to deviate from scripted question wording when necessary to achieve survey objectives—prevents possible comprehension problems by establishing shared meaning, particularly for questions concerned with objective phenomena (e.g., number of rooms in living quarters). On the other hand, Ong, Hu, West, and Kirlin (2018) reported that such interaction during the interview may increase interviewer error.

The Question as a Source of Error

The wording of questions may result in unnecessary measurement error if respondents misinterpret or misunderstand the true meaning of the questions (Tourangeau et al., 2009). Some questions may not have a fixed meaning (Groves, 2004), and some may have different meanings in a conversation compared with a survey context (Schober, 1999). The questions may suffer from various issues such as poor grammar and syntax and semantic issues; being double barreled; using words with ambiguous or vague meaning; using terms or words that respondents are not familiar with; or being worded in such a way as to lead respondents to the "right" answer, while lengthy questions may cause respondents to forget the actual question (Tourangeau et al., 2009). As a result, respondents may in some cases be uncertain of the true meaning of the questions being posed to them.

One strategy researchers have used to examine question-based measurement error is to examine behaviors and responses to questions that deliberately introduce a source of error. For example, some surveys have used questions with unclear terms. Oksenberg, Cannell, and Kalton (1991) reported that this kind of problem in questions can significantly affect responses. Numerous unanticipated differences in question interpretation may also be introduced when respondents speak a different first language and are interviewed in their second language. In addition, respondents from different cultural backgrounds may vary in the likelihood that they will misinterpret any given question (Warnecke et al., 1997).

Differences in respondent culture, often operationalized using race or ethnicity, may lead to variability in understanding of survey questions or increased confusion about them. Researchers sometimes mistakenly assume that measurement is similar between different cultural groups. Perales, Baffour, and Mitrou (2015) asserted that "indigenous cultural imperatives may result in understanding of survey questions and response categories that can be different from other sectors" (p. 3). They suggested that, to improve the quality of survey data, the survey questions should adapt to the needs and culture of respondents. Research has shown ethnic background can affect survey quality because respondents' cultural background may affect the response patterns and interpretation of the questions (Dolnicar & Grün, 2007).

The Interviewer as a Source of Error

Interviewer error is defined as "variation in answers that can be associated with the people who did the interview" (Fowler & Mangione, 1990, p. 24). It can be associated with coverage and nonresponse errors when making initial contact with potential respondents and with measurement error when conducting the interview (West & Blom, 2017). Although interviewers are considered a key factor in promoting response accuracy (Bell et al., 2016), empirical evidence suggests that slight deviations in question wording do not necessarily affect accuracy negatively (Dykema, Lepkowski, & Blixt, 1997). Interviewer error may vary depending on the question (West, Conrad, Kreuter, & Mittereder, 2017). Experienced interviewers in particular may be better able to manage the interaction with respondents and, in doing so, minimize measurement error (Garbarski et al., 2016).

Researchers have tried to reduce measurement error by matching interviewers with respondents. Webster (1996) reported that matching interviewer and respondent ethnicity increases the response rate and the item response effort. Similarly, Davis and Silver (2003) reported that in telephone surveys, matching the respondents' race with the interviewer's leads to better reporting results and less item nonresponse to sensitive questions; however, answers may not necessarily be improved. Firstly, some respondents may prefer interviewers from a different cultural background (Davis et al., 2013), and ethnicity matching may have a negative effect because respondents are more likely to produce answers acceptable to that cultural group (Fowler & Mangione, 1990). Similarly, Groves (2004) and Weisberg (2005) noted that matching may increase error because respondents tend to report more extreme answers to questions about culture. Research also has shown conflicting results regarding interviewer gender: Fowler and Mangione (1990) reported that gender matching leads to better data quality, whereas Groves and Magilavy (1986) underscored that there is no effect of interviewer gender. Matching respondents and interviewers on gender may have a significant effect only in some countries (Sahgal & Horowitz, 2011) and with certain questions where social desirability may be an issue (Lipps & Lutz, 2017). Although research suggests gender matching may lead to more accurate responses, men appear to be affected more by interviewer gender for some question topics (Catania et al., 1996). Early research has shown that poorly educated respondents are also more likely to respond differently based on interviewer gender (Cannell, Oksenberg, & Converse, 1977; Schuman & Presser, 1977).

The Respondent as a Source of Error

Measurement error can in addition be attributed to respondents, as they are burdened with the responsibility of understanding the intent of each survey question, recalling relevant memories, combining the information to produce a summary judgment, and accurately reporting their answer using the response format provided by the question (Tourangeau et al., 2009). Ideally, all respondents would attentively go through the steps of comprehension, retrieval, judgment, and response selection and provide high-quality data. In reality, however, factors such as cognitive sophistication and motivation can discourage engagement in optimal behavior, induce compromise, and result in provision of a "merely satisfactory" answer (Krosnick, 1991, p. 215).

Using Respondent Behaviors as an Indicator of Error

Behavior coding—coding behaviors that take place during a survey interview—is one method used to assess respondent cognitive processing of survey questions (Holbrook, Cho, & Johnson, 2006). These can include both respondent and interviewer behaviors; the coding can be done by humans from observation of the interview (although this is rarely done in practice), audio recordings of the interview, or written transcripts of audio recordings, or by computers (e.g., using automated text analysis tools). Behavior coding can also be employed by researchers to identify problematic questions when respondents ask for clarification, as well as problematic interviewer behaviors (Fowler & Cannell, 1996). A clarification may be needed when respondents do not feel they understand precisely what a question is asking and request additional information in an effort to resolve the confusion (Schaeffer & Maynard, 1996). Respondents are more likely to require clarification when they do not comprehend a question (Fowler, 1992) or the question does not relate to their past experiences (Lepkowski et al., 2000). However, behavior coding may not be useful if respondents do not exhibit certain behaviors, such as asking for clarification.

One common respondent behavior captured by behavior coding is requests for clarification. If a question is not clear (e.g., asks respondent to report an opinion about a nonexistent policy or whether they had been diagnosed with a nonexistent illness), respondents should ask for clarification. However, respondents may be motivated to report an opinion without asking for further clarification, even if they had not given any thought to it previously (Schwarz, 1996). Cahalan, Mitchell, Gray, Westat, and Tsapogas (1994) reported that only 2 percent of respondents asked for clarification on well-written questions when participating in the National Survey of Recent College Graduates in 1993. In contrast, Schwarz (1996) asserted that about 30 percent of respondents will answer questions on nonexisting issues. Respondents do not always interrupt the survey process for querying clarification; they may decide not to interrupt or require only one clarification and then answer an unclear question without showing any confusion or hesitation. In some instances, they may simply engage in satisficing behavior by providing an answer that is acceptable, even if not correct (Krosnick, 1991).

Another respondent behavior that is often captured by behavior coding is providing a qualified response (e.g., I'm not sure, but....) or a "don't know" response. People who provide a qualified response or do not know how to answer are more likely to have misinterpreted the question compared with respondents asking for clarification (Dykema et al., 1997). However, Lepkowski et al. (2000) underscored that respondents answering "don't know" or who request clarification tend to provide less accurate responses. Interruptions seem to be significantly correlated with inaccuracy of the question, such that respondents tend to interrupt the interview process when the question is unclear (Dykema et al., 1997), and respondents usually have comprehension difficulties when the questions are abstract and lengthy (Johnson et al., 2006). Research has shown that less educated respondents are more likely to interrupt the interview process and ask for clarification because they may need more help (Groves, 2004). Respondents also tend to express comprehension problems more often with conversational versus standardized interviewing (Conrad & Schober, 1999), perhaps because they feel less constrained to follow the interview script and freer to express difficulties, similar to the respondent–interview interaction during cognitive interviewing.

Consequently, there seem to be two reasons why respondents might not ask for clarification of a problematic question: (1) respondents may be under the impression that they understand the question adequately, even though that may not be true (Tourangeau et al., 2009), and (2) respondents are aware they have not understood the question but nonetheless provide an answer for self-presentation purposes (i.e., to avoid seeming clueless; Schwarz, 1996).

Social desirability pressures can have a profound impact on some respondents (Tourangeau & Yan, 2007). As mentioned earlier, the fact that some respondents answer questions instead of asking for additional information suggests that their goal may be to avoid appearing uninformed. Hence, they may express an opinion even if they have never thought about or do not have an opinion about a topic (Schuman & Presser, 1980). Although social desirability has been associated mostly with personal characteristics, there is strong evidence that culture can influence perceptions of social desirability (Johnson & Van de Vijver, 2003). In the United States, social desirability may have a larger effect on some minorities because they may in some circumstances regard the interview as a test and fear providing "wrong" answers (Davis & Silver, 2003).

If respondents do not fully comprehend survey questions, we can have no confidence in the quality of the information being reported. Researchers must ensure that all participants have a common understanding of the questions being asked and the response options being provided. In addition to racial and ethnic identification, respondents' first language is an important element of culture and, in addition to interviewer performance, may be a significant indicator of whether respondents ask for clarification on problematic questions. The remainder of this chapter examines how the language in which an interview is conducted and respondent acculturation influence respondent reactions to deliberately problematic questions.

Vygotsky (1962) underscores the importance of language in cognitive development. Understanding respondents' cognitive processing during the interview may be complex but necessary if we want to assess survey quality. People from various countries tend to think differently due to differences in their languages. Language is a significant indicator of question perception because each language has different syntactic properties, grammatical structures, and semantic categories, so language determines what information is retrieved (Peytcheva, 2018). Park and Goerman (2018) reported that respondents in the United States not speaking in English are more likely to face difficulties answering questions adequately, and Perales et al. (2015) asserted more generally that the use of second language in the interview process may hinder the understanding of the survey questions. Researchers have additionally identified issues with applying cognitive interview techniques to certain linguistic groups and in cognitive interviews with non-English speakers; it is hard for non-English speakers to paraphrase, ask for clarification, and think aloud (Park & Goerman, 2018). Hence, the first hypothesis was the following:

> **H_1: Respondents from recent immigrant groups (e.g., Mexican and Korean Americans) who prefer to be interviewed in English will be less likely to ask for clarification when confronted with problematic survey questions than respondents from these groups who prefer to be interviewed in their ethnic native language (e.g., Spanish or Korean).**

Scholars have conceived of and described culture in different ways. For example, Hofstede (1980) defines culture as "the collective programming of the mind which distinguishes the members of one human group from another" (p. 21), whereas others conceive of culture based on how groups interact with or adapt to their physical and social environments (Triandis, 2007). Acculturation is defined as "the process by which immigrants adopt the attitudes, values, customs, beliefs, and behavior of a new culture" (Abraído-Lanza, White, & Vásquez, 2004, p. 535). Thornton et al. (2010) discussed differences in perceptions of question meaning based on cultural context such that respondents should first comprehend the question to evaluate what information to provide and what the researcher needs to study—in other words, the pragmatic meaning. The pragmatic meaning of a question cannot be reached only by words because the context in which the question is asked is also very important (Uskul, Oyserman, & Schwarz, 2010).

Several studies have examined the effect of culture on response style; however, only a few studies have investigated variance within the same cultural group. One approach is to focus on levels of acculturation to a host culture among immigrants (Davis, Resnicow, & Couper, 2011). Measuring acculturation in bicultural respondents is very complex because the adoption of the second culture influences cognitive development (Tadmor & Tetlock, 2006). In everyday life, we can see how people from different cultural backgrounds may have different understandings in conversation based on the expressions, nuances, and colloquialisms used. For example, in English we say, "My name is," while in Spanish the exact translation of *Me llamo es* is "they call me." Therefore, it is essential that researchers employ terminology that is adequate for all cultures and do not assume that effective communications can be constructed in a similar manner for all populations (Marin, Gamba & Marin, 1992). Johnson (1998) discussed in detail the concept of equivalence in cross-cultural research, concluding there are two main dimensions for equivalence: (1) interpretive equivalence, which refers to "subjective cross-cultural comparability of meaning," and (2) procedural equivalence, which is concerned with "the objective development of comparable survey measures across cultural groups" (p. 38). Furthermore, Bailey and Marsden (1999) found that the interpretation of survey questions depends on the context, regardless of respondent cultural background. However, Qiufen (2014) concluded that even though there are differences in interpretation between and within groups, researchers can find significant similarities in question interpretation from people with similar cultural backgrounds, such that respondents make the same assumptions and follow similar trains of thought.

Acculturated Latino respondents in the United States experience more comprehension issues compared with native-born whites and African Americans, as do less educated respondents (Cho, Holbrook, & Johnson, 2013). Similarly, acculturated Asians tend to provide responses similar to Canadian Caucasian respondents, while less acculturated Asians provided less emotionally expressive answers when reporting their symptoms (Lai & Linden, 1993). In line with these findings, Johnson, Shavitt, and Holbrook (2010) reported that nonwhite respondents tend to agree and provide more acquiescent responses. We assume respondents who are more likely to agree are less likely to request clarification for questions that are specifically designed to be problematic. In theory, all respondents should request clarification when confronted with a poorly designed question. As discussed earlier, however, some respondents will not request clarification and instead will answer an ambiguous question for several possible reasons, including comprehension errors (e.g., they believe they clearly understood the question, even if that is not possible), social desirability pressures (e.g., they wish to avoid appearing uninformed), or satisficing (e.g., providing an acceptable response rather than an optimal one). Less acculturated respondents may avoid asking for clarification for any of the aforementioned reasons. Therefore, the second hypothesis was the following:

> **H_2: Among respondents from recent immigrant groups (e.g., Mexican and Korean Americans), those who are more acculturated to American culture will be more likely to request clarification when confronted with problematic survey questions.**

Deliberately Problematic Questions

Difficult or problematic questions can be a very useful tool in survey methodology because they can be used to measure question reliability. Respondents often answer questions even when they are not familiar with or know nothing about the policy, event, or object about which the question is asking. Researchers may include problematic questions in the survey instrument that feature nonexisting words or topics to test whether respondents will have an opinion (Bishop, Oldendick, Tuchfarber, & Bennett, 1980). Intuitively, one might expect that all respondents would request clarifications when confronted with deliberately problematic questions. In fact, previous research has demonstrated that some respondents are more likely to provide an opinion for problematic questions than others, with race being a significant indicator, such that African Americans are less likely to query (Bishop et al., 1980; Bishop, Tuchfarber, & Oldendick, 1986). If respondents provide an opinion to problematic questions that they cannot be expected to understand, they may also answer legitimate, nonproblematic questions that they do not fully understand. Therefore, we employed problematic questions to understand which groups of respondents ask for clarification when needed.

Data and Methods

The survey employed in this study was completed in June 2010 by the Survey Research Laboratory at the University of Illinois at Chicago. The primary goal of the survey was to measure racial and ethnic variability in survey question processing and response behaviors. All respondents were Chicago residents between 18 and 70 years old. Stratified sampling was used for this study; each stratum represented a targeted race and ethnic group. Participants were first contacted via telephone. After being screened for eligibility, individuals were invited to visit the Survey Research Laboratory to participate in face-to-face interviews. All interviews were audio and video recorded. Respondents were given $40 and a parking voucher for participation. The survey included 151 Mexican American and 150 Korean American respondents from whom the data reported here were obtained. Due to the complex procedures used to obtain a sufficient sample of each race and ethnic group, it is not possible to estimate a response rate based on American Association for Public Opinion Research guidelines.

Respondents could choose whether they were interviewed in English or Spanish or Korean, depending on their ethnic group. The goal was to conduct half of the interviews of Mexican Americans in Spanish and half of the interviews of Korean Americans in Korean, with the rest conducted in English. All respondents were matched with an interviewer of the same race because there is evidence that respondents are more likely to provide more accurate information when their race matches that of their interviewer (Davis, Couper, Janz, Caldwell, & Resnicow, 2009). From our sample, 75 Mexican respondents were interviewed in English and 75 in Spanish. Similarly, half of all Korean respondents chose English as their preferred language, and the other half selected Korean. The questionnaire in English was constructed by the principal investigators and reviewed by the Survey Research Laboratory's Questionnaire Review Committee. Special attention was given to Spanish and Korean translations. For each language, one translation expert conducted an initial translation, and then a team of experts reviewed the translation to identify problematic words or phrases and come to a resolution on the final translation.

The analysis focuses on the respondents' reactions to four problematic questions that were purposely included at different points throughout the questionnaire, as a method of validation for respondents' behaviors and answers. Specifically, we measured whether respondents asked for clarification when they were asked a question about a fictitious topic. The four deliberately problematic questions were (1) "Has a doctor ever told you that you have a hyperactive emissarium?"; (2) "Have you ever tried to cut down on the amount of tracines in your diet?"; (3) "How worried are you about your ordinal health?"; and (4) "Do you favor the Health Opportunity Act of 2006?" Questions 1, 2, and 4 each had two response options ("yes" or "no" or "favor" or "oppose"), whereas Question 3 had a 4-point scale: "very worried," "somewhat worried," "only a little worried," and "not at all worried." All four problematic questions deliberately mentioned nonexistent topics to examine whether respondents would ask for clarification. The respondents could not provide an informed answer if they did not ask for clarification, so we measured whether language and acculturation significantly affected their reactions to those questions.

Subsequent to field work, all interviews were behavior coded. Table 2-1 shows the subset of verbal behavior codes that involved respondent requests for clarification at the question level. These values were summed into a single measure indicating whether respondents asked for any type of clarification after being asked each question. We examined as dependent variables whether respondents requested clarification for each of the four problematic survey questions of interest, and we also created a summed index that represents the total number of questions for which respondents asked for clarification.

Logistic hierarchical models and hierarchical linear modeling[1] were used for the analysis in recognition that the variables of interest were measured at multiple levels, including the respondent level and the interviewer level. The independent variables were grouped based on both interviewer and respondent characteristics. Logistic hierarchical models were used to analyze the dichotomous dependent variables, and hierarchical linear modeling was used for the index of all problematic questions. On the interviewer level, there were three covariates: (1) whether the interviewer is the same gender as the respondent, (2) whether the absolute difference in age between the interviewer and respondent is 5

[1] We used hierarchical models so we could capture effects on two levels: (1) interviewer level and (2) respondent level. The main advantage of hierarchical models is that they are highly accurate because they can isolate the interviewer effect and the respondent, thus we can investigate both within group and between group relationships in a single analysis.

Table 2-1. Explanation of verbal behavior codes

Verbal Behavior Code List	Explanation
Interruption with question	Respondent interrupts initial question reading with a question.
Clarification (Unspecified)	Respondent indicates uncertainty about the question, but it is unclear whether the problem is related to the construct or the context (e.g., "What is the question asking?" or "What?").
Clarification (Construct/ statement)	Respondent makes a statement indicating uncertainty about question meaning (e.g., "I'm not sure what 'depressed' means.").
Clarification (Construct/ question)	Respondent asks for clarification of question meaning (e.g., "What do you mean by 'depressed'?" or "Depressed?").
Clarification (Context)	Respondent indicates an understanding of the meaning of the construct but indicates uncertainty about the question meaning within the context of the question as stated (e.g., "What do you want to know about being depressed?"; "How often do you pay with cash at restaurants?" Response: "Does that include debit cards?").
Clarification (Not enough information)	Respondent indicates that there is not enough information given in the question to answer. (Key phrases include "It depends on the situation."; "It is case by case."; and "I don't have enough information.").
Clarification (Response format)	Respondent indicates uncertainty about the format for responding (e.g., "I'm not sure how to answer that."; "What else, is that all you are offering me?"; or "Are you asking for a percentage?").
Clarification (Response option meaning)	Respondent asks for clarification of a response option meaning (e.g., "What is the meaning of 'sometimes'?").

years or less, and (3) whether the interviewer has previous experience working with the Survey Research Laboratory. The covariates measured at the respondent level were gender, age, ethnicity, education, language, and acculturation. Education was used as a factor variable, and the reference group was high school graduates. The respondents could choose the language in which they would be interviewed. We found that most of the respondents born in the United States chose to be interviewed in English, while those born in Mexico or Korea preferred Spanish or Korean, respectively ($r = .71$). Hence, language preference is strongly associated with country of birth and, consequently, culture.

As for acculturation, the index used consisted of the 17-item Stephenson Multigroup Acculturation Scale (SMAS), which includes questions about friends, acquaintances, food, current affairs, and history (Stephenson, 2000). Only Mexican and Korean respondents answered these questions because there was no reason for native-born white and African Americans to respond to acculturation questions. The SMAS Cronbach's alpha internal reliability coefficients for Mexicans and Koreans were 0.81 and 0.88, respectively. Table 2-2 shows the independent variables used in the analysis. There are four models that represent each question and a final model in which the dependent variable is the index. All analyses were conducted using the R programming language, using the libraries tidyverse and lme4.

Results

Tables 2-3 through 2-5 provide descriptive statistics for the study variables. We looked at the correlations between the independent variables and determined that none of the models suffered from multicollinearity.

Figure 2-1 shows the percentage of respondents asking for clarification, which varied for each question. A relatively small percentage asked for clarification for each of these items. Specifically, for Question 1 ("Has a doctor ever told you that you have a hyperactive emissarium?"), 17 percent of the respondents asked for clarification. For Question 2 ("Have you ever

Table 2-2. Explanation of independent variables

Variable Name	Explanation
Interviewer Level	
I_worked	Previous interviewer work experience with the Survey Research Laboratory. (0 = no; 1 = yes)
Ad_age	The absolute age difference between the interviewer and the respondent. (range = 0–47)
Samesex	Same sex as respondent. (0 = no; 1 = yes)
Respondent Level	
Female	Respondents' gender. (0 = male; 1 = female)
Age	Respondents' age. (range = 18–70)
Mexican	Respondents' ethnicity. It is a dummy variable. (0 = Koreans; 1 = Mexicans)
Educ	Respondents' education. It is a factor variable, where the base category is high school degree. The other groups are (1) less than high school, (2) some college, (3) four-year college degree, and (4) graduate degree.
Language	The language of the questionnaire (0 = English; 1 = Korean or Mexican)
Acculturation	Higher values indicate greater adjustment to American culture. (range = 47–96)

Table 2-3. Descriptive statistics of continuous independent variables

Variable	Minimum	Mean	Median	Max	*SD*	*n*
Ad_age	0.10	16.38	14.16	47.27	12.21	301
Age	18	39.82	38	69	15.49	301
Acculturation	47	72.43	73	96	9.30	228

Table 2-4. Distribution of dichotomous independent variables

	No		Yes	
Variable	*n*	%	*n*	%
I_worked	273	91	28	9
Samesex	149	50	152	50
Female	127	45	157	55
Language	134	47	150	53

Table 2-5. Distribution of the factor variable "education"

	Less than High School		High School Degree		Some College		4-Year College Degree		Graduate Degree	
	n	%	*n*	%	*n*	%	*n*	%	*n*	%
Education	65	22	55	18	70	23	85	28	26	9

Figure 2-1. Distribution of the index of all problematic questions, by race

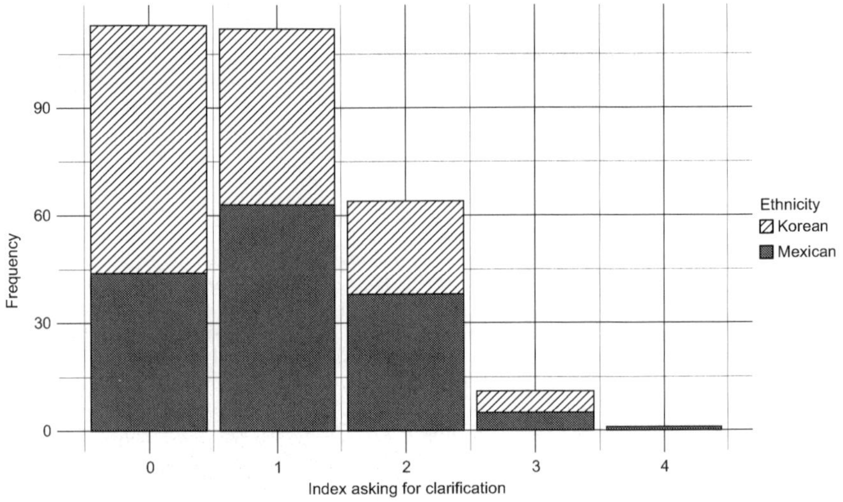

tried to cut down on the amount of tracines in your diet?"), 39 percent asked for clarification. For Question 3 ("How worried are you about your ordinal health?"), 25 percent asked for clarification. For Question 4 ("Do you favor the Health Opportunity Act of 2006?"), 12 percent asked for clarification. These findings are similar to those reported earlier by Schwarz (1996) but higher compared with Bishop et al. (1980, 1986). Because of the nature of the questions, it is possible respondents did not consider that a clarification was required. For example, for Question 1, respondents may have answered "no" without asking for clarification because they know that their doctor never told them they had a hyperactive emissarium. This may explain the relatively small percentage that asked for clarification. However, we notice that fewer respondents posed a query for Question 4, for which a clarification was needed to provide an opinion. By looking at the distribution of the dependent variable, it is apparent that a large number of respondents did not ask any clarifications, while very few people asked for clarification on all four questions.

Four logistic hierarchical models are presented in Table 2-6 to examine the variables associated with providing appropriate responses to each problematic survey question. A final model examined associations between the same set of variables and the index measure of the number of problematic questions that respondents answered appropriately. None of the variables at the interviewer level proved to be significant. At the respondent level, gender, age, and acculturation were also not significantly associated with requests for clarification, while education was only significant ($p < .01$) for respondents with some college education (compared to high school graduates) for Question 1. The direction of the relationship is positive such that respondents with some college education tended to ask for clarification more often. Mexican respondents were more likely to ask for clarification ($p < .01$) compared with Koreans only for Question 1: "Has a doctor ever told you that you have a hyperactive emissarium?" Language was the only significant covariate ($p < .01$) for the index of all four problematic questions because respondents interviewed in Korean or Spanish were more likely to ask for clarification.

Given this set of findings, we partially confirmed the first hypothesis (i.e., people interviewed in Spanish or Korean are more likely to provide higher data quality when confronted with problematic questions), and we rejected the second hypothesis because respondents adjusting to American culture were not more likely to ask for clarification.

Table 2-6. Logistic hierarchical and hierarchical linear models examining requests for clarifications to problematic questions

	Question 1	Question 2	Question 3	Question 4	All Questions
(Intercept)	−0.66 (0.35)*	0.28 (0.47)	−0.23 (0.42)	−0.23 (0.42)	−0.62 (0.80)
I_worked	−0.21 (0.10)**	0.16 (0.17)	−0.03 (0.13)	−0.03 (0.13)	−0.08 (0.29)
ad_age	0.00 (0.00)	0.00 (0.01)	0.00 (0.00)	0.00 (0.00)	0.02 (0.01)
samesex	−0.02 (0.05)	0.01 (0.07)	−0.03 (0.06)	−0.03 (0.06)	−0.06 (0.12)
female	−0.01 (0.05)	−0.05 (0.07)	−0.09 (0.06)	−0.09 (0.06)	−0.18 (0.12)
age	−0.00 (0.00)	−0.00 (0.00)	−0.00 (0.00)	−0.00 (0.00)	−0.01 (0.01)
educless than high school	0.01 (0.08)	−0.15 (0.11)	−0.16 (0.10)	−0.16 (0.10)	−0.21 (0.19)
educsome college	0.14 (0.08)*	−0.12 (0.11)	−0.07 (0.09)	−0.07 (0.09)	0.00 (0.18)
educfour year college degree	0.06 (0.08)	−0.10 (0.11)	−0.01 (0.09)	−0.01 (0.09)	−0.08 (0.18)
educgraduate degree	0.07 (0.10)	−0.14 (0.14)	0.20 (0.12)	0.20 (0.12)	0.05 (0.23)
Mexican	0.22 (0.06)***	0.13 (0.11)	−0.11 (0.08)	−0.11 (0.08)	0.19 (0.19)
language	0.25 (0.08)***	0.09 (0.11)	0.14 (0.10)	0.14 (0.10)	0.53 (0.19)***
acculturation	0.00 (0.00)	0.00 (0.01)	0.01 (0.00)	0.01 (0.00)	0.01 (0.01)
AIC	265.24	398.24	343.83	343.83	624.99
BIC	316.62	449.61	395.21	395.21	676.36
Log Likelihood	−117.62	−184.12	−156.92	−156.92	−297.50
Num. obs.	227	227	227	227	227
Num. groups: interviewer id	16	16	16	16	16
Var: interviewer id (Intercept)	0.00	0.01	0.00	0.00	0.04
Var: Residual	0.13	0.23	0.19	0.19	0.67

***$p < .01$, **$p < .05$, *$p < .1$

AIC = Akaike information criterion; BIC = Bayesian information criterion.

Note: Models Question 1 through Question 4 employed logistic regression, and All Questions employed hierarchical linear modeling.

Discussion

The purpose of this chapter was to examine interviewer- and respondent-level variables that can predict whether respondents require a query on deliberately problematic questions in a cross-cultural study and to test two hypotheses regarding the effects of language and acculturation. Asking for clarification is considered necessary before providing an opinion on problematic questions because it shows that respondents carefully listen to the question, try to understand the meaning of it, and are not only trying to satisfy the interviewer. In general, we did not find many significant effects, maybe because relatively few people asked for clarification in the first place, and we cannot easily predict the respondents who will do so. Although there was variability among interviewers, we found that interviewer experience and matching interviewers and respondents in terms of ethnicity were not significant.

After controlling for interviewer-level variables, few characteristics also proved to be significant at the respondent level. When examining the index of all four problematic questions, only language was found to be associated with requests for clarification: those who were interviewed in Korean or Spanish were more likely to ask for question clarifications. This evidence partially supports Hypothesis 1, but language was not significant for all models. However, it has a positive direction consistent with our hypothesis in all but one model. The findings are in line with previous research; Peytcheva (2018) found that the language in which the instrument was administered affected responses. Previous research has shown contradictory results of the effect of education. For the current research, education was significant only for two questions, such that more educated respondents were more likely to ask for clarification. Our findings are in line with some of the previous research (Bishop et al., 1980, 1986; Olson, Smyth, & Ganshert, 2019). Nevertheless, Johnson et al. (2018), contrary to previous research, found that more educated respondents tend to face more comprehensive issues.

Contrary to Hypothesis 2, acculturation did not appear to be associated with the likelihood that respondents would request clarification of problematic questions. Although none were significant, we found negative coefficients in each model, such that less acculturated respondents were more likely to require a query, which is contrary to previous research indicating that nonacculturated Spanish-speaking respondents in the United States are more likely to produce item nonresponse by answering "don't know" (Lee, Keusch, Schwarz, Liu, & Suzer-Gurtekin, 2018). This difference may be explained by the different scales used in each study. Usually, acculturation scales target specific groups (Celenk & Van de Vijver, 2011); however, there are significant differences in acculturation measures even within the same cultural groups (Unger, Ritt-Olson, Wagner, Soto, & Baezconde-Garbanati, 2007). Additionally, in the current study, we did not take into consideration the birth country of respondents, and we assessed acculturation for all respondents with different cultural backgrounds using the same measure.

In general, the problem was much broader than we initially thought. Few people asked for clarification of problematic questions, a trend that may affect data quality for legitimate questions as well. Specifically, researchers should be concerned about two issues: (1) respondents providing an opinion on issues, events, or policies that they are not familiar with and (2) respondents providing an answer to a question that they could not have completely understood. Researchers should be extremely conscious when designing their instruments because respondents will not always request assistance when confronted with problematic questions. Therefore, they should focus on careful design and pretesting of questionnaires. Well-designed and tested questionnaires are essential for multinational, multiregional, and multicultural respondents (Harkness, Edwards, Hansen, Miller, & Villar, 2010).

Researchers should pretest instruments with each of the cultural groups that will participate in the research. Once a survey is launched, it is very challenging to predict whether respondents will need assistance with some of the questions, and it is usually too late to make substantive changes. This applies to all ethnicities examined in the current study.

However, the limitations to this study require further consideration. One limitation is that there were only four deliberately problematic questions included here. Additional questions, samples, and strategies will be necessary to more thoroughly examine the predictors of respondent requests for clarification. In the current study, we were unable to examine the effect of question characteristics. Another limitation is that, because the research was conducted only with two ethnicities, Korean and Mexican, our findings are likely not generalizable to other cultural groups. Each culture differs from the others, and although Mexican and Korean cultures come from different continents, they have some similarities. Furthermore, the sample size in our study is relatively small because only 301 respondents were available for these analyses. In the future, we plan to expand our research and compare how likely Americans are to provide an opinion in response to problematic questions compared with people from different cultural backgrounds. We also plan to compare responses to these deliberately problematic questions with other survey questions included in this study to investigate the effects of poor question structure on response latencies and further explore cultural similarities and differences in the survey response process.

References

Abraído-Lanza, A. F., White, K., & Vásquez, E. (2004). Immigrant population and health. In N. Anderson (Ed.), *Encyclopedia of health and behavior* (pp. 533–537). Newbury Park, CA: SAGE.

Bailey, S., & Marsden, P. V. (1999). Interpretation and interview context: Examining the General Social Survey name generator using cognitive methods. *Social Networks*, *21*(3), 287–309.

Bell, K., Fahmy, E., & Gordon, D. (2016). Quantitative conversations: The importance of developing rapport in standardized interviewing. *Quality & Quantity*, *50*, 193–212.

Bishop, G. F., Oldendick, R. W., Tuchfarber, A. J., & Bennett, S. E. (1980). Pseudo-opinions on public affairs. *Public Opinion Quarterly*, *44*(2), 198–209.

Bishop, G. F., Tuchfarber, A. J., & Oldendick, R. W. (1986). Opinions on fictitious issues: The pressure to answer survey questions. *Public Opinion Quarterly*, *50*(2), 240–250.

Cahalan, M., Mitchell, S., Gray, L., Westat, A. C., & Tsapogas, J. (1994, August). *Recorded interview behavior coding study: National Survey of Recent College Graduates*. Proceedings of the American Statistical Association, Section on Survey Research Methods, Toronto.

Cannell, C., Oksenberg, L., & Converse, J. (1977). *Experiments in interviewing techniques: Field experiments in health reporting 1971–1977.* Ann Arbor, MI: University of Michigan Survey Research Center, National Center for Health Services Research.

Catania, J. A., Binson, D., Canchola, J., Pollack, L. M., Hauck, W., & Coates, T. J. (1996). Effects of interviewer gender, interviewer choice, and item wording on responses to questions concerning sexual behavior. *Public Opinion Quarterly*, *60*(3), 345–375.

Celenk, O., & Van de Vijver, F. J. (2011). Assessment of acculturation: Issues and overview of measures. *Online Readings in Psychology and Culture*, *8*(1), 10.

Cho, Y. I., Holbrook, A., & Johnson, T. P. (2013). Acculturation and health survey question comprehension among Latino respondents in the US. *Journal of Immigrant and Minority Health*, *15*(3), 525–532.

Conrad, F. G., & Schober, M. F. (1999). Conversational interviewing and data quality. *Proceedings of the Federal Committee on Statistical Methodology Research Conference, Tuesday B Sessions* (pp. 21–30). Arlington, VA: Federal Committee on Statistical Methodology.

Davis, D. W., & Silver, B. D. (2003). Stereotype threat and race of interviewer effects in a survey on political knowledge. *American Journal of Political Science, 47*(1), 33–45.

Davis, R. E., Caldwell, C. H., Couper, M. P., Janz, N. K., Alexander, G. L., Greene, S. M., ... Resnicow, K. (2013). Ethnic identity, questionnaire content, and the dilemma of race matching in surveys of African Americans by African American interviewers. *Field Methods, 25*(2), 142–161.

Davis, R. E., Couper, M. P., Janz, N. K., Caldwell, C. H., & Resnicow, K. (2009). Interviewer effects in public health surveys. *Health Education Research, 25*(1), 14–26.

Davis, R. E., Resnicow, K., & Couper, M. P. (2011). Survey response styles, acculturation, and culture among a sample of Mexican American adults. *Journal of Cross-Cultural Psychology, 42*(7), 1219–1236.

Dolnicar, S., & Grün, B. (2007). Cross-cultural differences in survey response patterns. *International Marketing Review, 24*(2), 127–143.

Dykema, J., Lepkowski, J. M., & Blixt, S. (1997). The effect of interviewer and respondent behavior on data quality: Analysis of interaction coding in a validation study. In L. Lyberg, P. Biemer, M. Collins, E. de Leeuw, C. Dippo, N. Schwarz, & D. Trewin (Eds.), *Survey measurement and process quality* (pp. 287–310). New York, NY: John Wiley & Sons.

Fowler, F. J., Jr. (1992). How unclear terms affect survey data. *Public Opinion Quarterly, 56*, 218–231.

Fowler, F. J., Jr., & Cannell, C. F. (1996). Using behavioral coding to identify cognitive problems with survey questions. In N. Schwarz & S. Sudman (Eds.), *Answering questions: Methodology for determining cognitive and communicative processes in survey research.* San Francisco, CA: Jossey-Bass.

Fowler, F. J., Jr., & Mangione, T. W. (1990). *Standardized survey interviewing: Minimizing interviewer-related error.* Newbury Park, CA: SAGE.

Garbarski, D., Schaeffer, N. C., & Dykema, J. (2016). Interviewing practices, conversational practices, and rapport: Responsiveness and engagement in the standardized survey interview. *Sociological Methodology, 46*(1), 1–38.

Groves, R. M. (2004). *Survey errors and survey costs*. New York, NY: John Wiley & Sons.

Groves, R. M., & Magilavy, L. J. (1986). Measuring and explaining interviewer effects in centralized telephone surveys. *Public Opinion Quarterly, 50*(2), 251–266.

Harkness, J. A., Edwards, B., Hansen, S. E., Miller, D. R., & Villar, A. (2010). Designing questionnaires for multipopulation research. In J. A. Harkness, M. Braun, B. Edwards, T. P. Johnson, L. Lyberg, P. Ph. Mohler, B. Pennell, & T. W. Smith (Eds.), *Survey methods in multinational, multiregional, and multicultural contexts* (pp. 191–202). Hoboken, NJ: Wiley.

Hofstede, G. (1980). *Culture's consequences: Comparing values, behaviors, institutions, and organizations across nations*. Thousand Oaks, CA: SAGE.

Holbrook, A. L., Cho, Y. I., & Johnson, T. P. (2006). The impact of question and respondent characteristics on comprehension and mapping difficulties. *Public Opinion Quarterly, 70*, 565–595.

Johnson, T. P. (1998). Approaches to equivalence in cross-cultural and cross-national survey research. *ZUMA-Nachrichten Spezial, 3*, 1–40.

Johnson, T. P., Cho, Y. I., Holbrook, A. L., O'Rourke, D., Warnecke, R. B., & Chavez, N. (2006). Cultural variability in the effects of question design features on respondent comprehension of health surveys. *Annals of Epidemiology, 16*, 661–668.

Johnson, T. P., Holbrook, A., Cho, Y. I., Shavitt, S., Chavez, N., & Weiner, S. (2018). Examining the comparability of behavior coding across cultures. In T. P. Johnson, B. E. Pennell, I. Stoop, & B. Dorer (Eds.), *Advances in comparative survey methods: Multinational, multiregional, and multicultural contexts (3MC)* (pp. 271–292). Hoboken, NJ: Wiley & Sons.

Johnson, T. P., Shavitt, S., & Holbrook, A. L. (2010). Culture and response styles in survey research. In D. Matsumoto & F. Van de Vijver (Eds.), *Cross-cultural research methods in psychology* (pp. 130–178). New York, NY: Cambridge University Press.

Krosnick, J. A. (1991). Response strategies for coping with the cognitive demands of attitude measures in surveys. *Applied Cognitive Psychology, 5*(3), 213–236.

Lai, J., & Linden, W. (1993). The smile of Asia: Acculturation effects on symptom reporting. *Canadian Journal of Behavioural Science/Revue Canadienne des Sciences du Comportement, 25*(2), 303.

Lee, S., Keusch, F., Schwarz, N., Liu, M., & Suzer-Gurtekin, Z. T. (2018). Cross-cultural comparability of response patterns of subjective probability questions. In T. P. Johnson, B.-E. Pennell, I. Stoop, & B. Dorer (Eds.), *Advances in comparative survey methods: Multinational, multiregional, and multicultural contexts (3MC)* (pp. 457–476). Hoboken, NJ: John Wiley & Sons.

Lepkowski, J. M., Siu, V., & Fisher, J. (2000). Event history analysis of interviewer and respondent survey behavior. In A. Ferligoj & A. Mrvar (Eds.), *Developments in survey methodology* (pp. 3–20). Metodološki Zvezki, 15. Ljubljana, Slovenia: FDV.

Lipps, O., & Lutz, G. (2017). Gender of interviewer effects in a multitopic centralized CATI panel survey. *Methods, Data, Analyses: A Journal for Quantitative Methods and Survey Methodology (MDA), 11*(1), 67–86.

Marin, G., Gamba, R. J., & Marin, B. V. (1992). Extreme response style and acquiescence among Hispanics: The role of acculturation and education. *Journal of Cross-Cultural Psychology, 23*(4), 498–509.

Oksenberg, L., Cannell, C., & Kalton, G. (1991). New strategies for pretesting survey questions. *Journal of Official Statistics, 7*(3), 349–365.

Olson, K., Smyth, J. D., & Ganshert, A. (2019). The effects of respondent and question characteristics on respondent answering behaviors in telephone interviews. *Journal of Survey Statistics and Methodology, 7*(2), 275–308.

Ong, A. R., Hu, M., West, B. T., & Kirlin, J. A. (2018). Interviewer effects in food acquisition surveys. *Public Health Nutrition, 21*(10), 1781–1793.

Ongena, Y. P., & Dijkstra, W. (2006). Methods of behavior coding of survey interviews. *Journal of Official Statistics, 22*(3), 419–451.

Park, H., & Goerman, P. L. (2018). Setting up the cognitive interview task for non-English speaking participants in the U.S. In T. P. Johnson, B.-E. Pennell, I. Stoop, & B. Dorer (Eds.), *Advances in comparative survey methods: Multinational, multiregional, and multicultural contexts (3MC)* (pp. 457–476). Hoboken, NJ: John Wiley & Sons.

Perales, F., Baffour, B., & Mitrou, F. (2015). Ethnic differences in the quality of the interview process and implications for survey analysis: The case of indigenous Australians. *PLoS ONE, 10*(6), 1–20.

Peytcheva, E. (2018). Can the language of survey administration influence respondent's answers? In T. P. Johnson, B.-E. Pennell, I. Stoop, & B. Dorer (Eds.), *Advances in comparative survey methods: Multinational, multiregional, and multicultural contexts (3MC)* (pp. 457–476). Hoboken, NJ: John Wiley & Sons.

Qiufen, Y. U. (2014). Understanding the impact of culture on interpretation: A relevance theoretic perspective. *Intercultural Communication Studies, 23*(3).

Sahgal, N., & Horrowitz, J. H. (2011, May 13). Interviewer gender effects in international surveys: An analysis of Muslim publics in six countries. *Comparative research on world suffering, extremism & evangelicalism.* Presented at the meeting of American Association for Public Opinion Research, Phoenix, AZ.

Schaeffer, N. C., & Maynard, D. W. (1996). From paradigm to prototype and back again: Interactive aspects of cognitive processing standardized survey interviews. In N. Schwarz & S. Sudman (Eds.), *Answering questions: Methodology for determining cognitive and communicating processes in survey research* (pp. 75–88). San Francisco, CA: Jossey-Bass.

Schober, M. F. (1999). Making sense of questions: An interactional approach. In M. Sirken, D. Herrmann, S. Schechter, N. Schwarz, J. Tanur, & R. Tourangeau (Eds.), *Cognition and survey research* (pp. 77–93). Hoboken, NJ: Wiley & Sons.

Schuman, H., & Presser, S. (1977). Attitude measurement and the gun control paradox. *Public Opinion Quarterly, 41*(4), 427–438.

Schuman, H., & Presser, S. (1980). Public opinion and public ignorance: The fine line between attitudes and nonattitudes. *American Journal of Sociology, 85*(5), 1214–1225.

Schwarz, N. (1996). Cognition and communication: Judgmental biases, research methods, and the logic of conversation. Mahwah, NJ: Lawrence Erlbaum Associates.

Stephenson, M. (2000). Development and validation of the Stephenson Multigroup Acculturation Scale (SMAS). *Psychological Assessment, 12*(1), 77.

Tadmor, C. T., & Tetlock, P. E. (2006). Biculturalism: A model of the effects of second-culture exposure on acculturation and integrative complexity. *Journal of Cross-Cultural Psychology, 37*(2), 173–190.

Tourangeau, R., Rips, L. J., & Rasinski, K. (2009). *The psychology of survey response.* Cambridge, UK: Cambridge University Press.

Tourangeau, R., & Yan, T. (2007). Sensitive questions in surveys. *Psychological Bulletin, 133*(5), 859–883.

Thornton, A., Achen, A., Barber, J. S., Binstock, G., Garrison, W. M., Ghimire, D. J., … Yount, K. (2010). Creating questions and protocols for an international study of ideas about development and family life. In J. A. Harkness, M. Braun, B. Edwards, T. P. Johnson, L. Lyberg, P. Ph. Mohler, B. Pennell, & T. W. Smith (Eds.), *Survey methods in multinational, multiregional, and multicultural contexts* (pp. 59–74). Hoboken, NJ: Wiley.

Triandis, H. C. (2007). Culture and psychology: A history of the study of their relationship. In S. Kitayama & D. Cohen (Eds.), *Handbook of cultural psychology* (pp. 59–76). New York, NY: Guilford Press.

Unger, J. B., Ritt-Olson, A., Wagner, K., Soto, D., & Baezconde-Garbanati, L. (2007). A comparison of acculturation measures among Hispanic/Latino adolescents. *Journal of Youth and Adolescence, 36*(4), 555–565.

Uskul, A. K., Oyserman, D., & Schwarz, N. (2010). Cultural emphasis on honor, modesty, or self-enhancement: Implications for the survey-response process. In J. A. Harkness, M. Braun, B. Edwards, T. P. Johnson, L. Lyberg, P. Ph. Mohler, B.-E. Pennell, & T. W. Smith (Eds.), *Survey methods in multinational, multiregional, and multicultural contexts* (pp. 191–202). Hoboken, NJ: Wiley.

Vygotsky, L.S. (1962). *Thought and language.* Cambridge, MA: MIT Press.

Warnecke, R. B., Johnson, T. P., Chavez, N., Sudman, S., O'Rourke, D. P., Lacey, L., & Horm, J. (1997). Improving question wording in surveys of culturally diverse populations. *Annals of Epidemiology, 7*(5), 334–342.

Webster, C. (1996). Hispanic and Anglo interviewer and respondent ethnicity and gender: The impact on survey response quality. *Journal of Marketing Research, 33*(1), 62–72.

Weisberg, H. F. (2005). *The total survey error approach.* Chicago, IL: University of Chicago Press.

West, B. T., & Blom, A. G. (2017). Explaining interviewer effects: A research synthesis. *Journal of Survey Statistics and Methodology, 5*(2), 175–211.

West, B. T., Conrad, F. G., Kreuter, F., & Mittereder, F. (2017). Nonresponse and measurement error variance among interviewers in standardized and conversational interviewing. *Journal of Survey Statistics and Methodology, 6*(3), 335–359.

A Longitudinal Perspective on the Effects of Household Language on Data Quality in the American Community Survey

Heather Kitada Smalley

Introduction

Linguistic diversity in the United States is dynamic and reflective of changes in immigration patterns. As the premier statistical organization for the federal government, the US Census Bureau is tasked with collecting data on language use for people living within the United States for diverse applications from sociolinguistic studies to support of legislation. As a result of studies on language use, the Census Bureau plans to offer the 2020 Decennial Census in seven new languages (Arabic, French, Haitian Creole, Japanese, Polish, Portuguese, and Tagalog) to join the already used English, Chinese, Korean, Russian, Spanish, and Vietnamese versions (Prior, 2019; Wang, 2019). With these new translations comes the need to study the effects of language on data quality.

The goal of this chapter is to examine the effects of household language on data quality in the American Community Survey (ACS) via the Public Use Microdata Sample (PUMS) from 2006 through 2017. This research combined multiple fields of study including sociolinguistics, mode effect, statistical modeling for complex surveys, and big data. We present novel data visualization tools that highlight temporal and spatial trends, as well as statistical models that account for the complexities of the sample. All data and analysis methods are freely available, reproducible, and accessible through the American FactFinder and R interfaces.

Background

Although English is the most commonly used and de facto language for governmental purposes, the United States has no official language. Questions regarding languages spoken and the degree of English proficiency have been included in the census in some form since 1890 and have evolved over time to mirror legislative needs (Shin & Kominski, 2010). Section 203 of the Voting Rights Act of 1965 mandated the creation of voting materials in minority languages (Ortman & Shin, 2011). This Act was reinforced in 2000 by Executive Order 13166, which aimed to bridge language barriers to accessing federal programs for individuals with limited English proficiency (LEP; Pan, Leeman, Fond, & Goerman, 2014). These types of legislation necessitated the creation of questions in the census and the ACS to study language trends and distributions.

Forecasting models confirm the increasing trend in the number of non-English-speaking households and the resulting need for linguistic support. The diversity and frequency of languages spoken parallel immigration patterns, reflecting a transition from immigrants speaking predominantly English and Indo-European languages in the late 19th to early 20th centuries (Stevens, 1999) to continually increasing numbers of Spanish and Asian/Pacific Islander language speakers starting in the middle of the 20th century (Bean & Stevens, 2003). Using Census Bureau National Population Projections along with assumptions for population growth and levels of international migration, Ortman and Shin (2011) forecasted language trends using both linear and logistic models. These models suggested that (1) English would continue to be the majority language spoken; (2) Spanish, Portuguese, Russian, Hindi, Chinese, Vietnamese, Tagalog, and Arabic language prevalence would increase, with Spanish continuing to be the most frequently spoken non-English language; and (3) French, Italian, German, Polish, and Korean would decline. In addition to migration patterns, English language acquisition, transmission, and proficiency are often viewed as key indicators of an immigrant's and their descendants' social and cultural assimilation in the United States (Akresh, Massey, & Frank, 2014; Alba, Logan, Lutz, & Stults, 2002; Mouw & Xie, 1999; Ortman & Stevens, 2008; Rumbaut, 1997; Rumbaut, Massey, & Bean, 2006). Yet holistic translation techniques need to be applied to surveys to acquire high-quality data.

Functional equivalence in multilingual survey instruments is of paramount concern (Genkova, 2015; Johnson, 1998). Translations require care at the lexical (wording), syntactic (grammar and naturalness in target language), and pragmatic (sociocultural context and appropriateness) levels (Pan, Sha, Park, & Schoua-Glusberg, 2009). Two primary techniques for survey translation include adoption and adaptation (Harkness, Pennell, & Schoua-Glusberg, 2004; Harkness & Schoua-Glusberg, 1998). The goal of the adoption method is to obtain the most direct translation from the source to the target language alone. It does not allow for differences in cultural interpretation. By contrast, the adaptation method not only involves lexical translation but also incorporates flexibility that allows for changes to achieve a similar stimulus to the desired question construct to ensure the intended meaning is preserved for diverse respondents. The Census Bureau advocates for the committee approach in their Translation Guidelines to aid in the goal of attaining functional equivalence between the source and target language versions (Pan & de la Puente, 2005). However, this goal can be hindered by the fact that the source survey materials are developed in English and are closed to modifications during the translation process (Pan & Fond, 2014). Thus, during the translation process, cognitive interview pretesting is used to assess the efficacy of the instruments (Goerman, Caspar, Sha, McAvinchey, & Quiroz, 2007; Pan, 2004; Pan, Landreth, Park, Hinsdale-Shouse, & Schoua-Glusberg, 2010; Park, Sha, & Pan, 2014; Sha, Pan, & Lazirko, 2013). This method has illuminated conceptual problems in the Spanish-language translation of the ACS for Spanish-speaking respondents (Carrasco, 2003). Furthermore, intrinsic differences in cultural communication norms may affect total survey error (TSE) and ultimately result in biased results.

A TSE frame describes and classifies sources of variability that contribute to differences between a population parameter of interest and the estimated statistic obtained from the survey (Weisberg, 2009). TSE is first partitioned into sampling and nonsampling errors, the latter of which is further broken down into coverage error, nonresponse error, measurement error, and processing error (Groves, 1987, 2004). Of these, nonresponse error and measurement error are especially vulnerable to shifts in cultural perceptions of survey studies. Pan (2003) argued that with "the increase of cultural diversity in survey population, cultural factors, including cultural value systems and social circumstances of personal experience, have been recognized as a strong influence on survey quality and participation" (p. 2). In regard to unit nonresponse, degree of social responsibility, perceived legitimacy of society institutions, and social cohesion can affect a respondent's participation (Groves & Couper, 2012). These factors can have strong negative effects on participation for immigrants who have little or no experience with surveys in their home country (Pan, 2004). Moreover, answering surveys is inherently a social activity that is governed by social and cultural communication standards, the differences of which are made more apparent when coupled with survey mode effect.

Survey modes of administration vary in degree of cognitive tasks and social interaction (de Leeuw, 1992; Sudman, Bradburn, Schwarz, & Gullickson, 1997), which contribute to systematic differences in response distribution among modes. This phenomenon (known as mode effect) is most commonly found to be significant in comparisons between self-administered and interview-type modes and is predominantly due to the presence of an interviewer (Bowling, 2005; Tourangeau & Smith, 1996). When engaging with an interviewer, respondents may feel compelled to provide perceived socially desirable responses (Walker & Restuccia, 1984). However, social desirability is subjective and related to a respondent's cultural experiences. A key assumption of survey research is that respondents are able to "express their opinions and preferences openly and directly" (Pan, 2003, p. 7). Yet, within the continuum of directness, "Western cultures tend to be direct in expressing their opinions" (Pan, 2003, p. 7), whereas respondents who come from cultures that value indirect communication (e.g., some Asian and African cultures) may become uncomfortable when forced to give direct answers in surveys. Cross-cultural studies on social desirability have used individualism–collectivism, expressiveness, and self-disclosure frameworks to describe respondents' willingness to engage and share personal information with an interviewer who is a stranger (Johnson & Van de Vijver, 2003). In some cases, the effects of social desirability and willingness to respond may result in a modified response or a lack of response to questions that are perceived to be irrelevant. Thus, self-administered modes may appear favorable because they allow respondents to have a sense of anonymity and the security to provide more honest answers. Nonetheless, self-administered modes may come with increased item nonresponse because of complex skip patterns without the aid of an interviewer to help with correct navigation. Hence, mode choice comes with trade-offs between costs, nonresponse, and measurement errors. The balance of these trade-offs has led to the increased popularity of mixed-mode studies (De Leeuw, Hox, Dillman, & European Association of Methodology, 2008; Dillman, Smyth, & Christian, 2014) that aim to balance mode characteristics, resulting in better quality data. This study presents a rare opportunity to examine the effects of both linguistic diversity and survey mode of administration.

Data Application

The ACS and its Public Use Microdata Area (PUMA) data are well used and documented elsewhere (US Census Bureau, 2014). The complex design and methodology components described in this section summarize elements that are relevant to the subsequent analyses presented.

About the ACS

The ACS is an annual product of the US Census Bureau that has provided social, demographic, economic, and housing data at both the individual and household levels since its inception in 2005. Originally these data were collected only on the long form of the decennial census, once every 10 years. The increased frequency of these surveys allows for a better understanding of trends and improved time series data. Estimates from the ACS can be obtained for 1- and 5-year increments; 3-year estimates are also available for years between 2007 and 2013. Laypeople, unaffiliated with the US Census Bureau, may obtain these estimates at the aggregated level through the American FactFinder and may obtain individual questionnaire-level data for people or housing units via the PUMS. The PUMS represents a subsample of responses from the ACS, where a single year of data records is approximately 1 percent of the US population. Individual records have been de-identified to protect personally identifiable information. The PUMS data are often used by researchers and policy makers for analyses because of their granularity and flexibility (Kinney & Karr, 2017).

The smallest obtainable geographic units within the PUMS dataset are the artificial boundaries known as the PUMA. PUMAs are built on census tracts, and counties and have been designed to partition a state such that at least 100,000 people are contained within them. In fact, "nearly every town and county in the country" is represented by a respondent in the PUMS files (US Census Bureau, 2018). The ACS is composed of two separate samples from housing units and group quarters. The Census Bureau's Master Address File is used to construct the sampling frame for the ACS (Bates, 2013). Viable housing units are sampled independently from each of the 3,143 counties using a stratified sampling technique. A two-stage sampling process is used to obtain responses from housing units. In the first stage, blocks are assigned to the sampling strata, sampling rates are calculated, and the sample is selected. The second stage of sampling serves to capture data from those who have not responded to the previous mode of contact by using differential subsampling rates based on expected rates of completed interviews at the tract level, mailability of the address, and harder-to-reach populations (Asiala, 2005; US Census Bureau, 2012).

A mixed-mode methodology and a schedule of multiple contacts are used to improve data quality. The Census Bureau monitors the ACS quality measures, which include sample size, coverage rates, response rates, and item allocation rates, to ensure accuracy and reliability of the data (US Census Bureau, 2002, 2004, 2015). Each ACS iteration comprises 12 monthly independently sampled panels with overlapping cycles of data collection, each of which lasts for 3 months. During these 3 months, three sequential phases of data collection are deployed: mail and Internet, phone, and personal visits. Given that mail and Internet modes are the most cost-effective options, respondents are encouraged to respond through several contacts via these methods. The mail phase consists of up to six postal mailing attempts: prenotice letter, initial mail package, first reminder postcard, replacement mail package (containing an ACS questionnaire), second reminder postcard, and an additional postcard. These multiple mailing attempts, along with a statement regarding one's legal obligation to answer the survey, have been shown to improve response rates (Dillman, 1978). The first three mailings' (prenotice, initial mail package, and first reminder postcard) respondents are given directions on how to log in and respond to the survey via the Internet. It is not until the replacement mail package that respondents are provided with a physical printed copy of the survey and a prepaid envelope in which to return it. Each mailing also includes information about the toll-free telephone questionnaire assistance (TQA), which can be used if a respondent has any questions or needs help completing their survey. If a sampling unit still has not responded to the survey through the mail or Internet and the household has a valid associated phone number, they are eligible to receive the questionnaire over the phone. Computer-assisted telephone interviews (CATIs) are used to automate the data collection process, prevent out-of-range responses, and navigate question skips. Finally, if a unit still fails to respond, they may be selected for the personal visit phase. In this final phase, trained interviewers equipped with laptops are sent into the field to conduct computer-assisted personal interviews (CAPIs). Furthermore, although multiple modes are implemented throughout survey administration to mitigate the weaknesses inherent in each mode, there may be concerns about subsequent mode effects resulting in instability. The estimation and impact of these effects are further complicated by the use of multiple languages within different modes.

The ACS Language Assistance program has been developed to improve accessibility for the ACS and the quality of data obtained from non-English-speaking households. It is standard for all initial mailing materials of the ACS within the United States to be sent in English but also to provide resources for additional support of other languages (Table 3-1). The prenotice letter is accompanied by a multilingual informational brochure with text in English, Spanish, Russian, Chinese, Korean, and Vietnamese. The multilanguage brochure has been shown to significantly improve response rates in experiments for these supported language groups (Joshipura, 2010). The TQA number is also provided so that respondents can receive help directly from an in-language speaker to answer the survey in each of these languages. If a respondent calls the TQA and speaks to an agent during business hours, they may be prompted to answer the questionnaire over the telephone using an automated survey instrument. It should be noted that even though a respondent in this scenario answers the questionnaire over the telephone, they are considered a "mail" response because they were initially part of that group. In addition, if a respondent accesses the ACS online, they have the ability to answer in either English or Spanish. Similarly, if a respondent receives a physical paper survey, the questionnaire is in English, but there is a message on the cover in Spanish that instructs respondents how to receive a paper questionnaire in Spanish. Historically, these requests for Spanish language questionnaires have comprised less than 1 percent of those in the mail phase, which is approximately 200 questionnaires per panel (Fish, 2013). Furthermore, additional support may be requested for Chinese and Korean speakers in the form of language assistance guides. These guides contain full translations of the questionnaires, which are useful for both respondents and interviewers. Bilingual interviewers are hired for the CATI and CAPI phases. Although the CATI and CAPI instruments are in English and Spanish,

Table 3-1. American Community Survey modes of survey administration and languages per mode

Mode	Language of Questionnaire/Interview
Internet (via mail sample)	English or Spanish
Mail	English or Spanish (if requested)
Telephone[a] (via mail sample)	English, Chinese, Korean, Russian, Spanish, and Vietnamese
CATI and CAPI	Instrument in English and Spanish Personal interviews provided in Arabic, Chinese, English, French, German, Greek, Haitian Creole, Italian, Japanese, Korean, Navajo, Polish, Portuguese, Russian, Spanish, Tagalog, Urdu, and Vietnamese[b]

CATI = computer-assisted telephone interview; CAPI = computer-assisted personal interview.

[a] Support provided by calling TQA (telephone questionnaire assistance).

[b] This list depends on the capabilities of bilingual interview staff.

bilingual staff have been able to conduct interviews in more than 30 languages other than English, including Arabic, Chinese, French, German, Greek, Haitian Creole, Italian, Japanese, Korean, Navajo, Polish, Portuguese, Russian, Spanish, Tagalog, Urdu, and Vietnamese. The efficacy of the ACS Language Assistance program, with regard to bridging language barriers, is of considerable interest. In 2005, Griffin (2006) found that bilingual interviewers were well used, interviewing 86 percent of all Spanish-speaking households and 8 percent of Chinese-speaking households who received the CAPI mode.

Language Use and Data Quality

The consistent use of three language questions in the decennial censuses and the ACS has provided useful time series data on the dynamic state of language use in the United States. These questions are part of the person-level sections of the ACS. As shown in Figure 3-1, the first question asks, "Does this person speak a language other than English at home?" with a binary response choice of "yes" or "no." If the respondent answers "yes," the following question asks, "What is this language?" and is accompanied by a one-word open-ended write-in box. Finally, the questionnaire asks, "How well does this person speak English?" with a 4-point Likert response scale with "very well," "well," "not well," and "not at all" as options. Although Singer and Ennis (2002) found that respondents' self-assessment of their proficiency was highly variable, for each housing unit, values were obtained by aggregating the responses from individuals living in the unit.

This chapter explores the effects of three factors on data quality: the household language (HHL), whether the unit is limited English-speaking status (LNGI), and what mode the unit used to respond to the ACS (RESMODE). Although thousands of languages are spoken in the United States, the HHL variable is condensed into five major language groups: English, Spanish, Other Indo-European, Asian and Pacific Island, and a final group that encompasses other languages. Let us further classify the latter four groups as language-other-than-English (LOTE) households. A housing unit may then be categorized as limited English-speaking status, formerly known as "linguistically isolated" until 2010, if no member of the household 14 years old or older (1) speaks only English or (2) speaks a non-English language and speaks English "very well." This distinction is important because it indicates housing units that need additional assistance with English outside of their homes. Because of the varying language support provided for the ACS, we

Figure 3-1. A reproduction of the language questions from the 2017 American Community Survey

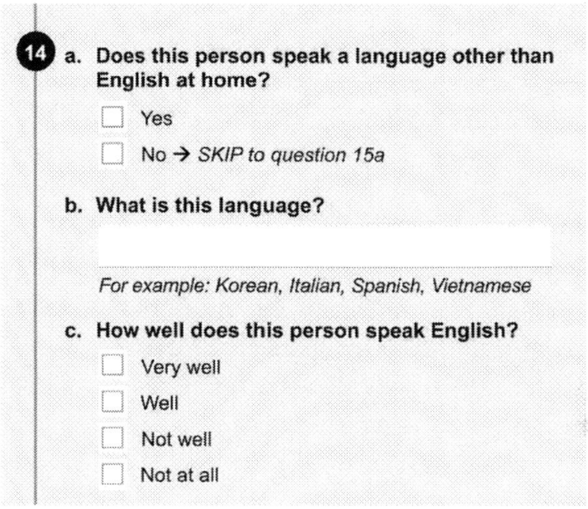

14 a. **Does this person speak a language other than English at home?**

☐ Yes

☐ No → *SKIP to question 15a*

b. **What is this language?**

For example: Korean, Italian, Spanish, Vietnamese

c. **How well does this person speak English?**

☐ Very well

☐ Well

☐ Not well

☐ Not at all

Source: US Census Bureau (2019).

would expect to see differential language distributions across the modes of survey administration coded as mail, CATI/CAPI, and Internet. McGovern and Griffin (2003) demonstrated that "linguistically isolated" households are less likely to respond by mail than households speaking English only. This finding is especially true for Spanish linguistically isolated households, which respond at greater rates when interview modes are used. Ideally, the effects of different questionnaires and interview translations used by the ACS could be studied; however, currently the PUMS does not contain a variable that distinguishes in which language the survey was completed. A proxy variable can be created for this by assuming that LOTE households that have LEP will choose to respond in their preferred language when it is available. Although this is not necessarily true, research suggests that a respondent may be more likely to respond if the mode of communication is in their language (Chan & Pan, 2011).

In this setting, we focus on data quality by assessing item nonresponse and response distribution. The occurrence of an item nonresponse in the ACS data record can be deduced by whether a value needed to be imputed to create a complete data record. Two types of imputation methods can be used: assignment and allocation. In the assignment case, the missing value can be derived by taking logical steps from other provided responses within the questionnaire. If logical assignment cannot be used, allocation can be performed, which uses hot-deck or nearest neighbor imputation (Chen & Shao, 2000; Lohr, 2019). Allocation indicators for each item are built into the PUMS data and are used to calculate their respective item allocation rates. Furthermore, examining whether distributions vary across items and across different modes of administration may provide evidence for mode effect that can be detrimental to longitudinal comparisons and even render trends inestimable.

Methods

This chapter uses the 1-year national PUMS data records at the household level from 2006 through 2017 to study trends in language diversity and prevalence over time and space, the effects of non-English-speaking households on data quality, and how they interact with the effect of survey mode of administration. We combined 12 years of PUMS data to expand on the work of McGovern and Griffin (2003), which originally used data from the Census 2000 Supplemental Survey and the 2001 Supplementary Survey to ask (1) which languages have the greatest numbers of linguistically isolated households, (2) how linguistically isolated households were interviewed, and (3) how complete the data collected from linguistically isolated households were. The novelty and contribution of our work lie in the graphical tools and statistical modeling techniques that account for the complexities of the sample to identify and test for trends within these data.

Comma-separated values (CSV) files for each year of PUMS data for households and individuals are approximately 1 and 4 gigabytes, respectively. Thus, combining several years of data quickly exhausts the capabilities of many statistical computing software tools. Because of the size of these data, we used data wrangling and split-apply-combine techniques for big data (Wickham, 2011). In addition, thoughtful consideration was given to constructing data visualization tools to illuminate spatial and temporal trends, particularly for subgroups, in an exploratory data analysis (EDA) (Tufte, 2001). Choropleths were created by joining Census TIGER/Line shapefiles (Walker, 2019) using GEOIDs geographic identifiers at the PUMA level with 2017 PUMS data to visualize the language diversity distribution across the United States. Finally, all statistical modeling was done in R with the survey package to incorporate the complex survey design and weighting structure (Lumley, 2011). A survey design object must first be declared to employ further survey model functionality. This object contains the data as well as the sampling design and weights. Although a household weighting factor variable (WGTP) was contained in the dataset for calculating aggregate statistics, it alone was not sufficient for estimating standard errors. These household weights align demographic characteristics with those determined by the Population Estimates Program of the Census Bureau. Thus, to compute the proper standard errors to use for inference, such as hypothesis testing and confidence interval construction in this complex setting (Binder, 1983), we used a replicate weight methodology. This methodology is akin to resampling techniques, such as the bootstrap, that enable the estimation of variability for a statistic by obtaining multiple samples from a single sample, while still retaining information about the complex survey design (Asparouhov & Muthén, 2010). Eighty columns of replicate weights (WGTP1–WGTP80) were provided with the PUMS data using the successive differences replication (SDR) method (Fay & Train, 1995; Judkins, 1990). The standard error equation for a statistic X using the SDR method is given by

$$SE(X) = \sqrt{C_r \sum_{r=1}^{R} (X_r - X)^2}$$

where there are R replicate estimates of the statistic X_r and $C_r = 4/R$ is a multiplier that scales the variance. For the PUMS data, $R = 80$ and $C_r = 4/80 = 0.05$, which is referred to as the scale in R. Although we used SDR to construct the weights, it is available in neither SAS nor R. However, the jackknife method for variance estimation can be used instead because it is similar and widely available (Dirmyer, 2017; Keathley, Navarro, & Asiala, 2010). This weighting scheme can be coded into R for the PUMS data to define the survey design object (Figure 3-2). Note the use of regular expressions, or regex, to manipulate strings (Friedl, 2006). In this case, regex is used to identify column names for the 80 replicate weights.

Once the survey design object has been defined, the effects are estimated, tested, and modeled with functions built into the survey package, such as svytotal, svyby, svychisq, and svyglm. It should be made clear that the data collected were not from experiments, that is, respondents were not randomly assigned to modes or languages. Therefore, the results of all modeling should be interpreted with caution. We sought to understand patterns inherent in the sample without making causal or broad inferences. For instance, the Rao-Scott adjusted chi-squared test was used to assess the significance of the

Figure 3-2. Segment of R code specifying a survey design object using the survey package

```
svrepdesign(weights = ~WGTP,
 repweights = 'WGTP[1-9]+',
 scale = 4/80,
 rscales = ncol('WGTP[1-9]+'),
 mse = T,
 combined.weights = T,
 type = 'JK1',
 data = PUMS)
```

difference in mode of response across language groups, while accounting for the complex nature of the sample (Rao & Scott, 1981, 1984; Scott, 2007). Although contingency tables are useful for determining associations between two categorical variables, they do not allow for modeling relationships involving multiple covariates simultaneously. Survey generalized linear models (GLMs) are used to model the main effects of mode and household language, as well as their interactions, which are all treated as factors. Interactions in statistical models occur when the effect of one or more variables depends on the level of another variable. In addition, survey GLMs are different from traditional GLMs because they account for weighting and complex sampling in coefficient and standard error estimation. Survey GLMs can be used for both numeric and binary responses, and both numeric and binary approaches can be used to model the allocation indicators or overall allocation scores. When modeling allocation indicator variables, a survey logistic regression technique was used with a quasibinomial family (Morel, 1989). In addition, we computed an allocation rate for each individual household by taking the ratio between the number of imputed values and the number of items with eligible responses (i.e., non-NA values). These rates were used as a response variable and are considered to be independent within and across years.

Results

Exploratory Data Analysis

First, using the most currently accessible data, we sought to understand the trends in language diversity and prevalence from 2006 through 2017 and the distribution of non-English speakers across the country. Using weighted values, we estimated that the number of households speaking a LOTE increased 17.3 percent from 2006 through 2017, for a total of 25.8 million households (Figure 3-3, Left). This continual increase is largely driven by a 16.9 percent increase in the number of Spanish-speaking households (to 14.7 million), which is by far the largest LOTE group. Although the Indo-European languages group remains the second largest non-English-speaking group, its membership has stagnated at around 5.2 million households. Conversely, the number of Asian/Pacific Islander language households has shown the greatest increase (34.3 percent, to 4.4 million). In addition, if we consider only households that have LEP status, we see very different trends (Figure 3-3, Right). Overall, the number of LEP households has been relatively stable around 5.3 million. However, both Spanish and Indo-European LEP numbers experienced slight 8 percent decreases to 3.2 million and 0.8 million households, respectively. In contrast, the number of Asian/Pacific Islander LEP households increased by 20 percent, to 1.1 million, surpassing Indo-European as the second most common LOTE-LEP language group. Although we computed 95 percent confidence intervals for all of the total estimates and illustrated significant differences between all estimates, we omitted them from the plot for ease of comparison and trend identification.

Choropleth maps using US PUMAs revealed spatial relationships for both language and LEP in 2017. The most popular language spoken other than

Figure 3-3. Trends in language diversity and prevalence and distribution of non-English speakers across the country, 2006–2017

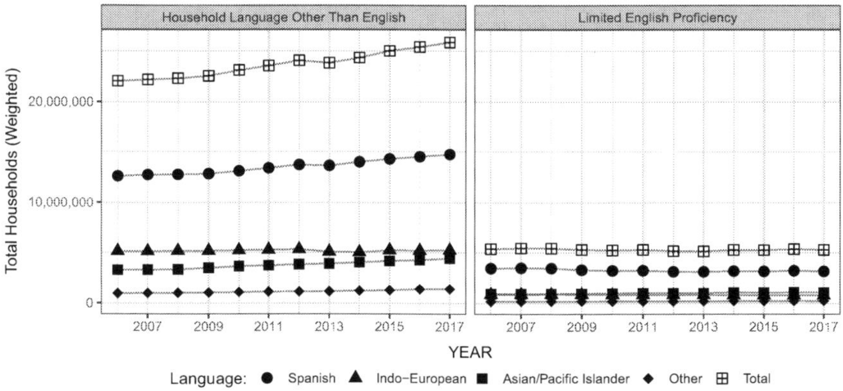

(Left) Weighted totals of non-English-speaking households from 2006 through 2017 show that the overall increase was driven predominantly by increases in Spanish and Asian/Pacific Islander language speaking households.
(Right) Considering only households with LEP status, the weighted totals of households split by language group appear to be relatively constant from 2006 through 2017.

English was computed for each PUMA (Figure 3-4). It is immediately evident that Spanish is the most common LOTE across PUMAs. There is also a clear pattern of Indo-European languages being most commonly spoken in many PUMAs starting in the Northeast and continuing throughout the Midwest.

Furthermore, the distribution of LEP household counts by PUMA has a strong left skew: LEP households are mainly concentrated along the Southern border and in large metropolitan cities (Figure 3-5). These graphics may help provide an indication of areas in need of linguistic support.

Statistical Modeling

The statistical models we used incorporated weighting and a complex sampling design, which highlighted the significant effect that household language has on both mode choice and data quality via allocation rates. The distribution of the four sequential modes (Internet, mail, CATI, and CAPI), which are associated with varying degrees of language assistance, follows a natural pattern for the language groups. For instance, Chinese speakers are more likely to respond to modes that offer Chinese assistance (Chan & Pan, 2011). We calculated conditional probability distributions for each language group within each year to emphasize these differences (Figure 3-6). In general, these distributions show mail to be the most popular mode of response until 2013, when it was overtaken by the Internet mode; however, this is not the case

Figure 3-4. Choropleth map of Public Use Microdata Areas colored by the most popular language group other than English, using 2017 Public Use Microdata Sample data

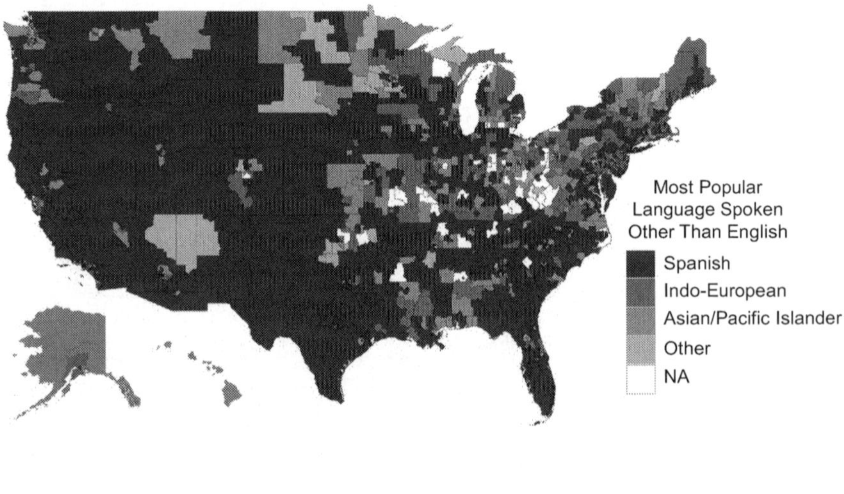

Figure 3-5. Choropleth map of Public Use Microdata Areas shaded by the number of limited English proficiency households, using 2017 Public Use Microdata Sample data

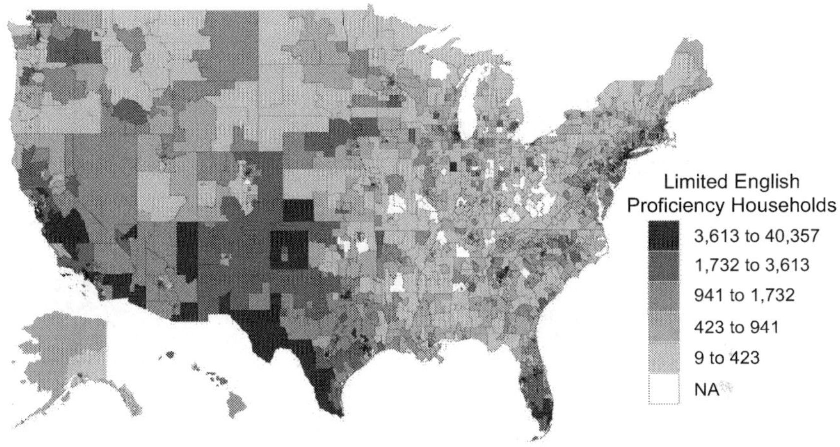

for Spanish-speaking households. For these households, the interview methods (CATI and CAPI) are used at a much higher rate than for the other language groups. This difference drives the significance in the Rao-Scott adjusted chi-squared tests comparing response modes against household language for all years, which all resulted in *p* values less than .0001.

English proficiency was then added to induce additional dimensionality and perspective on conditional mode distribution across language groups (Figure 3-7). The interaction of English proficiency and household language

Figure 3-6. Conditional distributions for response mode across each language group and year have significant differences

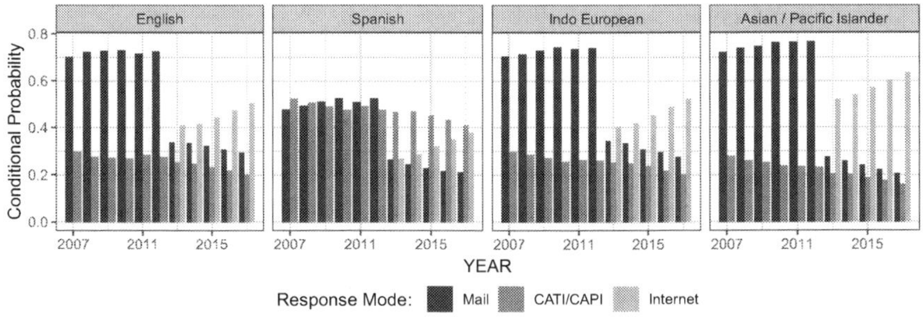

CATI = computer-assisted telephone interview; CAPI = computer-assisted personal interview.

Figure 3-7. Conditional distributions on both household language and English proficiency exhibit significantly different modes of response distributions

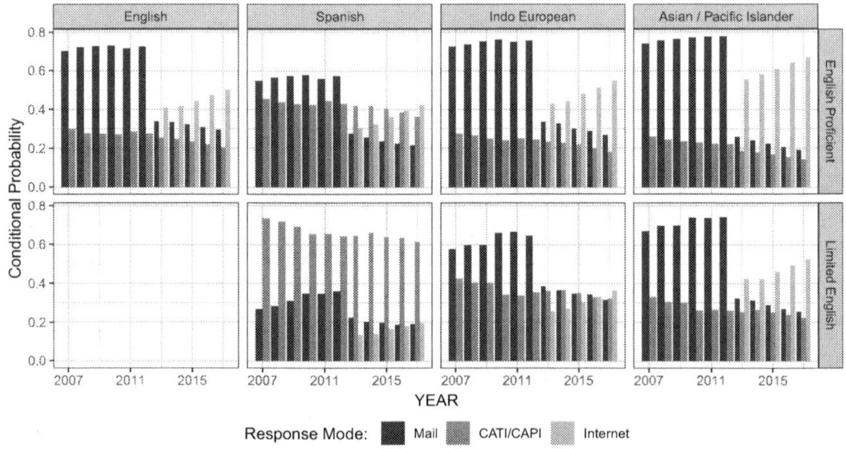

CATI = computer-assisted telephone interview; CAPI = computer-assisted personal interview.

proves to be significant in predicting mode of response. For instance, Spanish LEP households favor interview modes or, rather, do not respond to the self-administered modes of mail and Internet with a clear majority.

Finally, when modeling allocation rates, we found many significant effects for household language and English proficiency levels for both main effects and their interaction. Lower allocation rates are viewed as favorable because they suggest that there is less need for imputation and thus fewer missing data. Estimated marginal means with 95 percent confidence intervals show surprising patterns in allocation rates over time (Figure 3-8). When comparing mail and the CATI/CAPI modes that have existed since the start of the ACS, we see that neither mode is dominant across all language groups and times. Initially, respondents from the mail mode have the lowest average allocation rates, but the lowest average allocation rate shifts to CATI/CAPI after 2012. However, again we observe that Spanish LEP households have the highest allocation rates in the mail mode compared with all other groups and combinations throughout the study from 2006 through 2017. Lower allocation rates for this group may be observed in the CATI/CAPI group because of the aid of bilingual interviewers. In addition, the data first include the Internet response mode in 2013, which clearly has the best allocation rate.

Figure 3-8. Average allocation rates across household language groups split by mode of response and level of English proficiency with bands for 95 percent confidence intervals

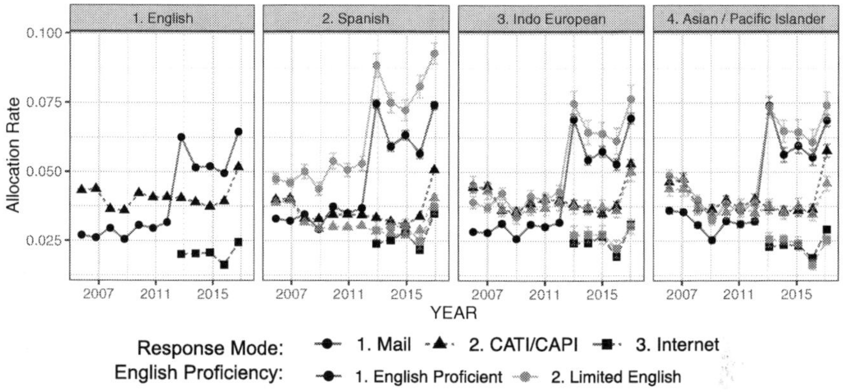

CATI = computer-assisted telephone interview; CAPI = computer-assisted personal interview.
Note: Mode types are distinguished with different symbols, whereas the level of English proficiency is shaded.

This finding could be because the Internet questionnaires have programmed skips to help respondents navigate the survey properly.

English language with the mail mode of response was used as the baseline group for comparison in all models (Tables 3-2 and 3-3). From 2006 through 2012, the CATI/CAPI mode had significantly higher allocation rates, which reversed from 2013 through 2017, when its allocation rates were significantly lower. The effect of Internet mode on allocation rates was significantly lower in all years. In addition, the main effects for all language groups other than English showed significantly higher allocation rates than their English counterparts.

The effects of the interactions between household language and response mode on allocation rates were less consistent, but all estimates had negative point estimates. This result affirms the efforts of the Census Bureau to provide sufficient language assistance, especially by hiring and training bilingual interviewers to better acquire responses. Moreover, although it would have been informative to include an indicator for English proficiency to test for its main effect, two-way interactions, and the three-way interaction, this model did not converge.

Table 3-2. Coefficient estimates for main effects and interactions of household languages and response modes both treated as factors from 2006 through 2012

Coefficients		Effect Estimates						
Response Mode	**Household Language**	**2006**	**2007**	**2008**	**2009**	**2010**	**2011**	**2012**
(Intercept)		0.027	0.026	0.029	0.026	0.031	0.030	0.031
CATI/CAPI	—	0.016 ***	0.017 ***	0.007 ***	0.010 ***	0.012 ***	0.011 ***	0.009 **
—	Spanish	0.008 ***	0.008 ***	0.007 ***	0.006 ***	0.009 ***	0.008 ***	0.008 ***
—	Indo-European	0.003 ***	0.003 ***	0.003 ***	0.001 **	0.002 ***	0.002 ***	0.001 ***
—	Asian/Pacific Islander	0.012 ***	0.012 ***	0.004 ***	0.002 ***	0.003 ***	0.003 ***	0.002 ***
—	Other	0.008 ***	0.009 ***	0.007 ***	0.005 ***	0.006 ***	0.007 ***	0.008 ***
CATI/CAPI	Spanish	–0.012 ***	–0.012 ***	–0.011 ***	–0.010 ***	–0.018 ***	–0.015 ***	–0.015 ***
CATI/CAPI	Indo-European	–0.001	–0.002 **	–0.003 ***	–0.002 *	–0.006 ***	–0.003 ***	–0.003 ***
CATI/CAPI	Asian/Pacific Islander	–0.010 ***	–0.010 ***	–0.003 **	–0.002 *	–0.007 ***	–0.006 ***	–0.004 ***
CATI/CAPI	Other	–0.004 *	–0.007 ***	–0.005 **	–0.005 **	–0.010 ***	–0.011 ***	–0.010 ***

CATI = computer-assisted telephone interview; CAPI = computer-assisted personal interview.

Significance codes for *p* values: *** = 0; ** = .001; * = .01; '.' = .05; ' ' = .1.

Note: Standard errors were computed with a jackknife procedure and repeated weights.

Table 3-3. Coefficient estimates for main effects and interactions of household languages and response modes both treated as factors from 2013 through 2017

Coefficients		Effect Estimates				
Response Mode	**Household Language**	**2013**	**2014**	**2015**	**2016**	**2017**
(Intercept)		0.062	0.051	0.052	0.049	0.064
CATI/CAPI	—	−0.022 ***	−0.013 ***	−0.015 ***	−0.010 ***	−0.013 ***
Internet	—	−0.042 ***	−0.031 ***	−0.031 ***	−0.033 ***	−0.040 ***
—	Spanish	0.014 ***	0.010 ***	0.013 ***	0.011 ***	0.013 ***
—	Indo-European	0.007 ***	0.004 ***	0.006 ***	0.005 ***	0.006 ***
—	Asian/Pacific Islander	0.011 ***	0.007 ***	0.009 ***	0.007 ***	0.006 ***
—	Other	0.014 ***	0.012 ***	0.011 ***	0.014 ***	0.016 ***
CATI/CAPI	Spanish	−0.023 ***	−0.019 ***	−0.020 ***	−0.018 ***	−0.017 ***
Internet	Spanish	−0.010 ***	−0.005 ***	−0.005 ***	−0.005 ***	−0.002 *
CATI/CAPI	Indo-European	−0.010 ***	−0.007 ***	−0.008 ***	−0.007 ***	−0.005 ***
Internet	Indo-European	−0.003 **	0.000	0.000	−0.001	0.000
CATI/CAPI	Asian/Pacific Islander	−0.014 ***	−0.011 ***	−0.010 ***	−0.011 ***	−0.003 *
Internet	Asian/Pacific Islander	−0.008 ***	−0.004 **	−0.006 ***	−0.005 ***	−0.002
CATI/CAPI	Other	−0.018 ***	−0.016 ***	−0.016 ***	−0.018 ***	−0.017 ***
Internet	Other	−0.007 **	−0.005 *	−0.003	−0.008 **	−0.005

CATI = computer-assisted telephone interview; CAPI = computer-assisted personal interview.

Significance codes for p values: *** = 0; ** = .001; * = .01; '.' = .05; ' ' = .1.

Standard errors were computed with a jackknife procedure and repeated weights. Note the inclusion of the Internet mode.

Discussion and Limitations

The implications of these findings both support the work of the US Census Bureau Language Assistance Program and offer insight into areas on which to focus additional effort. The results of this study reinforce the findings of McGovern and Griffin (2003), while providing a perspective on spatial and temporal trends. Overall, resounding evidence suggests that there is a relationship between household language and mode of response to the ACS. Interactions between these effects then carry forward to influence allocation rates. Yet we should be cautious when communicating inference from these statistical models because of a lack of randomness in mode assignment. As stated in the design and methodology, survey modes are offered to respondents in succession from the Internet mode, to mail, then to CATI, and, finally, CAPI. Brochures are offered in multiple languages that provide non-English-speaking respondents with additional resources, such as a toll-free TQA phone number for assistance in their language or directions for how to obtain language guides or a printed Spanish questionnaire. However, this approach makes the strong assumption that those selected for contact are willing to perform additional steps to receive help. The validity of this assumption is challenged by the clear difference in mode of response distribution across languages. Therefore, the effect of household language and English proficiency may be confounded with mode of response. In addition to the lack of mode assignment, there may be a bias in the estimation of mode effect for the mail group because respondents who answer the questionnaire over the phone by calling the TQA number are included in the mail group and not separated into the CATI group or a separate telephone group. This mixing of interview and self-administer type modes may create distinctly different responses for subgroups within the mail group. Furthermore, care should be given when including additional socioeconomic variables in the model that may be correlated with language groups that commonly represent distinct demographic groups.

Conclusion

The work presented in this chapter provides a quantitative perspective on sociolinguistics in cross-cultural survey studies. As a result of increases and shifts in language diversity in the United States, the work of the Census Bureau has followed suit to provide increased accessibility for minority language speakers in the decennial census and the ACS. However, providing translations is not as simple as a lexical change but rather requires consideration of cultural communication norms and experience. It is these cultural differences that may adversely affect data quality, which is particularly evident across different modes of survey administration resulting in mode effect. The social engagement with an interviewer has been found to both positively and negatively affect data quality measures such as nonresponse and measurement error (Lavrakas, 2008). In the ACS, allocation rates represent the proportion of missing answers for an individual and are used as the metric for item nonresponse.

Using the publicly available microdata for the ACS, we have shown that the sequential aspect of survey mode phases and varying degrees of translation aid across modes led to significant differences in mode distribution across language groups throughout the course of the study from 2006 through 2017. The self-selection of mode and lack of random assignment may cause confounding of language and cultural subgroups with mode. Assuming identifiability, statistical models show that allocation rates are significantly lower for English speakers overall, but the interaction between whether a household speaks English and interview modes tends to improve their allocation rates compared with their language counterparts who chose to respond to the ACS by mail. However, allocation rates for the mail group after 2012 also appear to trend upward unexpectedly.

These data provide a wealth of fruitful opportunities for continued research in this area, for instance, joining the PUMS population and housing data sets to yield an additional depth of information. Comparing allocation rates for housing and personal items across modes and languages would be interesting. Beyond allocation rates, understanding the effects of language and modes on response distributions would shed light on possible sources of measurement error for personal and housing questionnaire items. In addition, a variable could be created to classify the different question types, such as check box, radio button, or fill in, for each item to compare how allocation rates and response distributions vary in these settings. Furthermore, all of these topics can incorporate spatial and temporal features to assess trends.

References

Akresh, I. R., Massey, D. S., & Frank, R. (2014). Beyond English proficiency: Rethinking immigrant integration. *Social Science Research*, *45*, 200–210.

Alba, R., Logan, J., Lutz, A., & Stults, B. (2002). Only English by the third generation? Loss and preservation of the mother tongue among the grandchildren of contemporary immigrants. *Demography*, *39*(3), 467–484.

Asiala, M. (2005). American Community Survey research report: Differential sub-sampling in the computer assisted personal interview sample selection in areas of low cooperation rates. DSSD 2005 American Community Survey Documentation Memorandum Series #ACS05-DOC2. Washington, DC: US Census Bureau.

Asparouhov, T., & Muthén, B. (2010). Resampling methods in Mplus for complex survey data. *Structural Equation Modeling, 14*(4), 535–569.

Bates, L. (2013). Editing the MAF extracts and creating the unit frame universe for the American Community Survey. DSSD 2013 American Community Survey Universe Creation Memorandum Series #ACS13-UC-1. Washington, DC: US Census Bureau.

Bean, F. D., & Stevens, G. (2003). *America's newcomers and the dynamics of diversity.* New York, NY: Russell Sage Foundation.

Binder, D. A. (1983). On the variances of asymptotically normal estimators from complex surveys. *International Statistical Review/Revue Internationale de Statistique, 51*(3), 279–292.

Bowling, A. (2005). Mode of questionnaire administration can have serious effects on data quality. *Journal of Public Health, 27*(3), 281–291.

Carrasco, L. (2003). The American Community Survey (ACS) en Español: Using cognitive interviews to test the functional equivalency of questionnaire translations. *Survey Methodology, 2003*, 17.

Chan, A. Y., & Pan, Y. (2011). The use of cognitive interviewing to explore the effectiveness of advance supplemental materials among five language groups. *Field Methods, 23*(4), 342–361.

Chen, J., & Shao, J. (2000). Nearest neighbor imputation for survey data. *Journal of Official Statistics, 16*(2), 113.

De Leeuw, E. D. (1992). *Data quality in mail, telephone and face to face surveys.* Plantage Doklaan, Amsterdam: TT Publikaties.

De Leeuw, E. D., Hox, J. J., Dillman, D. A., & European Association of Methodology. (2008). *International handbook of survey methodology.* New York, NY: Lawrence Erlbaum Associates.

Dillman, D. (1978). *Mail and telephone surveys: The total design method.* New York, NY: John Wiley and Sons.

Dillman, D. A., Smyth, J. D., & Christian, L. M. (2014). *Internet, phone, mail, and mixed-mode surveys: The tailored design method.* New York, NY: John Wiley & Sons.

Dirmyer, R. (2017, April). The truth is out there: Leveraging census data using PROC SURVEYLOGISTIC. Paper presented at SAS Global Forum 2017, Orlando, FL. Retrieved from http://support.sas.com/resources/papers/proceedings17/0802-2017.pdf

Fay, R. E., & Train, G. F. (1995). Aspects of survey and model-based postcensal estimation of income and poverty characteristics for states and counties. In *Proceedings of the Section on Government Statistics* (pp. 154–159). Alexandria, VA: American Statistical Association.

Fish, S. (2013, December 17). Percent of Spanish questionnaire requests out of mailout sample. 2013 American Community Survey Office, Special Studies Staff Memorandum Series #SSS13-3. Washington, DC: US Census Bureau.

Friedl, J. E. (2006). *Mastering regular expressions.* Sebastopol, CA: O'Reilly Media.

Genkova, P. (2015). Methodical problems in cross cultural studies: Equivalence—An overview. *Psychology, 5*(5), 338–346.

Goerman, P., Caspar, R., Sha, M., McAvinchey, G., & Quiroz, R. (2007). *Census bilingual questionnaire research final round 2 report.* Statistical Research Division Report Series No. SSM2007/27. Suitland, MD: US Census Bureau.

Griffin, D. (2006). *Requests for alternative language questionnaires.* American Community Survey Discussion Paper. Washington, DC: US Census Bureau.

Groves, R. M. (1987). Research on survey data quality. *Public Opinion Quarterly, 51,* S156–S172.

Groves, R. M. (2004). *Survey errors and survey costs* (Vol. 536). New York, NY: John Wiley & Sons.

Groves, R. M., & Couper, M. P. (2012). *Nonresponse in household interview surveys.* New York, NY: John Wiley & Sons.

Harkness, J., Pennell, B. E., & Schoua-Glusberg, A. (2004). Survey questionnaire translation and assessment. In S. Presser, J. Rothgeb, M. Couper, J. Lessler, E. Martin, J. Martin, & E. Singer (Eds.), *Methods for testing and evaluating survey questionnaires* (pp. 453–473). Hoboken, NJ: John Wiley & Sons.

Harkness, J., & Schoua-Glusberg, A. (1998). Questionnaires in translation. *ZUMA-Nachrichten Spezial, 3*, 87–127.

Johnson, T. P. (1998). Approaches to equivalence in cross-cultural and cross-national survey research. *ZUMA-Nachrichten Spezial, 3*, 2–40. Retrieved from http://www.gesis.org/fileadmin/upload/forschung/publikationen/zeitschriften/zuma_nachrichten_spezial/znspezial3.pdf

Johnson, T. P., & Van de Vijver, F. J. (2003). Social desirability in cross-cultural research. *Cross-Cultural Survey Methods, 325*, 195–204.

Joshipura, M. (2010, August). Evaluating the effects of a multilingual brochure in the American Community Survey. Paper presented at the *65th Annual American Association for Public Opinion Research Conference.* Chicago, IL.

Judkins, D. R. (1990). Fay's method for variance estimation. *Journal of Official Statistics, 6*(3), 223–239.

Keathley, D., Navarro, A., & Asiala, M. E. (2010). An analysis of alternate variance estimation methods for the American Community Survey group quarters sample. In *JSM Proceedings, Survey Research Methods Section* (pp. 1448–1461). Alexandria, VA: American Statistical Association.

Kinney, S. K., & Karr, A. (2017). Public-use vs. restricted-use: An analysis using the American Community Survey. US Census Bureau Center for Economic Studies Paper No. CES-WP-17-12. Washington, DC: Bureau of the Census.

Lavrakas, P. J. (2008). *Encyclopedia of survey research methods.* Thousand Oaks, CA: SAGE.

Lohr, S. L. (2019). *Sampling: Design and analysis.* Boca Raton, FL: Chapman and Hall/CRC.

Lumley, T. (2011). *Complex surveys: A guide to analysis using R* (Vol. 565). New York, NY: John Wiley & Sons.

McGovern, P. D., & Griffin, D. H. (2003). *Quality assessment of data collected from non- English speaking households in the American Community Survey.* Washington, DC: Bureau of the Census.

Morel, J. G. (1989). Logistic regression under complex survey designs. *Survey Methodology, 15*(2), 203–223.

Mouw, T., & Xie, Y. (1999). Bilingualism and the academic achievement of first-and second- generation Asian Americans: Accommodation with or without assimilation? *American Sociological Review, 64*(2), 232–252.

Ortman, J. M., & Shin, H. B. (2011, August). Language projections: 2010 to 2020. In *Annual meetings of the American Sociological Association* (Vol. 20). Las Vegas, NV: American Sociological Association.

Ortman, J. M., & Stevens, G. (2008, April). Shift happens, but when? Inter- and intragenerational language shift among Hispanic Americans. In *Annual Meetings of the Population Association of America* (pp. 17–19). New Orleans, LA: Population Association of America.

Pan, Y. (2003, November). The role of sociolinguistics in the development and conduct of federal surveys. *Proceedings of the Federal Committee on Statistical Methodology Research Conference* (pp. 1–13). Arlington, VA: Federal Committee on Statistical Methodology.

Pan, Y. (2004). Cognitive interviews in languages other than English: Methodological and research issues. In *JSM Proceedings, Section on Survey Research Methods* (pp. 4859–4865). Alexandria, VA: American Statistical Association.

Pan, Y., & de La Puente, M. (2005). Census Bureau guideline for the translation of data collection instruments and supporting materials: Documentation on how the guideline was developed. *Survey Methodology.* Retrieved from https://www.census.gov/srd/papers/pdf/rsm2005-06.pdf

Pan, Y., & Fond, M. (2014). Evaluating multilingual questionnaires: A sociolinguistic perspective. *Survey Research Methods, 8*(3), 181–194.

Pan, Y., Landreth, A., Park, H., Hinsdale-Shouse, M., & Schoua-Glusberg, A. (2010). Cognitive interviewing in non-English languages: A cross-cultural perspective. In J. A. Harkness, M. Braun, B. Edwards, T. P. Johnson, L. Lyberg, P. Ph. Mohler, B.-E. Pennell, & T. W. Smith (Eds.), *Survey methods in multinational, multiregional, and multicultural contexts* (pp. 91–113). Hoboken, NJ: John Wiley & Sons.

Pan, Y., Leeman, J., Fond, M., & Goerman, P. (2014). Multilingual survey design and fielding: Research perspectives from the US Census Bureau. Survey Methodology, Center for Statistical Research & Methodology Research Report Series (Survey Methodology #2014-01). Washington, DC: US Census Bureau. Retrieved from https://www.census.gov/srd/papers/pdf/RSM2014-01.pdf

Pan, Y., Sha, M. M., Park, H., & Schoua-Glusberg, A. (2009). 2010 Census language program: Pretesting of Census 2010 questionnaire in five languages. Statistical Research Division Research Report Series (Survey Methodology #2009-01). Washington, DC: US Census Bureau.

Park, H., Sha, M. M., & Pan, Y. (2014). Investigating validity and effectiveness of cognitive interviewing as a pretesting method for non-English questionnaires: Findings from Korean cognitive interviews. *International Journal of Social Research Methodology, 17*(6), 643–658.

Prior, R. (2019, April 3). US Census forms to be online in 7 new languages, from Arabic to Tagalog. CNN. Retrieved from www.cnn.com/2019/04/03/us/us-census-languages-trnd/index.html

Rao, J. N., & Scott, A. J. (1981). The analysis of categorical data from complex sample surveys: Chi-squared tests for goodness of fit and independence in two-way tables. *Journal of the American Statistical Association, 76*(374), 221–230.

Rao, J. N., & Scott, A. J. (1984). On chi-squared tests for multiway contingency tables with cell proportions estimated from survey data. *Annals of Statistics, 12*(1), 46–60.

Rumbaut, R. G. (1997). Paradoxes (and orthodoxies) of assimilation. *Sociological Perspectives, 40*(3), 483–511.

Rumbaut, R. G., Massey, D. S., & Bean, F. D. (2006). Linguistic life expectancies: Immigrant language retention in Southern California. *Population and Development Review, 32*(3), 447–460.

Scott, A. (2007). Rao-Scott corrections and their impact. In *JSM Proceedings, Section on Survey Research Methods* (pp.3514–3518). Alexandria, VA: American Statistical Association.

Sha, M., Pan, Y., & Lazirko, B. (2013). Adapting and improving methods to manage cognitive pretesting of multilingual survey instruments. *Survey Practice, 6*(4), 1–8.

Shin, H. B., & Kominski, R. (2010). *Language use in the United States, 2007.* Washington, DC: US Department of Commerce, Economics and Statistics Administration, US Census Bureau.

Singer, P., & Ennis, S. (2002). *Census 2000 content reinterview survey: Accuracy of data for selected population and housing characteristics as measured by reinterview.* Washington, DC: US Census Bureau, Demographic Statistical Methods Division.

Stevens, G. (1999). A century of US censuses and the language characteristics of immigrants. *Demography, 36*(3), 387–397.

Sudman, S., Bradburn, N., Schwarz, N., & Gullickson, T. (1997). Thinking about answers: The application of cognitive processes to survey methodology. *PsycCRITIQUES, 42*(7): 652.

Tourangeau, R., & Smith, T. W. (1996). Asking sensitive questions: The impact of data collection mode, question format, and question context. *Public Opinion Quarterly, 60*(2), 275–304.

Tufte, E. R. (2001). *The visual display of quantitative information* (Vol. 2). Cheshire, CT: Graphics Press.

US Census Bureau. (2002). *Meeting 21st century demographic data needs—Implementing the American Community Survey: Report 2: Demonstrating survey quality.* Washington, DC: US Department of Commerce.

US Census Bureau. (2004). *Meeting 21st century demographic data needs—Implementing the American Community Survey: Report 7: Comparing quality measures: The American Community Survey's three-year averages and Census 2000's long form sample estimates.* Washington, DC: US Department of Commerce.

US Census Bureau. (2012). *Accuracy of the data.* Retrieved from https://www2.census.gov/programs-surveys/acs/tech_docs/accuracy/ACS_Accuracy_of_Data_2012.pdf?#

US Census Bureau. (2014). *American Community Survey design and methodology report.* Retrieved from https://www.census.gov/programs-surveys/acs/methodology/design-and-methodology.html

US Census Bureau. (2015). *Sample size and data quality, American Community Survey.* Retrieved from www.census.gov/acs/www/methodology/sample_size_and_data_quality/

US Census Bureau. (2018). *About PUMS.* Retrieved from www.census.gov/programs-surveys/acs/technical-documentation/pums/about.html

US Census Bureau. (2019). *The American Community Survey questionnaire.* Retrieved December 12, 2019, from https://www2.census.gov/programs-surveys/acs/methodology/questionnaires/2019/quest19.pdf?

Walker, A. H., & Restuccia, J. D. (1984). Obtaining information on patient satisfaction with hospital care: Mail versus telephone. *Health Services Research, 19*(3), 291–306.

Walker, K. (2019). tigris: Load Census TIGER/Line shapefiles. R package version 0.8.2. Retrieved from https://CRAN.R-project.org/package=tigris

Wang, H. L. (2019). For the first time, US census to collect responses in Arabic among 13 languages. NPR. Retrieved from www.npr.org/2019/03/31/629409884/for-the-first-time-u-s-census-to-collect-responses-in-arabic-among-13-languages

Weisberg, H. F. (2009). *The total survey error approach: A guide to the new science of survey research.* Chicago, IL: University of Chicago Press.

Wickham, H. (2011). The split-apply-combine strategy for data analysis. *Journal of Statistical Software, 40*(1), 1–29.

Quantitative Evaluation of Response Scale Translation Through a Randomized Experiment of Interview Language With Bilingual English- and Spanish-Speaking Latino Respondents

Sunghee Lee, Mengyao Hu, Mingnan Liu, and Jennifer Kelley

Introduction

Survey data collection using multiple languages has increased dramatically with a greater interest in research concerning populations that speak different languages. Questionnaire translation, once viewed as only integral for international surveys (e.g., Ervin & Bower, 1952), is now needed even for surveys within a single country. In the United States, for example, it has become a standard practice to conduct surveys in both English and Spanish languages for scientific population-based data collection. Spanish has become a standard interview language in the United States for two reasons. First, the number of Latinos living in the United States has increased sharply. Persons reporting Latino origin grew from 35.3 million to 50.5 million between 2000 and 2010, corresponding to 13 and 16 percent of the total US population, respectively (Ennis, Ríos-Vargas, & Albert, 2011). What sets Latinos apart from non-Latinos is their language use. According to the 2010 American Community Survey, close to 8 out of 10 Latinos aged 5 years or older spoke Spanish at home. Among those who spoke Spanish at home, nearly half reported speaking English less than "very well," which the US Census Bureau uses as a working definition of "linguistically isolated" (Ryan, 2013; Siegel, Martin, Bruno, Martin, & Siegel, 2001; see Chapter 3 for background information on the term "linguistically isolated," now referred to as "limited English speaking"). Second, English proficiency is associated with various educational, economic, health, and social behaviors (Institute of Medicine, 2003; Yu, Nyman, Kogan, Huang, & Schwalberg, 2004). Hence, interviewing only in English incurs unexpected incorrect representation of the US population (Korey & Lascher, 2006; Lee, Nguyen, Jawad, & Kurata, 2008).

While conducting interviews in multiple languages improves the scope of the population covered in a given survey, it also introduces challenges to the measurement properties that are not present in monolingual surveys (Smith, 2009). In a multilingual survey, the differences in responses across languages may reflect not only true differences in the concept that a question seeks to measure but also measurement artifacts due to translation. This chapter introduces a way to evaluate the translation of response scales using an experiment implemented in a questionnaire targeting bilingual English- and Spanish-speaking Latino respondents in the United States.

Translation and Measurement Equivalence

Translation is a necessary and crucial step in multilingual surveys. In most translation practices, a questionnaire is prepared in one language (source language) and then translated into other languages (target languages) (Harkness, 2003). Given that languages are not isomorphic, translation is more than a mechanical process that finds semantically and lexically close texts. It often involves careful adaptation for use in the cultures associated with the target languages. The rationale behind this practice is to retain measurement properties equivalent across languages. Measurement equivalence in multilingual surveys can be described in many ways. For example, Johnson (1998, Table 1) lists 52 types of equivalence ranging from vocabulary equivalence to theoretical equivalence. In this chapter, we use *functional equivalence* to describe measurement equivalence. Per Scheuch (1968), functional equivalence extends beyond comparability in the meaning and implies equivalence for the purpose of analysis. When a question is not functionally equivalent between the source and target languages, the measured construct or concept may not be comparable.

Translation may hamper measurement equivalence in multilingual surveys by affecting respondents' cognitive processes when answering questions. More specifically, translation may affect how respondents interpret the questions, what information they retrieve from their memories, how they use the retrieved information for rendering the appropriate judgment, and finally how they map their judgment onto the response scales (Yan & Hu, 2018).

Translation of Response Scales

Because response scales are closely tied to respondents' cognitive processes, translation of *response scales* is of critical importance (Mohler, Smith, & Harkness, 1998). Given that respondents may perceive the meaning or magnitude of a specific response category in a given response scale specific to each language, translation may affect how respondents interpret and map their answers onto the scale. Because respondents may use the response scales presented with questions to help interpret the meaning of the questions, response scale translation may also affect how respondents understand the questions. Overall, lack of measurement equivalence introduced by response scale translation is likely to distort the response distribution, making analysis noncomparable (Keller et al., 1998).

For a target language, there is no consensus on how to effectively translate response scales. In fact, the extant literature includes frequent observations in which, for a given response scale in the source language, various versions exist in the same target language. The difficulty of translating response scales has been explicitly reported for the Likert agreement scale in Japanese, German, and Swahili. For example, Shishido, Iwai, & Yasuda (2009) reported that "agree" and "disagree" have been translated as *sansei* ("agree") and *hantai* ("disagree") and as *sou omou* ("I think so") and *sou omowanai* ("I don't think so") in Japanese surveys and that Japanese respondents expressed their opinions more clearly on *sou omou* ("I think so") and *sou omowanai* ("I don't think so") than on the other versions. German does not offer a formally matched expression of "disagree"; Hebrew and Swahili do not have a well-matched expression of "neither agree nor disagree" (Harkness, Pennell, & Schoua-Glusberg, 2004; Harkness, Villar, & Edwards, 2010; Yan & Hu, 2018). Similar difficulties are reported for the "excellent-very good-good-fair-poor" response scale, where response categories in a source language are translated differently depending on the target language.

Yan and Hu (2018) examined translations of the "excellent" to "poor" scale in several national surveys. They found that the category "fair" was translated as 一般 ("average") in Chinese, *mittelmäßig* ("middle" or "mediocre") in German, and *ganska dålig* ("somewhat poor") in Swedish, resulting in incomparable results across cultures. Although difficulties of translating response categories are not widely reported for Spanish, some researchers discuss response categories as a source of noncomparability in reports between Latino and non-Latino respondents in the United States (Bzostek,

Goldman, & Pebley, 2007; Kandula, Lauderdale, & Baker, 2007; Viruell-Fuentes, Morenoff, Williams, & House, 2011) and sensitivity of the Likert scale presentation in Spanish (Arce-Ferrer, 2006). Response scale translation may also change the structure of the scales that respondents perceive implicitly (e.g., changing unipolar into bipolar scales and changing balanced scales into unbalanced scales). For example, for the self-rated health question using an "excellent-very good-good-fair-poor" scale, "poor" has been translated into a word meaning "not good" in some surveys and "bad" in other surveys using the same target language (Behr, Dept, & Krajčeva, 2018). As respondents assign meanings to numeric values (Schwarz, Knauper, Hippler, Noelle-Neumann, & Clark, 1991), if we match the translated response categories to numbers, "not good" could be understood as zero on a unipolar scale of goodness, while "bad" could be understood as a negative value on a bipolar scale of bad to good (Yan & Hu, 2018). This structural change may bias the survey estimates because "poor" actually means worse health when translated into a word meaning "bad" rather than "not good."

Translation Evaluation

There are various approaches for evaluating questionnaire translation as discussed in the Cross-Cultural Survey Guidelines published by the University of Michigan. Qualitative approaches, such as experts' review, feedback from translators, cognitive interviews, and behavioral coding (e.g., Dept, Ferrari, & Wäyrynen, 2010; Gordoni & Schmidt, 2010; Hunt & Bhopal, 2004; Willis et al., 2010), are commonly used. Qualitative approaches are the necessary first step to ensuring translation quality, and their dominance reflects practical constraints on resources in survey research (Tourangeau, 2004). Translation evaluation can also take a quantitative approach, which may provide a higher level of generalizability and reproducibility (Harkness et al., 2004). However, quantitative research on translation is rather sparse.

Quantitative approaches for assessing translation can be classified into two categories: (1) experiments designed to collect assessment data and (2) statistical models with existing data. Most quantitative studies use the latter (e.g., Davidov & De Beuckelaer, 2010; Saris, 2003; also see Braun & Johnson, 2010; Van de Vijver, 2003; and Van de Vijver & Leung, 1997 for an overview of the modeling approaches). Data for statistical models may but typically do not involve randomized experiments on translation. While conceivable, experiments with bilingual respondents who are fluent in both source and target languages have been rarely used for translation evaluation (Smith,

2004). When these bilingual respondents are randomly assigned to either language for a survey interview, they are comparable except for the interview language. Hence, equivalence between source and target languages can be tested directly by comparing estimates between languages. Moreover, if there are multiple versions of translation of a particular response scale in a target language, they can also be assessed to compare their levels of equivalence with the source language.

Goal of This Research

To address the need to evaluate response scale translation quantitatively, this chapter uses data from an experiment on interview language conducted in a population-based survey that targeted racial and ethnic minorities in the United States. The interview language experiment was implemented for bilingual Latinos who reported speaking English and Spanish about the same amount of time, providing unique data that allow us to examine measurement equivalence in translated questionnaires quantitatively.

We focused on the translation of quantifier-based ordinal response scales. As noted earlier, translation of these response scales is difficult because they combine both negation and quantification, and the available lexical and structural options for the scales differ across languages (Harkness et al., 2004). Moreover, when translated, the vagueness of quantifiers may elicit nonequivalent measurement structures.

Data and Method

Data Source

We used data from the National Latino and Asian American Study (NLAAS) fielded between May 2002 and November 2003. NLAAS was conducted specifically to overcome the lack of population-based data for Latino and Asian Americans in the United States. Targeting adults aged 18 years old or older in those racial and ethnic groups, the study used a stratified area-probability sampling. To account for high linguistic isolation rates of the target population, NLAAS interviews were conducted in Spanish, Chinese, Vietnamese, and Tagalog in addition to English by fully bilingual interviewers. The questionnaire was first developed in English and translated into other languages. The sample comprised 2,554 Latino and 2,095 Asian American adults. Pennell et al. (2004) and Takeuchi, Gong, and Gee (2012) offered detailed accounts of NLAAS and Alegria et al. (2004) of cultural adaptation and translation processes in NLAAS.

At the beginning of the interview, Latino respondents were asked about their English and Spanish usage. Among them, 827 reported speaking only Spanish, 521 mostly Spanish, 332 Spanish and English about the same amount of time, 627 mostly English, and 227 only English. NLAAS regarded those 332 who reported speaking English and Spanish about the same amount of time as bilingual and randomly assigned them to either Spanish or English for interviews. As a result, 182 bilingual Latino respondents completed interviews in English and 150 in Spanish. This study used data from this interview language experiment. Note that this experiment was implemented only for bilingual Latino respondents.

There were two types of translation for response scales in NLAAS. The first involved translating a scale in English into one version in Spanish. The second type translated a scale in English into two versions in Spanish. (Note that it is unclear from the NLAAS documents whether two Spanish versions for one English scale were designed intentionally.) We labeled the former as "one-on-one translation" and the latter as "one-on-two translation." Most response scales in NLAAS followed one-on-one translation. We chose four response scales in this study for two reasons. First, they are widely used in questionnaires in general. Second, each of the chosen scales was used for multiple questions on the same topic. Having multiple items reduces the chance of misinterpreting an attribute of a single item as evidence for translation equivalence and provides more analysis options.

Under one-on-one translation, we examined two response scales: (1) a 4-point excellent-to-poor scale that translated "excellent-good-fair-poor" into *excelente-bien-regular-pobre* and was used for a set of six language proficiency questions and (2) a 4-point Likert agreement scale that translated "strongly agree-somewhat disagree-strongly disagree" into *mayormente de acuerdo-algo de acuerdo-algo en desacuerdo-mayormente en desacuerdo* and was used for 10 family cohesion questions.

Two response scales fell under the one-on-two translation: (1) a 4-point frequency scale and (2) a 4-point quantity scale. The frequency scale of "often-sometimes-rarely-never" was translated into either *muchas veces-alguna veces-casi nunca-nunca* or *muchas veces-alguna veces-pocas veces-nunca*, using different Spanish words (*casi nunca* or *pocas veces*) for "rarely." The version with *casi nunca* was used for four questions about demands by social networks, while the version with *pocas veces* was used for four immigration and discrimination questions. The English version of the quantity scale was "a lot-some-a little-not at all" and was translated into either *mucho-algo-poco-nada* or *mucho-regular-poco-nada*. "Some" was translated into either *algo* or *regular*. The version with *algo* was used for seven questions on the effects of a terrorist attack, and *regular*was used for four questions about reliance on social networks. With the one-on-two translation, we can examine not only translation equivalence but also comparability in equivalence across translation versions. See Appendix 4-1 for the wording of the questions used in the study. Alegria et al. (2004) documented the backgrounds on how these questions were developed for NLAAS.

Analysis Plan

We analyzed each response scale separately. We first compared response distributions by interview language for each scale and by different Spanish translation versions for the one-on-two translation scales. Similar response distributions between English and Spanish indicate translation equivalence in the first comparison. With one-on-two translation scales, similarities in response distributions between two versions of the Spanish response scales imply that the two translated versions are comparable regardless of their individual equivalence to the English scale. For this, the relative difference in each response category was calculated by dividing the difference in estimates between Spanish and English interviews by the estimates based on English interviews and compared between the two Spanish versions. The Spanish version with smaller relative differences was considered to be more equivalent to the English version. We used a relative difference rather than an absolute difference because the latter does not provide as much information when the response distributions are uneven across response categories (e.g., skewness toward one end or concentration around one category) and illustrates the impact less clearly.

Because each scale was used for multiple topically related questions, we also computed Cronbach's α on each response scale for each language and compared it between interview languages through χ^2 tests, as illustrated in Feldt, Woodruff, and Salih (1987). If translation retained the equivalence, Cronbach's α should not be different between English and Spanish. We also conducted analysis of variance (ANOVA), suggested by Van de Vijver and Leung (1997) as an extension of Cleary and Hilton (1968). This method detects item bias caused by translation. For the ANOVA analysis, we first created a score summary variable for each scale in three steps: summed responses of all topically related items into a total score within a respondent, computed the quartile of the summary score, and assigned each respondent to a quartile. Hence, the score summary variable has four levels. We then modeled responses of each item on two main effects—the interview language and the score summary variable—as well as their interaction. In these models, the score summary variable was not of interest because individual item scores were part of the total score. Instead, the effect of the language was of interest because interview language should not play a role in explaining the variance of individual item scores due to its random assignment. If interview language was significant in the estimated model, it would indicate lack of translation equivalence. This ANOVA approach allowed us to test whether interview language contributed to the variance of the individual item scores, while controlling for the person's standing in the total score. Note that Cronbach's α and the ANOVA approach described here were feasible because each response scale had multiple items on the same topic.

Because sample sizes were relatively small, the focus of the study was not necessarily to detect statistical significance. Rather, it was to demonstrate how such experimental data can be used for evaluating a translation quantitatively. We attempted to understand potential changes in measurement due to translation with commonly used response scales and, when more than one translation version was used, to propose a better version. Because of the experimental nature of the data, the results presented here did not consider population-level weight adjustments.

We note that the randomization of interview language should have produced two groups of respondents with similar characteristics. In comparing sociodemographic characteristics, specifically, age (18–30 years old, 31–50 years old, 51 years old or older), gender (male, female), education (less than high school, high school, some college, college or more), nativity (US born, foreign born), and Latino subgroups (Mexican, Puerto Rican, others), we found most were comparable between the English and Spanish interview language groups. However, the proportion of the age category 18–30 years was not even; there was a larger proportion in the English interview groups compared with the Spanish interview groups (44.0 percent vs. 34.0 percent, $p = .035$, respectively). This discrepancy led us to assume an uneven breakoff pattern by younger respondents interviewed in Spanish. The smaller sample size of the Spanish interviews compared with the English interviews (150 vs. 182) may be indirect evidence. Because there is no information about the breakoffs in the NLAAS data or documents, this assumption was not verified. Instead, to maintain the comparability, we adjusted for any potential differences between language groups with respect to the previously listed characteristics in all analyses by standardizing their marginal distributions using the English group as a benchmark. All analyses were conducted in SAS, except for the comparison of Cronbach's α, which used an R package "cocron" (Diedenhofen & Musch, 2016).

Results

One-on-One Translation

Excellent-to-Poor Scale

How bilingual Latino respondents rated their own speaking, reading, and writing aspects of Spanish and English language proficiency is presented by interview language in Figure 4-1. For all measures except the Spanish writing aspect, respondents interviewed in English chose "excellent" at a consistently higher rate than those interviewed in Spanish. This choice made those interviewed in English appear more proficient in both English and Spanish, even though, in reality, these respondents were comparable in their language use. Although we do not discuss this response scale in this chapter, it is notable that the same pattern emerged for questions on physical and mental health, which used a 5-point excellent-to-poor scale ("excellent-very

Figure 4-1. Distribution of Spanish and English proficiency on speaking, reading, and writing, by interview language

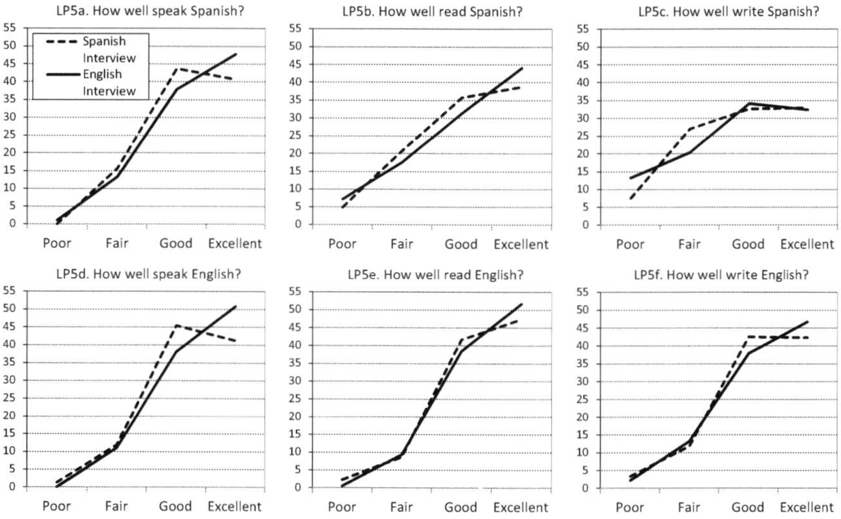

good-good-fair-poor" translated into *excelente-muy-bien-bien-regular-pobre*): bilingual respondents interviewed in English chose "excellent" and "very good" categories at a higher rate than those interviewed in Spanish, making English-language respondents look as though they were healthier than Spanish-language respondents (results not shown).

Given that speaking, reading, and writing aspects all measure the concept of language proficiency, they should be related for a given language. To test this idea, we compared Cronbach's α by interview language. Cronbach's α for Spanish proficiency measured higher among those interviewed in Spanish at .913, compared with .885 among those interviewed in English, but the difference was not statistically significant ($\chi^2 = 1.56$ [$df = 1$]; $p = .212$). For English proficiency measures, Cronbach's α was comparable at .930 and .938 for the Spanish and English interviews, respectively. In the ANOVA models, interview language was significant in explaining English speaking scores as a main effect as well as through an interaction with the score summary. The English reading score was higher for bilingual Latino respondents who were interviewed in English rather than in Spanish. (See Appendix 4-2 for detailed results of all ANOVA models.)

Agreement Scale

On the 4-point agreement scale used for 10 family cohesion questions, the "strongly agree" category was chosen most frequently for both interview languages. However, this tendency was more pronounced for Spanish than English interviews, as shown by comparing proportions of "strongly agree" between languages in Table 4-1. Even with the small sample size, language of interview was significant at $p < .05$ for questions such as "Things work well for us as a family (FC3)" and "We really do trust and confide in each other (FC4)," for which Spanish interviewees used "strongly agree" by 14.8 and 11.5 percentage points higher than English interviewees, respectively, and at $p < .1$ for "We share similar values and beliefs as a family (FC2)" and "Family togetherness is very important (FC10)," with 9.2 and 8.2 percentage point differences, respectively.

Cronbach's α across family cohesion questions was not significantly different between interview languages (.931 for English and .929 for Spanish). Language in ANOVA introduced earlier showed a significant effect on one item (FC3) through an interaction ($p = .016$). Among those in the third and fourth quartiles of the total score, those interviewed in Spanish showed a significantly higher score on this item than those interviewed in English.

Table 4-1. Proportion of "strongly agree" for family cohesion questions, by interview language

Question: Now I'd like to know how strongly you agree or disagree with the following statements about your family.	Interview Language		Difference: Spanish–English	*p* value
	Spanish % (*SE*) *n* = 149	English % (*SE*) *n* = 182		
FC1. Family members respect one another.	70.0 (4.0)	63.7 (3.6)	6.2	.244
FC2. We share similar values and beliefs as a family.	69.1 (4.0)	59.9 (3.6)	9.2	.085
FC3. Things work well for us as a family.	69.7 (4.0)	54.9 (3.7)	14.8	.007
FC4. We really do trust and confide in each other.	71.9 (3.9)	60.4 (3.6)	11.5	.031
FC5. Family members feel loyal to the family.	74.0 (3.9)	66.5 (3.5)	7.5	.149
FC6. We are proud of our family.	82.5 (3.2)	75.8 (3.2)	6.7	.139
FC7. We can express our feelings with our family.	66.6 (4.1)	61.5 (3.6)	5.0	.357
FC8. Family members like to spend free time with each other.	59.5 (4.3)	52.2 (3.7)	7.3	.194
FC9. Family members feel very close to each other.	67.1 (4.1)	65.9 (3.5)	1.2	.830
FC10. Family togetherness is very important.	81.9 (3.3)	73.6 (3.3)	8.2	.078

One-on-Two Translation

Frequency Scale

For the frequency scale of "often-sometimes-rarely-never" where "rarely" was translated into two Spanish versions, *casi nunca* and *pocas veces*, we examined the relative difference for each response category between the English version and each Spanish version and compared the relative differences between the two Spanish versions in Figure 4-2A. The differences were particularly large for the "often" and "sometimes" categories with the Spanish scale using *casi nunca* rather than *pocas veces*. The average of the question-level relative difference was 41.0 percent with *casi nunca* compared with 22.3 percent with *pocas veces*.

While Cronbach's α was not comparable between languages when using *casi nunca* ($\alpha = .688$ vs. $\alpha = .545$ for Spanish and English, respectively; $\chi^2 = 3.41$ [$df = 1$]; $p = .064$), it was comparable with *pocas veces* ($\alpha = .729$ vs. $\alpha = .717$ for Spanish and English, respectively). From ANOVA, the interview language and its interactions with the score summary variable showed a significant effect on three of the four items using *casi nunca* (SN5, SN9, and

Figure 4-2. Percentage relative difference for items with frequency and quantity scales between Spanish and English interviews, by Spanish translation version

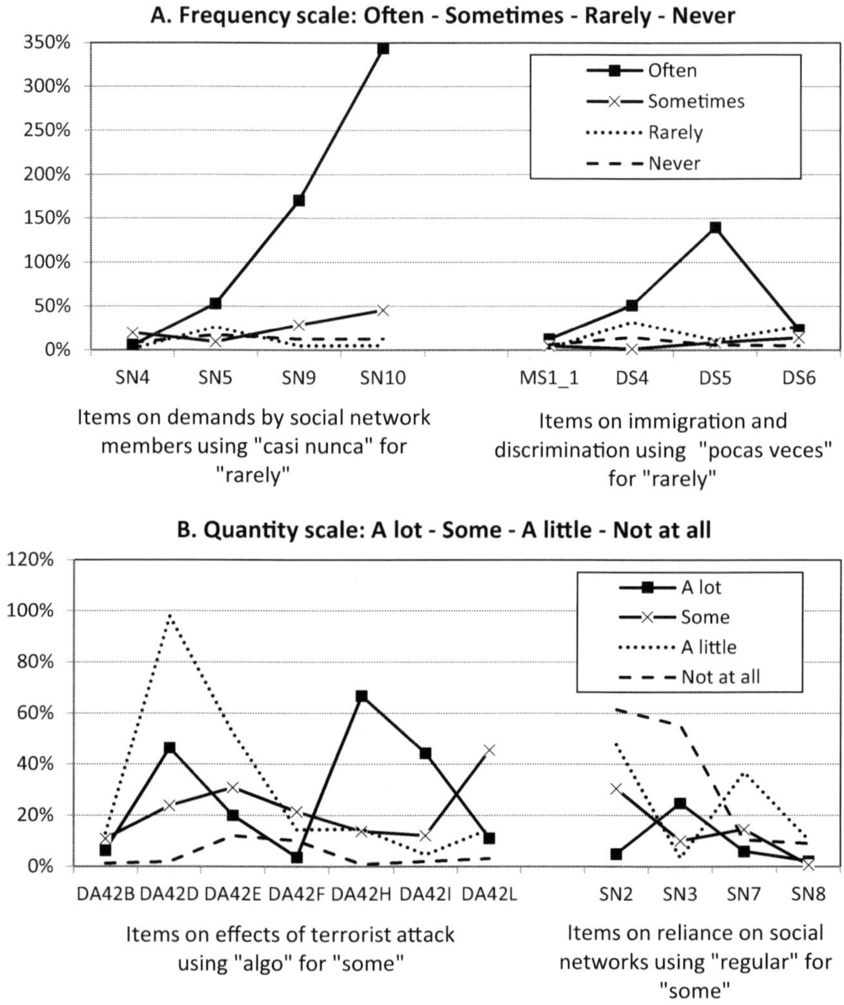

SN10), suggesting item bias due to translation. However, none of the items using the scale with *pocas veces* was subject to a significant language effect.

Quantity Scale

Eleven questions used the "a lot-some-a little-not at all" quantity scale, for which "some" was translated into either *algo* or *regular*. The relative difference reported in Figure 4-2B was consistently larger for the Spanish response scale using *algo* than the scale using *regular*. The overall mean of the relative difference was 31.1 percent for the scale with *algo* and 20.5 percent for the scale with *regular*. The difference in Cronbach's α between English and Spanish interview languages was significant for questions using *algo* ($\alpha = .649$ vs. $\alpha = .758$ for Spanish and English, respectively; $\chi^2 = 4.25$ [$df = 1$]; $p = .039$) but not for *regular* ($\alpha = .678$ vs. $\alpha = .702$ for Spanish and English, respectively). However, based on ANOVA, language showed a significant effect on one item using *algo* (DA42b) as a main effect and one item using *regular* only through its interaction with the score summary variable (SN3).

Discussion

Our analysis illustrates an assessment of measurement equivalence between English and Spanish questionnaires through an experiment that randomized interview language with bilingual English- and Spanish-speaking Latino Americans. Overall, the results show a language effect. On the "excellent-good-fair-poor" scale used for language proficiency questions, bilingual Latinos chose positive responses more frequently when interviewed in English than in Spanish. When interviewed in English, bilingual Latinos' language proficiency in both English and Spanish appeared higher. Clearly, the translated Spanish response scales did not align with the English scale on the continuum of true language proficiency. It could be that *excelente* in Spanish conveys a more desirable state than "excellent" in English.

With the agreement scale used for family cohesion questions, bilingual Latinos reported "strongly agree" at a consistently higher rate when interviewed in Spanish than in English. This trend may be related to extreme response style (ERS). It is hypothesized in the literature that Latinos are more engaged in ERS than non-Latino whites (Hui & Triandis, 1989; Marín, Gamba, & Marín, 1992; Weech-Maldonado, Elliott, Oluwole, Schiller, & Hays, 2008). While our study included only Latinos, it is imaginable that the ERS tendency of Latinos is partially due to the priming effect of the interview language. That is, when interviewed in Spanish as opposed to in English, bilingual Latinos are more likely to exhibit ERS because the Spanish language itself activates Latino-specific cultural norms promoting ERS. Further, the nature of the topic, family cohesion, is more culturally salient to Latinos than non-Latino whites because of *familismo*, one of the important Latino cultural values (Marín & Marín, 1991; Toro-Morn, 2012; Zea,

Quezada, & Belgrave, 1993). Therefore, Latino cultural norms associated with the Spanish language may have influenced how bilingual Latinos responded to questions about family cohesion when these questions were asked in Spanish.

For the "often-sometimes-rarely-never" frequency scale or the "a lot-some-a little-not at all" quantity scale, this study offers quantitative evidence for better translations in Spanish. Between *casi nunca* and *pocas veces* in place of the English category "rarely," the scale with *pocas veces* produced more similar results to English than the scale with *casi nunca*. When choosing a Spanish quantifier for "some" on the "a lot-some-a little-not at all" scale, *regular* appeared somewhat more advantageous for measurement comparability than *algo*.

Of course, for the reasons behind the lack of translation equivalence shown in this chapter, one may argue that bilingual respondents bring in different cultural norms associated with the language they are interviewed in because language primes respondents' cognition (Bond, 1983; Marian & Kaushanskaya, 2004; Ross, Xun, & Wilson, 2002; Trafimow, Silverman, Fan, & Fun Law, 1997; Triandis, Davis, Vassiliou, & Nassiakou, 1965). Research has shown that bilingual people process information differently than monolingual people (Holmes, 2008), which makes it reasonable to conclude that the effect shown in this chapter may be caused by cultural differences combined with linguistic differences. In fact, the purpose of this study was not to distinguish these two. Instead, the interview language effect can be seen as a result of translation, which may activate respondents' cultural norms when they answer survey questions.

Translation is an inherent task for cross-cultural and cross-national research and is a topic that has received much attention from cross-cultural survey researchers. Unfortunately, despite the importance and broad impact, there are many inconsistent translations with no clear guidelines. Still, translation is mostly assessed through qualitative approaches. Smith (2004) recommended quantitatively evaluating the qualitative translation to ensure measurement comparability, which, in turn, lowers the chances of producing misleading results in cross-cultural studies. Similarly, Scheuch (1968) argued that literal equivalence achieved through qualitative translation procedures may not guarantee functional equivalence. This study demonstrated how experimental data with bilingual speakers provide quantifiable and objective evidence, which can enhance translation procedures.

This study has several important implications. First, it shows the importance of response scale translation and its unintended negative effects on measurement equivalence. Direct comparisons of estimates between interview languages may lead to biased results. Second, it shows difficulties with response scale translation. Inconsistent translations (e.g., *algo* or *regular* for "some") can lead to different response distributions. Third, it suggests better translation of some response scales. For instance, "some" on a frequency scale may be better translated using *regular* rather than *algo* in Spanish questionnaires when targeting US Latinos.

Other developments are underway to quantitatively assess translation and to make appropriate adjustments. Approaches such as anchoring vignettes (e.g., Hopkins & King, 2010; Hu, Lee, & Xu, 2018; Van Soest, Delaney, Harmon, Kapteyn, & Smith, 2011), item response theory (e.g., Azocar, Areán, Miranda, & Muñoz, 2001; Ellis, Minsel, & Becker, 1989), and unfolding models (e.g., Javaras & Ripley, 2007) are great examples. If using these approaches, evaluations need to be preplanned because they require specific types of data.

References

Alegria, M., Takeuchi, D., Canino, G., Duan, N., Shrout, P., Meng, X.-L., … Gong, F. (2004). Considering context, place and culture: The National Latino and Asian American Study. *International Journal of Methods in Psychiatric Research, 13*(4), 208–220. Retrieved from http://www.ncbi.nlm.nih.gov/pubmed/15719529

Arce-Ferrer, A. J. (2006). An investigation into the factors influencing extreme-response style. *Educational and Psychological Measurement, 66*(3), 374–392. https://doi.org/10.1177/0013164405278575

Azocar, F., Areán, P., Miranda, J., & Muñoz, R. F. (2001). Differential item functioning in a Spanish translation of the Beck Depression Inventory. *Journal of Clinical Psychology, 57*(3), 355–365.

Behr, D., Dept, S., & Krajčeva, E. (2018). Documenting the survey translation and monitoring process. In T. P. Johnson, B.-E. Pennell, I. Stoop, & B. Dorer (Eds.), *Advances in comparative survey methods: Multinational, multiregional, and multicultural contexts (3MC)* (p. 457–476). Hoboken, NJ: John Wiley & Sons.

Bond, M. H. (1983). How language variation affects inter-cultural differentiation of values by Hong Kong bilinguals. *Journal of Language and Social Psychology, 2*(1), 57–66. https://doi.org/10.1177/0261927X8300200104

Braun, M., & Johnson, T. P. (2010). An illustrative review of techniques for detecting inequivalences. In J. A. Harkness, M. Braun, B. Edwards, T. P. Johnson, L. Lyberg, P. Ph. Mohler, B.-E. Pennell, & T. W. Smith (Eds.), *Survey methods in multinational, multiregional, and multicultural contexts* (pp. 373–393). Hoboken, NJ: John Wiley & Sons.

Bzostek, S., Goldman, N., & Pebley, A. (2007). Why do Hispanics in the USA report poor health? *Social Science & Medicine, 65*(5), 990–1003. https://doi.org/10.1016/J.SOCSCIMED.2007.04.028

Cleary, T. A., & Hilton, T. L. (1968). An investigation of item bias. *Educational and Psychological Measurement, 28*(1), 61–75. https://doi.org/10.1177/001316446802800106

Davidov, E., & De Beuckelaer, A. (2010). How harmful are survey translations? A test with Schwartz's human values instrument. *International Journal of Public Opinion Research, 22*(4), 485–510. https://doi.org/10.1093/ijpor/edq030

Dept, S., Ferrari, A., & Wäyrynen, L. (2010). Developments in translation verification procedures in three multilingual assessments: A plea for an integrated translation and adaptation monitoring tool. In J. A. Harkness, M. Braun, B. Edwards, T. P. Johnson, L. Lyberg, P. Ph. Mohler, B.-E. Pennell, & T. W. Smith (Eds.), *Survey methods in multinational, multiregional, and multicultural contexts* (pp. 157–173). Hoboken, NJ: John Wiley & Sons.

Diedenhofen, B., & Musch, J. (2016). cocron: A web interface and R package for the statistical comparison of Cronbach's alpha coefficients. *International Journal of Internet Science, 11*(1), 51–60.

Ellis, B. B., Minsel, B., & Becker, P. (1989). Evaluation of attitude survey translations an investigation using item response theory. *International Journal of Psychology, 24*(6), 665–684. https://doi.org/10.1080/00207598908247838

Ennis, S. R., Ríos-Vargas, M., & Albert, N. G. (2011). *The Hispanic population: 2010.* Retrieved from http://www.census.gov/prod/cen2010/briefs/c2010br-04.pdf

Ervin, S., & Bower, R. T. (1952). Translation problems in international surveys. *Public Opinion Quarterly, 16*(4), 595. https://doi.org/10.1086/266421

Feldt, L. S., Woodruff, D. J., & Salih, F. A. (1987). Statistical inference for coefficient alpha. *Applied Psychological Measurement, 11*(1), 93–103. https://doi.org/10.1177/014662168701100107

Gordoni, G., & Schmidt, P. (2010). The decision to participate in social surveys: The case of the Arab minority in Israel—An application of the theory of reasoned action. *International Journal of Public Opinion Research, 22*(3), 364–391. https://doi.org/10.1093/ijpor/edq022

Harkness, J. A. (2003). Questionnaire translation. In J. A. Harkness, F. J. R. Van de Vijver, & P. Ph. Mohler (Eds.), *Cross-cultural survey methods* (pp. 35–36). Hoboken, NJ: Wiley-Interscience.

Harkness, J., Pennell, B.-E., & Schoua-Glusberg, A. (2004). Survey questionnaire translation and assessment. In S. Presser, J. Rothgeb, M. Couper, J. Lessler, E. Martin, J. Martin, & E. Singer (Eds.), *Methods for testing and evaluating survey questionnaires* (pp. 453–473). Hoboken, NJ: John Wiley & Sons.

Harkness, J. A., Villar, A., & Edwards, B. (2010). Translation, adaptation, and design. In J. A. Harkness, M. Braun, B. Edwards, T. P. Johnson, L. Lyberg, P. Ph. Mohler, B.-E. Pennell, & T. W. Smith (Eds.), *Survey methods in multinational, multiregional, and multicultural contexts* (pp. 115–140). Hoboken, NJ: John Wiley & Sons.

Holmes, J. (2008). *An introduction to sociolinguistics* (3rd ed.). London, UK: Longman.

Hopkins, D., & King, G. (2010). Improving anchoring vignettes: Designing surveys to correct interpersonal incomparability. *Public Opinion Quarterly, 74*, 201–222.

Hu, M., Lee, S., & Xu, H. (2018). Using anchoring vignettes to correct for differential response scale usage in 3MC surveys. In T. P. Johnson, B.-E. Pennell, I. A. L. Stoop, & B. Dorer (Eds.), *Advances in comparative survey methods: Multinational, multiregional, and multicultural contexts (3MC),* (pp. 181–202). Hoboken, NJ: Wiley.

Hui, C. H., & Triandis, H. C. (1989). Effects of culture and response format on extreme response style. *Journal of Cross-Cultural Psychology, 20*(3), 296–309. https://doi.org/10.1177/0022022189203004

Hunt, S. M., & Bhopal, R. (2004). Self report in clinical and epidemiological studies with non-English speakers: The challenge of language and culture. *Journal of Epidemiology and Community Health, 58*(7), 618–622. https://doi.org/10.1136/jech.2003.010074

Institute of Medicine. (2003). *Unequal treatment: Confronting racial and ethnic disparities in health care*. Washington, DC: National Academies Press. https://doi.org/10.17226/12875

Javaras, K. N., & Ripley, B. D. (2007). An "unfolding" latent variable model for Likert attitude data. *Journal of the American Statistical Association, 102*(478), 454–463. https://doi.org/10.1198/016214506000000960

Johnson, T. P. (1998). Approaches to equivalence in cross-cultural and cross-national survey research. In J. A. Harkness (Ed.), *Cross-cultural survey equivalence. ZUMA-Nachrichten Spezial 3* (pp. 1–40). Mannheim, Germany: ZUMA. Retrieved from https://www.ssoar.info/ssoar/handle/document/49730

Kandula, N. R., Lauderdale, D. S., & Baker, D. W. (2007). Differences in self-reported health among Asians, Latinos, and non-Hispanic whites: The role of language and nativity. *Annals of Epidemiology, 17*(3), 191–198.

Keller, S. D., Ware, J. E., Gandek, B., Aaronson, N. K., Alonso, J., Apolone, G., … Wood-Dauphinee, S. (1998). Testing the equivalence of translations of widely used response choice labels: Results from the IQOLA Project. International Quality of Life Assessment. *Journal of Clinical Epidemiology, 51*(11), 933–944.

Korey, J. L., & Lascher, E. L. (2006). Macropartisanship in California. *Public Opinion Quarterly, 70*(1), 48–65. https://doi.org/10.1093/poq/nfj011

Lee, S., Nguyen, H. A., Jawad, M., & Kurata, J. (2008). Linguistic minorities in a health survey. *Public Opinion Quarterly, 72*(3) 470–486. https://doi.org/10.1093/poq/nfn036

Marian, V., & Kaushanskaya, M. (2004). Self-construal and emotion in bicultural bilinguals. *Journal of Memory and Language, 51*(2), 190–201. https://doi.org/10.1016/j.jml.2004.04.003

Marín, G., Gamba, R. J., & Marín, B. V. (1992). Extreme response style and acquiescence among Hispanics. *Journal of Cross-Cultural Psychology, 23*(4), 498–509. https://doi.org/10.1177/0022022192234006

Marín, G., & Marín, B. V. (1991). *Research with Hispanic populations*. Thousand Oaks, CA: Sage Publications.

Mohler, P. P., Smith, T. W., & Harkness, J. A. (1998). Respondents' ratings of expressions from response scales: A two-country, two-language investigation on equivalence and translation. In J. A. Harkness (Ed.), *ZUMA-Nachrichten Spezial 3* (pp. 159–184). Mannheim, Germany: ZUMA.

Pennell, B.-E., Bowers, A., Carr, D., Chardoul, S., Cheung, G.-Q., Dinkelmann, K., … Torres, M. (2004). The development and implementation of the National Comorbidity Survey Replication, the National Survey of American Life, and the National Latino and Asian American Survey. *International Journal of Methods in Psychiatric Research, 13*(4), 241–269.

Ross, M., Xun, W. Q. E., & Wilson, A. E. (2002). Language and the bicultural self. *Personality and Social Psychology Bulletin, 28*(8), 1040–1050. https://doi.org/10.1177/01461672022811003

Ryan, C. (2013). *Language use in the United States: 2011*. Washington, DC. Retrieved from https://www2.census.gov/library/publications/2013/acs/acs-22/acs-22.pdf

Saris, W. E. (2003). Multitrait-multimethod studies. In J. A. Harkness, F. Van de Vijver, & P. Ph. Mohler (Eds.), *Cross-cultural survey methods* (pp. 207–233). Hoboken, NJ: Wiley-Interscience.

Scheuch, E. K. (1968). The cross-cultural use of sample surveys: Problems of comparability. *Historical social research/Historische sozialforschung, 18*(2), 104–138.

Schwarz, N., Knauper, B., Hippler, H.-J., Noelle-Neumann, E., & Clark, L. (1991). Rating scales: Numeric values may change the meaning of scale labels. *Public Opinion Quarterly, 55*(4), 570–582. https://doi.org/10.1086/269282

Shishido, K., Iwai, N., & Yasuda, T. (2009). Designing response categories of agreement scales for cross-national surveys in East Asia: The approach of the Japanese General Social Surveys. *International Journal of Japanese Sociology, 18*(1), 97–111. https://doi.org/10.1111/j.1475-6781.2009.01111.x

Siegel, P., Martin, E. A., Bruno, R., Martin, E., & Siegel, P. (2001). Language use and linguistic isolation: Historical data and methodological issues. In *Statistical policy working paper 32: 2000 Seminar on integrating federal statistical information and processes* (Vol. 32, pp. 167–190). Washington, DC: Federal Committee on Statistical Methodology, Office of Management and Budget. Retrieved from https://www.census.gov/srd/papers/pdf/ssm2007-02.pdf

Smith, T. W. (2004). Developing and evaluating cross-national survey instruments. In S. Presser, J. M. Rothgeb, M. P. Couper, J. T. Lessler, E. Martin, J. Martin, & E. Singer (Eds.), *Methods for testing and evaluating survey questionnaires* (pp. 431–452). Hoboken, NJ: John Wiley & Sons.

Smith, T. W. (2009). Editorial: Comparative survey research. *International Journal of Public Opinion Research, 21*(3), 267–270. https://doi.org/10.1093/ijpor/edp038

Takeuchi, D. T., Gong, F., & Gee, G. (2012). The NLAAS Story: Some reflections, some insights. A commentary. *Asian American Journal of Psychology, 3*(2). https://doi.org/10.1037/a0029019

Toro-Morn, M. I. (2012). Familismo. In S. Loue & M. Sajatovic (Eds.), *Encyclopedia of immigrant health* (pp. 672–674). New York, NY: Springer Science + Business Media.

Tourangeau, R. (2004). Experimental design considerations for testing and evaluating questionnaires. In S. Presser, J. M. Rothgeb, M. P. Couper, J. T. Lessler, E. Martin, J. Martin, & E. Singer (Eds.), *Methods for testing and evaluating survey questionnaires* (pp. 209–224). Hoboken, NJ: John Wiley & Sons. https://doi.org/10.1002/0471654728.ch11

Trafimow, D., Silverman, E. S., Fan, R. M.-T., & Fun Law, J. S. (1997). The effects of language and priming on the relative accessibility of the private self and the collective self. *Journal of Cross-Cultural Psychology, 28*(1), 107–123. https://doi.org/10.1177/0022022197281007

Triandis, H. C., Davis, E. E., Vassiliou, V., & Nassiakou, M. (1965). *Some methodological problems concerning research on negotiations between monolinguals.* Urbana, IL: Department of Psychology, University of Illinois.

Van de Vijver, F. (2003). Bias and equivalence: Cross-cultural perspectives. In J. A. Harkness, F. Van de Vijver, & P. Ph. Mohler (Eds.), *Cross-cultural survey methods* (pp. 143–155). Hoboken, NJ: Wiley-Interscience.

Van de Vijver, F. J. R., & Leung, K. (1997). *Methods and data analysis for cross-cultural research.* Thousand Oaks, CA: SAGE.

Van Soest, A., Delaney, L., Harmon, C., Kapteyn, A., & Smith, J. P. (2011). Validating the use of anchoring vignettes for the correction of response scale differences in subjective questions. *Journal of the Royal Statistical Society. Series A, (Statistics in Society), 174*(3), 575–595. https://doi.org/10.1111/j.1467-985X.2011.00694.x

Viruell-Fuentes, E. A., Morenoff, J. D., Williams, D. R., & House, J. S. (2011). Language of interview, self-rated health, and the other Latino health puzzle. *American Journal of Public Health, 101*(7), 1306–1313. https://doi.org/10.2105/AJPH.2009.175455

Weech-Maldonado, R., Elliott, M. N., Oluwole, A., Schiller, K. C., & Hays, R. D. (2008). Survey response style and differential use of CAHPS rating scales by Hispanics. *Medical Care, 46*(9), 963–968. https://doi.org/10.1097/MLR.0b013e3181791924

Willis, G. B., Kudela, M. S., Levin, K., Norberg, A., Stark, D. S., Forsyth, B. H., … Hartman, A. M. (2010). Evaluation of a multistep survey translation process. In J. A. Harkness, M. Braun, B. Edwards, T. P. Johnson, L. Lyberg, P. Ph. Mohler, B.-E. Pennell, & T. W. Smith (Eds.), *Survey methods in multinational, multiregional, and multicultural contexts* (pp. 141–156). Hoboken, NJ: John Wiley & Sons.

Yan, T., & Hu, M. (2018). Examining translation and respondents' use of response scales in 3MC surveys. In T. P. Johnson, B.-E. Pennell, I. A. L. Stoop, & B. Dorer (Eds.), *Advances in comparative survey methods: Multinational, multiregional, and multicultural contexts (3MC)* (pp. 501–518). Hoboken, NJ: John Wiley & Sons.

Yu, S. M., Nyman, R. M., Kogan, M. D., Huang, Z. J., & Schwalberg, R. H. (2004). Parent's language of interview and access to care for children with special health care needs. *Ambulatory Pediatrics: The Official Journal of the Ambulatory Pediatric Association, 4*(2), 181–187. https://doi.org/10.1367/A03-094R.1

Zea, M. C., Quezada, T., & Belgrave, F. (1993). Latino culture values: Their role in adjustment to disability. *Journal of Social Behavior and Personality, 9*(5), 185–200.

Appendix 4-1. Question Names and Exact Wording

A. Excellent-to-Poor Scale

	English	Spanish
Scale	*Poor, Fair, Good, Excellent*	*Pobre, Regular, Bien, Excelente*
LP5a	How well do you speak Spanish?	¿Qué tan bien habla usted el español?
LP5b	How well do you read Spanish?	¿Qué tan bien lee usted el español?
LP5c	How well do you write in Spanish?	¿Qué tan bien escribe usted el español?
LP5d	How well do you speak English?	¿Qué tan bien habla usted el inglés?
LP5e	How well do you read English?	¿Qué tan bien lee usted el inglés?
LP5f	How well do you write in English?	¿Qué tan bien escribe usted el inglés?

B. Agreement Scale

	English	Spanish
Scale	*Strongly Agree, Somewhat Agree, Somewhat Disagree, Strongly Disagree*	*Mayormente de Acuerdo, Algo de Acuerdo, Algo en Desacuerdo, Mayormente en Desacuerdo*
FC Lead	Now I'd like to know how strongly you agree or disagree with the following statements about your family.	Ahora me gustaría saber qué tan de acuerdo o desacuerdo está con las siguientes descripciones sobre su familia.
FC1	Family members respect one another.	Los miembros de la familia se respetan unos a otros.
FC2	We share similar values and beliefs as a family.	Compartimos valores y creencias en común como familia.
FC3	Things work well for us as a family.	Las cosas resultan bien para nosotros como familia.
FC4	We really do trust and confide in each other.	Realmente compartimos y confiamos unos en otros.
FC5	Family members feel loyal to the family.	Sentimos mucha lealtad entre nosotros como familia.
FC6	We are proud of our family.	Estamos orgullosos de nuestra familia.
FC7	We can express our feelings with our family.	Podemos expresar nuestros sentimientos con nuestra familia.
FC8	Family members like to spend free time with each other.	A los miembros de la familia les gusta compartir el tiempo libre los unos con los otros.
FC9	Family members feel very close to each other.	Los miembros de la familia se sienten bien cercanos los unos de otros.
FC10	Family togetherness is very important.	La unión familiar es muy importante.

C. Frequency Scale

	English	Spanish
Scale	***Often, Sometimes, Rarely, Never***	***Muchas Veces, Alguna Veces, Casi Nunca, Nunca***
SN4	How often do your relatives or children make too many demands on you?	¿Con qué frecuencia exigen sus familiares demasiado de usted?
SN5	How often do your family or relatives argue with you?	¿Con qué frecuencia discuten o argumentan sus familiares con usted?
SN9	How often do your friends make too many demands on you?	¿Con qué frecuencia sus amigos(as) exigen demasiado de usted?
SN10	How often do your friends argue with you?	¿Con qué frecuencia discuten o argumentan sus amigos(as) con usted?

Scale	***Often, Sometimes, Rarely, Never***	***Muchas Veces, Alguna Veces, Pocas Veces, Nunca***
MS1_1	How often have you returned to [the country of origin of your parents/your country of origin]?	¿Con qué frecuencia ha regresado [the country of origin of your parents/your country of origin]?
DS4	How often do people dislike you because you are [ethnic/race group]?	¿Con qué frecuencia no le cae bien a la gente por ser de origen [ethnic/race group]?
DS5	How often do people treat you unfairly because you are [ethnic/race group]?	¿Con qué frecuencia le tratan injustamente por ser de origen [ethnic/race group]?
DS6	How often have you seen friends treated unfairly because they are [ethnic/race groups]?	¿Con qué frecuencia ha visto como tratan injustamente a sus amigos(as) por ser de origen [ethnic/race group]?

D. Quantity Scale

	English	Spanish
Scale	***A lot, Some, A little, Not at All***	***Mucho, Algo, Poco, Nada***
DA42 lead	As a result of the attacks, how much has your life been affected in the following areas –?	Debido a los ataques de terrorismo, ¿cuánto se ha visto afectada su vida en las siguientes áreas?
DA42b	Losing my job.	Perder mi trabajo.
DA42d	Reduction in my family income.	Tener una reducción en el ingreso familiar.
DA42e	Feeling more patriotic.	Sentirme más patriótico(a).
DA42f	Feeling less safe and secure.	Sentirme menos a salvo e inseguro(a).
DA42h	Been treated unfairly because of my race, ethnicity, or physical appearance.	Tener un trato injusto por mi raza, origen étnico, o apariencia física.
DA42i	Feeling less optimistic about the future.	Sentirme menos optimista acerca del futuro.
DA42l	Feeling that I no longer can cope with things.	Sentirme que no puedo hacerle frente a las cosas.

Scale	*A Lot, Some, A Little, Not at All*	*Mucho, Regular, Un Poco, Nada*
SN2	[Not including your husband/wife/ partner] how much can you rely on relatives who do not live with you for help if you have a serious problem?	[Sin incluir a su esposo/esposa/pareja] ¿cuánto puede contar con que los familiares que no viven con usted lo (la) ayuden si tiene un problema serio?
SN3	[Not including your husband/wife/ partner] how much can you open up to relatives who do not live with you if you need to talk about your worries?	[Sin incluir a su esposo/esposa/pareja] ¿cuánta confianza puede tener con los familiares que no viven con usted si necesita hablar de sus preocupaciones?
SN7	How much can you rely on your friends for help if you have a serious problem?	¿Cuánto puede contar con que sus amigos(as) lo (la) ayuden si tiene un problema serio?
SN8	How much can you open up to your friends if you need to talk about your worries?	¿Cuánta confianza tiene usted con sus amigos(as) si necesita hablar de sus preocupaciones?

Appendix 4-2. Coefficient Estimates of ANOVA for All Measures

(Bold indicates significant at $p < .1$)

A. Excellent-to-Poor Scale

	LP5a	LP5b	LP5c	LP5d	LP5e	LP5f
Intercept	**1.872**	**1.097**	**0.725**	**1.778**	**1.788**	**1.535**
Language: English vs. Spanish	0.078	−0.019	−0.166	0.119	**0.146**	0.072
Score summary: Total score quartiles	**0.504**	**0.720**	**0.790**	**0.556**	**0.576**	**0.633**
Language × score summary	−0.006	0.021	0.043	−0.026	**−0.051**	−0.033

B. Agreement Scale

	FC1	FC2	FC3	FC4	FC5	FC6	FC7	FC8	FC9	FC10
Intercept	0.180	−0.082	0.054	**−0.260**	−0.077	0.169	**−0.292**	**−0.405**	−0.162	0.224
Language: English vs. Spanish	−0.214	0.066	−0.242	−0.108	−0.217	−0.079	0.126	0.181	−0.242	−0.140
Score summary: Total score quartiles	**0.435**	**0.544**	**0.474**	**0.602**	**0.527**	**0.396**	**0.631**	**0.700**	**0.581**	**0.366**
Language × score summary	0.084	−0.018	**0.127**	0.056	0.080	0.027	−0.053	−0.049	0.078	0.071

C. Frequency Scale

	SN4	SN5	SN9	SN10
Intercept	**0.995**	**1.940**	**1.797**	**2.242**
Language: English vs. Spanish	−0.074	**−0.407**	**0.562**	**0.501**
Score summary: Total score quartiles	**0.673**	**0.417**	**0.529**	**0.425**
Language × score summary	0.006	**0.118**	**−0.160**	**−0.150**
	MS1_1	**DS4**	**DS5**	**DS6**
Intercept	**1.390**	**1.994**	**1.888**	**1.468**
Language: English vs. Spanish	−0.055	0.106	0.204	−0.089
Score summary: Total score quartiles	**0.469**	**0.469**	**0.540**	**0.590**
Language × score summary	0.039	−0.007	−0.051	0.023

D. Quantity Scale

	SN2	SN3	SN7	SN8
Intercept	**0.531**	**0.521**	**0.509**	**0.284**
Language: English vs. Spanish	−0.182	−0.159	0.086	0.142
Score summary: Total score quartiles	**0.464**	**0.473**	**0.667**	**0.712**
Language × score summary	0.091	**0.158**	−0.081	−0.070

	DA42b	DA42d	DA42e	DA42f	DA42h	DA42i	DA42l
Intercept	**2.568**	**2.214**	**0.722**	**0.837**	**3.223**	**1.883**	**3.422**
Language: English vs. Spanish	**−0.372**	−0.237	0.137	0.177	0.046	−0.133	−0.117
Score summary: Total score quartiles	**0.363**	**0.468**	**0.497**	**0.692**	**0.188**	**0.516**	**0.159**
Language × score summary	0.114	0.071	−0.008	−0.088	0.001	0.034	0.028

Language Differences Between Interviewers and Respondents in African Surveys

Charles Q. Lau, Stephanie Eckman, Luis Sevilla Kreysa, and Benjamin Piper

Introduction

In face-to-face surveys, the survey language has important implications for data quality. Linguistic issues are particularly relevant in Africa because of its linguistic diversity and complexity. Combined, there are over 2,000 African languages, more than 30 percent of the world's languages (Eberhard, Simons, & Fennig, 2019). Although there are some relatively linguistically homogeneous countries (e.g., predominantly Arabic-speaking countries in Northern Africa), most countries have a complex, multilingual structure. Many Africans are multilingual: 61 percent of Kenyan adults, for example, speak three or more languages (Logan, 2017). There are also different types of languages. People may grow up speaking the language of their tribe or local community but often learn languages of broader communication in school (for brevity, we refer to these languages as "local languages" and "broader languages"). These broader languages may be African (e.g., Swahili) or Western (e.g., English or French) and are often used in mass media, government communications, and workplaces (Bodomo, 1996). Although both local and broader languages are used to communicate, local languages tend to be used more for verbal communication, whereas broader languages are typically used for written communication.

The linguistic diversity in Africa presents several challenges for face-to-face surveys. Survey language can lead to undercoverage if the survey is not offered in a language the respondents speak (Andreenkova, 2018). Language also can shape the respondents' cultural and cognitive frames, affecting the response formation process (see Chapter 1). In this chapter, we focus on another challenge: problems that arise if respondents or data collectors are not proficient in the survey language (Ahlmark et al., 2014; Pearson, Garvin, Ford, & Balluz, 2010; Peytcheva, 2008).

In the simplest situation, respondents and data collectors share the same first language (also known as "home language" in Africa) and conduct the interview in that language, as is the situation in many surveys around the world. In Africa, however, the linguistic situation is more complicated for four reasons:

- The linguistic diversity of Africa means it may not be feasible to translate surveys into all languages, primarily because of cost but also because of the difficulty in securing qualified translators and data collectors. If the survey is not offered in a respondent's home language, the respondent can either (1) not participate in the survey and become a nonrespondent or (2) participate using a language other than their home language (if available).
- For most surveys, data collectors work in multiple areas within a country with different languages, and many data collectors are multilingual. If data collectors work in a region where their home language is not spoken, they may need to use their second or third language to complete an interview (if available).
- Our experience observing fieldwork in Africa suggests that some people view participating in a survey as a "formal" activity more suited to a language of broader communication than a local language. As a result, respondents and data collectors may gravitate toward using a language of broader communication.
- Surveys sometimes use terminology that is more natural in a language of broader communication. The surveys we analyze in this chapter, for example, ask questions about democracy and political attitudes. Because the word "democracy" does not exist in most African languages, data collectors are trained to use a language of broader communication, not a local language, for these questions. For these reasons, even if a respondent and data collector share the same first language, they may opt out of that local language and choose to conduct the survey in a language of broader communication.

In sum, respondents and data collectors may opt to use a language other than their home or first language. Respondents may also engage in "code switching" (i.e., changing languages within the survey)—using a broader language for complex questions and a local language for standard questions. Using a nonhome language in a survey, either because of choice or constraint, may have implications for data quality.

Given the limited literature on linguistic issues in African survey research, this chapter describes language patterns in face-to-face surveys in 36 African countries. Our goal is to provide a broad-brush, descriptive account that sets the stage for more complex analysis in future research. Our analysis extends the excellent descriptive work conducted by Logan (2017) on linguistic issues in the Afrobarometer project by pursuing three research goals:

1. Describe the languages used by respondents and data collectors in face-to-face surveys and develop a five-category taxonomy of language patterns.
2. Describe how the taxonomy functions in three countries from different regions and linguistic backgrounds (Cameroon, Kenya, and Mozambique).
3. Investigate which respondent characteristics (e.g., age, education, urban or rural location, gender) are associated with choosing different languages.

Data and Methods

Data

We analyze data from Afrobarometer Round 6, face-to-face, paper-and-pencil surveys conducted in 2014–2015 in 36 African countries. With surveys spanning two decades, the Afrobarometer initiative is the primary source of public opinion data on Africans' political attitudes, behaviors, and beliefs (see afrobarometer.org for more information). To produce comparable data, each country used a standardized sample design, questionnaire, and fieldwork procedures. The surveys were based on clustered, multistage area probability samples and used random walk procedures to select households. The sample design included stratification by geography (e.g., state, province) and urban–rural location. One individual was randomly selected in each household; to ensure adequate representation by gender, the random selection of respondents alternated between selecting men and women (Afrobarometer Network, 2014). Response rates varied by country, ranging from 30 percent (Tunisia) to 99 percent (Zambia; Isbell, 2017).

In Round 6, 53,935 interviews were completed with approximately 1,200 completed per country, except for Nigeria, Kenya, Uganda, South Africa, Ghana, Malawi, and Tanzania, which had approximately 2,400 interviews each. Of the 53,935 completed interviews, our analytic sample consisted of 53,596 cases; we excluded cases in which the respondent was younger than 18 or older than 120 ($n = 294$) and cases for which the variables on respondent or interviewer language were missing ($n = 45$).

Across the 36 countries, the interview had a median length of 59 minutes. The questionnaire asked about complex topics, including conflict and crime, democracy, elections, gender equality, governance, identity, macroeconomics and markets, political participation, poverty, public services, social capital, and tolerance.

Language Measure

The data include three language variables: (1) the respondent's first language, which the interviewer asked at the beginning of the questionnaire (example in Kenya: "Which Kenyan language is your home language?"); (2) the data collector's first language; and (3) the language of the interview. Across the 36 countries, there were 414 unique respondent home languages, 203 unique interviewer home languages, and 104 survey languages.

Using these variables, we created a five-category taxonomy that describes the combinations of respondent first language, data collector first language, and interview language (see Table 5-1). This table describes each category and provides an example from Kenya. The first two categories (common language and opt out of first) occur when a respondent and data collector share the same first language. The remaining three categories (data collector compromises, respondent compromises, third language as bridge) occur when a respondent and data collector do not share the same first language.

Languages Used in Afrobarometer (Research Goal 1)

Figure 5-1 shows the distribution of cases across the five categories in the taxonomy. The figure is sorted (ascending) by the percentage of interviews completed in the common language of the interviewer and respondent. The last row shows all countries combined. The figure shows that there is substantial variability across countries in how the language of the interview is chosen. In Côte d'Ivoire, Liberia, and Tanzania, interviews are never conducted in a common language shared by the interviewer and respondent. In 15 countries, the common language category is the majority category.

Table 5-1. Language taxonomy

		Example (from Kenya)		
		First Language		
Name	Description	Respondent	Data Collector	Interview Language
A. Respondent and Data Collector Share First Language				
Common Language	The respondent and interviewer share a first language. The interview is conducted in that language.	Dholuo	Dholuo	Dholuo
Opt Out of First	The respondent and interviewer share a first language, but they conduct the interview in another language.	Dholuo	Dholuo	Kiswahili
B. Respondent and Data Collector Do Not Share First Language				
Data Collector Compromises	The respondent and interviewer have different first languages. The interview is conducted in the *respondent's* first language.	Dholuo	Kikamba	Dholuo
Respondent Compromises	The respondent and interviewer have different first languages. The interview is conducted in the *interviewer's* first language.	Dholuo	Kikamba	Kikamba
Third Language as Bridge	The respondent and interviewer have different first languages, and they conduct the interview in another language.	Dholuo	Kikamba	Kiswahili

Overall, when the interviewer and respondent do not share a home language, the two are about equally likely to compromise (in 10 percent of cases, the data collector compromises; in 10 percent of cases, the respondent compromises).

Description of Three Countries (Research Goal 2)

To provide a closer look at how respondents and interviewers choose which language to use in the interview, we look in-depth at three countries: Cameroon, Kenya, and Mozambique. In Figure 5-1, Cameroon is the fourth country from the top, and Kenya and Mozambique are the fifth and sixth countries from the top. We explore these countries for various reasons. First, they represent multilingual countries where data collectors and respondents could share more than one common language to choose from when conducting an interview. Second, they each have different languages of

Figure 5-1. Taxonomy of language choice, by Afrobarometer country

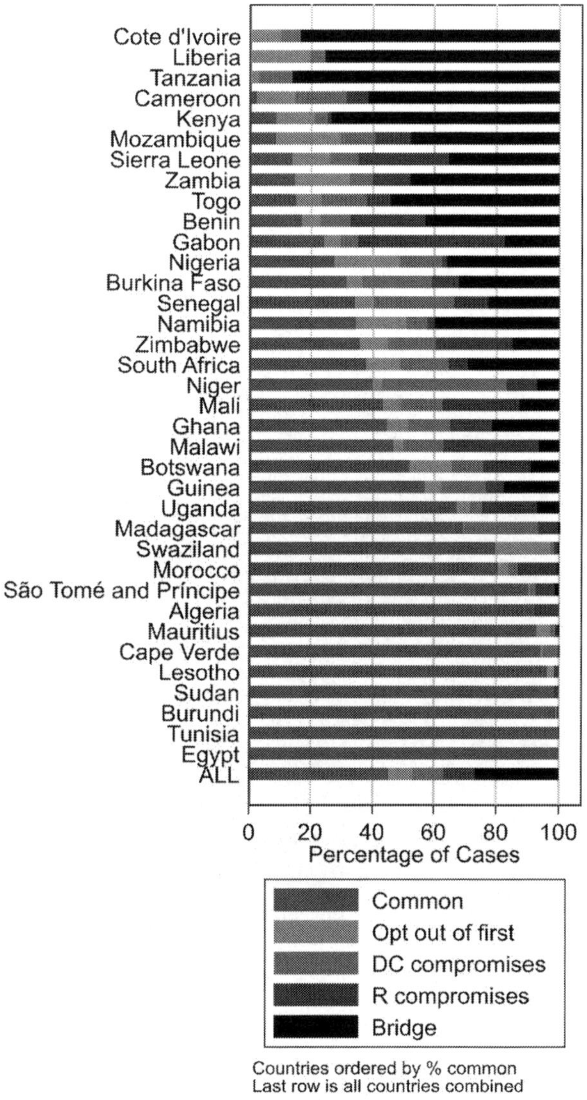

broader communication: English and French in Cameroon, Kiswahili and English in Kenya, and Portuguese in Mozambique. For each country, we cross-tabulated the language taxonomy with the survey language. This analysis makes the taxonomy more concrete and provides suggestive evidence for respondents and data collectors' language choices.

Table 5-2 shows the survey language by language taxonomy in Cameroon, Kenya, and Mozambique. For each country, we show the distribution of language taxonomy (e.g., in Kenya, 9 percent of all interviews used a common language, and 74 percent used a third language as a bridge). Then we report the specific languages used within each language taxonomy category. An example from Kenya: 18 percent of all interviews in which a common language was used were conducted in Gikuyu. Similarly, 51 percent of opt out of first interviews were conducted in English.

In the first column, the common language consists of respondents and data collectors speaking the same first language. In the case of Kenya and Cameroon, the common language category consisted of local languages—not broader languages. Nine percent of cases in Kenya and only 2 percent of cases in Cameroon fell into this category; it is rare for data collectors and respondents to speak the same language and do the interview in that language. In Kenya, interviews conducted in a common language were typically conducted in Dholuo (47 percent), Kikamba (21 percent), and Gikuyu (18 percent). In Cameroon, most interviews in a common language were conducted in Foufouldé (84 percent). In the case of Mozambique, fewer than 1 in 10 interviews (8 percent) was conducted in a shared first language; however, unlike Kenya and Cameroon, most surveys conducted in a common language were in a broader language (Portuguese).

Across the three countries, it was more common to find instances in which the data collector and respondent spoke a common language but chose to do the interview in a different language: respectively, 12 percent, 12 percent, and 21 percent of cases in Cameroon, Kenya, and Mozambique resulted in the opt out of first category. In nearly all these cases, they chose a broader language for the interview. This is interesting because, theoretically, the conversation could have been done in their first and common language, but a broader language may have been used because the survey was perceived as a more formal activity or the words in the questionnaire were easier to use in a broader language.

In instances in which the first language was not shared by the respondent and data collector, we see that the data collector compromises and respondent compromises categories were rare in Kenya (4 percent and 1 percent, respectively). In contrast, in Mozambique, the data collector compromised in 11 percent of cases, and the respondent compromised in 12 percent of cases. When the data collector compromised, the survey language was Portuguese 58 percent of the time; when the respondent compromised, they almost

Table 5-2. Survey language in Kenya, Mozambique, and Cameroon, by language taxonomy

Survey Language	Share First Language: (1) Common Language	Share First Language: (2) Opt Out of First	Do Not Share First Language: (3) Data Collector Compromises	Do Not Share First Language: (4) Respondent Compromises	Do Not Share First Language: (5) Third Language as Bridge
Cameroon					
Percentage of all cases (row %)	2	12	17	7	62
Languages					
English	0	8	0	78	8
French	0	76	88	0	82
Foufouldé	84	0	17	19	3
Pidgin	0	16	0	0	7
Ewondo	4	0	0	0	0
Other	12	0	0	2	0
Total	100	100	100	100	100
Kenya					
Percentage of all cases (row %)	9	12	4	1	74
Languages					
English	0	51	2	68	30
Kiswahili	0	48	57	0	69
Gikuyu	18	0	10	0	0
Dholuo	47	0	17	16	0
Luhya	0	1	2	0	0
Kikamba	21	0	4	4	0
Kalenjin	0	0	2	0	0
Kisii	0	0	1	0	0
Somali	13	0	1	12	0
Other	1	0	4	0	0
Total	100	100	100	100	100
Mozambique					
Percentage of all cases (row %)	8	21	11	12	48
Languages					
Portuguese	60	93	58	91	93

(Continued)

Table 5-2. Survey language in Kenya, Mozambique, and Cameroon, by language taxonomy (*Continued*)

	Share First Language	Do Not Share First Language			
Survey Language	(1) Common Language	(2) Opt Out of First	(3) Data Collector Compromises	(4) Respondent Compromises	(5) Third Language as Bridge
Makhuwa	11	2	7	1	2
Sena	4	0	11	1	1
Ndau	7	0	6	2	0
Changana	17	0	15	5	0
Other	0	4	3	0	4
Total	100	100	100	100	100

always (91 percent) used Portuguese. In Cameroon, data collectors compromised more than respondents did (17 percent versus 7 percent, respectively). When respondents compromised, they used English most often. In contrast, when data collectors compromised, they used French most often. This pattern suggests that the Cameroonian data collectors mostly speak English as their first language.

In all three countries, when the data collector and respondent had different first languages, they most often chose to use a third language as a bridge for communication (62 percent of the time in Cameroon, 74 percent in Kenya, and 48 percent in Mozambique). The bridge language was nearly always a broader language. In Kenya, among the cases that relied on a bridge language, 30 percent used English and 69 percent used Kiswahili. In Mozambique and Cameroon, the majority of cases relied on Portuguese and French, respectively.

Analysis of Language Choice (Research Goal 3)

The previous analyses focused on aggregate patterns of languages across countries and within three countries. Next, we seek to understand language patterns on a micro level, that is, between the respondent and data collector. To analyze Research Goal 3, we focused on two issues. First, when respondents and data collectors speak the same first language, why do some interviews occur in that first language (common language) and others occur in a different language (opt out of first)? Second, when respondents and data collectors do not speak the same first language, why do respondents compromise in some cases, whereas data collectors compromise in other cases?

Respondents and data collectors may opt out of their common language in favor of a different language for a variety of reasons. In some instances, they may opt out because the questionnaire was not translated into the first language. Alternatively, respondents and data collectors may be accustomed to using technical terms in a language of broader communication. The decision to opt out of first language could also reflect the interviewer's discomfort with reading the local language. Data collectors may be accustomed to speaking a mother tongue (e.g., Dholuo) but feel more comfortable reading in a broader language (e.g., English or Swahili). Finally, there may be social benefits for respondents in showing that they can participate in an interview in English or Swahili, for example.

For cases in which respondents and data collectors do not speak the same language, the available languages may constrain the decision of who (respondent or data collector) compromises. If a respondent is multilingual and the data collector speaks only one language (the respondent's second language), then the respondent compromises. Other dynamics may be at play, however. For instance, data collectors may attempt to accommodate respondents, out of politeness or to secure cooperation, by using the respondent's language. Alternatively, some interviewers may insist on their own first language to exert power over respondents or because they are more comfortable administering the survey in that language.

Answering these two questions requires knowledge of all languages spoken by the respondents and interviewers and all languages in which the questionnaire was available in each country. Information on the languages each party speaks would help us understand the choices available to the respondent and the data collector (the demand side of the language-choice decision). Unfortunately, the Afrobarometer Round 6 data only include information about first languages. Information on the questionnaire languages would help us understand the supply side. These details were not available to us at the time of this writing. Without both pieces of information, we cannot fully model the choices the respondent–data collector pairs make.

We can make progress toward answering the two questions posed earlier, however, by understanding the respondent characteristics that predict whether a case is opt out of first rather than common language (to answer the first question) and whether a case is respondent compromise rather than data collector compromise (to answer the second question).

Figure 5-2 shows parameters from two multilevel logistic regressions with opt out of first (left-hand panel) and respondent compromises (right-hand

Figure 5-2. Coefficients from multilevel logistic regression models predicting language choice

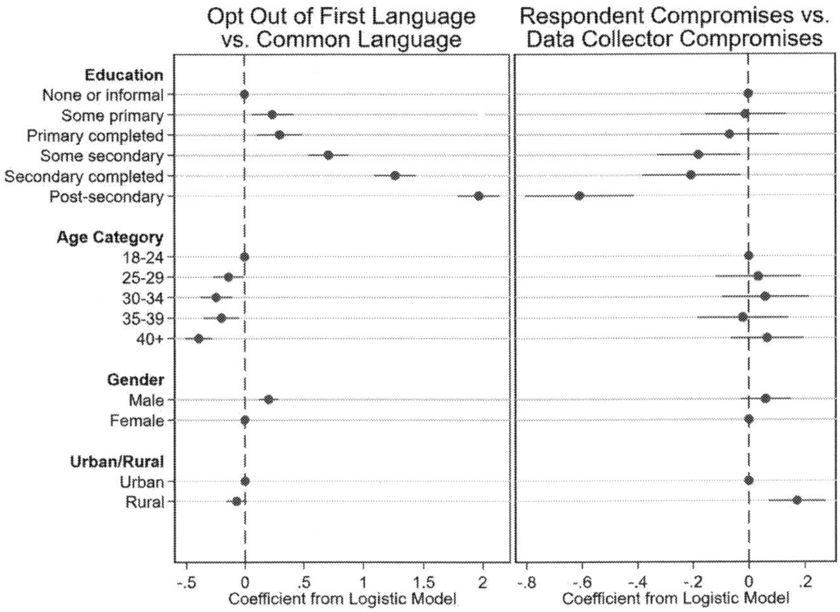

panel) conditions as the dependent variables. Both regressions use the following respondent characteristics as independent variables: education, age, gender, and urban or rural residence. The regressions pool all countries and include a random effect for country. The figure shows estimated beta coefficients from a logistic model (not odds ratios). Note that the figure includes points for the reference categories for completeness. We include 95 percent confidence intervals for the estimates. Estimates where the confidence interval does not cross zero are considered statistically significant.

In the left-hand panel, respondents with more education are more likely than their less educated peers to opt out of their first language. Similarly, younger respondents are more likely to opt out than older respondents. Men and urban residents are also more likely to opt out. In Table 5-2, we saw that most opt-out interviews were conducted in a broader (rather than local) language. These characteristics (more education, younger, male, and urban) are all markers of social advantage, suggesting that these respondents may have better skills in a broader language.

In the right-hand panel, we see that education is the only statistically significant predictor of whether a respondent, rather than the data collector, compromises. When respondents have post-secondary education, it is less likely that the respondent compromises and more likely that the interviewer compromises. Possibly, respondents have greater bargaining power for language choice as their education increases. Alternatively, more educated respondents may also know more languages, increasing their linguistic options. When respondents have lower levels of education, both forms of compromising are equally likely.

Discussion

This chapter provides a broad-brush, descriptive account of linguistic issues in a major study of public opinion surveys across 36 African countries. We developed a taxonomy to illustrate the relationships between three language variables: the interview language, the respondent's first language, and the data collector's first language. Our analysis reveals considerable variation across countries in language usage.

When respondents and data collectors share the same first language, we find that the parties sometimes opt out of that first language and choose to use another language for the interview—often a language of broader communication. This opting out phenomenon is interesting because the parties could have used a common language but chose not to. The reasons for opting out are not apparent from our data. We speculate that data collectors and respondents may choose to opt out because they view broader languages as more appropriate for a survey or because technical terms may be easier to discuss in a broader language. Opting out of a first language in favor of a language of broader communication may affect survey estimates. In the case of Afrobarometer surveys, choosing to conduct the survey in English (versus a local language) may lead respondents to report more favorable views toward the international community. Testing this idea would require an experiment that randomly assigns respondents to a local or broader language to evaluate the impact of language on survey estimates.

We also find scenarios where respondents and data collectors do not share the same first language; in this scenario, either the respondent compromises (using the data collector's first language) or the data collector compromises. The frequency of compromise is about the same for respondents and data collectors in the total sample, although it varies by country. As survey managers, we would prefer that respondents not compromise to avoid situations in which they do not fully understand the question or cannot express their answers. It would be especially troubling if lower levels of respondent education increased the likelihood of respondent compromising. But fortunately, our results showed this was not the case.

Our research highlights methodological challenges in conducting research on linguistic issues in African surveys. The biggest challenge in this analysis concerns measurement of languages. The data we analyzed have information only about the respondents' and data collectors' *first languages*. Many Africans are multilingual, so a mismatch in first languages between respondents and data collectors is not necessarily a sign that they cannot communicate effectively. Additional information on the languages spoken by respondents and data collectors would provide a more accurate portrait. Most useful would be a measure of second and third languages spoken by both parties. Here, measurements of both *proficiency* and *preferences* would be relevant. Proficiency is understanding the set of language choices. Preferences would help us understand language choices given a similar choice set. Further, measures of proficiency and preferences would be useful for both spoken and written ability. Whereas parties both need to speak the language, data collectors also need to read it. Data collectors may be more comfortable reading in a language of broader communication, but both parties may be more comfortable speaking in a local language.

Another measurement issue concerns the coding of interview language. Like most surveys, the Afrobarometer codes survey language as a single response. From our experience in the field, however, we know that respondents sometimes switch between languages within an interview. Future research—perhaps based on audio recordings of interviews—would benefit from more information about how often this happens and when.

After these measurement issues are addressed, one next step is to investigate the association between language choice and indicators of data quality. We may expect language choices (particularly respondent compromises) to affect acquiescence, item nonresponse, nondifferentiation in scales, and interview length. This research would need to address several factors. First, language is not randomly assigned: language is highly correlated with ethnicity, and there is evidence that interviewer ethnicity affects responses in the Afrobarometer (Adida, Ferree, Posner, & Robinson, 2015). Second, this research would ideally be conducted separately by country to capture the unique context of each country. Third, this research should include the full set of respondent and data collector characteristics. In the future, we plan to replicate and expand this analysis with another survey that contains additional information about respondents and interviewers.

References

Adida, C. L., Ferree, K. E., Posner, D. N., & Robinson, A. L. (2015). Who's asking? Interviewer coethnicity effects in African survey data. Afrobarometer Working Paper No. 158. Retrieved from https://afrobarometer.org/sites/default/files/publications/Working%20papers/afropaperno158.pdf

Afrobarometer Network. (2014). Afrobarometer Round 6 survey manual. Retrieved from https://www.afrobarometer.org/sites/default/files/survey_manuals/ab_r6_survey_manual_en.pdf

Ahlmark, N., Algren, M. H., Holmberg, T. Norredam, M. L., Nielsen, S. S., Blom, A. B., ... Juel, K. (2014). Survey nonresponse among ethnic minorities in a national health survey–Mixed-method study of participation, barriers, and potentials. *Ethnicity and Health, 20*(6), 611–632. https://doi.org/10.1080/13557858.2014.979768

Andreenkova, A. (2018). How to choose interview language in different countries. In T. P. Johnson, B.-E. Pennell, I. A. L. Stoop, & B. Dorer (Eds.), *Advances in comparative survey methods: Multinational, multiregional, and multicultural contexts (3MC)* (pp. 293–324). Hoboken, NJ: John Wiley & Sons.

Bodomo, A. (1996). On language and development in Africa: The case of Ghana. *Nordic Journal of Africa Studies, 5*(2), 31–51.

Eberhard, D., Simons, G., & Fennig, C. (Eds.), (2019). *Ethnologue: Languages of the world.* (22nd ed.). Dallas, TX: SIL International.

Isbell, T. A. (2017). Data codebook for Round 6 Afrobarometer Survey. Retrieved from http://afrobarometer.org/data/merged-round-6-codebook-36-countries-2016

Logan, C. (2017). 800 languages and counting: Lessons from survey research across a linguistically diverse continent. Afrobarometer Working Paper No. 172. Retrieved from https://afrobarometer.org/publications/wp172-800-languages-and-counting-lessons-survey-research-across-linguistically-diverse

Pearson, W. S., Garvin, W. S., Ford, E. S., & Balluz, L. S. (2010). Analysis of five-year trends in self-reported language preference and issues of item non-response among Hispanic persons in a large cross-sectional health survey: Implications for the measurement of an ethnic minority population. *Population Health Metrics*, *8*, 7. https://doi.org/10.1186/1478-7954-8-7

Peytcheva, E. (2008, May). Language of administration as a cause of measurement error. Paper presented at the 63rd Annual Conference of the American Association for Public Opinion Research, New Orleans, LA.

Chapter 6

Void of the Voiceless: An Analysis of Residents With a Language Barrier in Germany, France, and the United Kingdom

Nicholas Heck-Grossek and Sonila Dardha

Introduction

Coverage error is an essential component of the total survey error (TSE) framework, particularly worth examining if excluded units differ systematically from the surveyed respondents (Biemer, 2010; Biemer et al., 2017; Groves, 2004; Groves et al., 2011). In nationally representative surveys where researchers aim to make inferences about the general population as a whole, systematically undercovering or undersampling specific groups may lead to biased estimates. A clear example of such exclusion is the community of migrants who reside in a country but do not speak the national language(s). Large-scale comparative surveys in Europe and beyond, like the European Social Survey (ESS), the Eurobarometer (EB), and the European Quality of Life Survey (EQLS), sample individuals from households on the premise that an eligible unit is one that speaks the official language(s) of the country, among other potential criteria. If a general population target means the resident population of a country, such surveys would exclude migrant residents simply because they do not speak the languages on which the questionnaire is translated and scripted. Overlooking such units becomes especially problematic if this group presents dissimilar sociodemographic composition, perceptions, attitudes, or behaviors compared with the rest of the population.

A large body of literature in the field of public health examines migrant minorities with a language barrier and how they differ from their majority counterparts. Previous research shows that a language barrier affects the patient–physician relationship (Diamond, Izquierdo, Canfield, Matsoukas, & Gany, 2019; Jaeger, Pellaud, Leville, & Klauser, 2019), and often the health status of those facing a language barrier is significantly different from the remainder of the population (Bousmah, Combes & Abu-Zaineh, 2019; Ding & Hargraves, 2009; Watson, Harrop, Walton, Young, & Soltani, 2019). Studies investigating sociological research questions present evidence that ethnic or racial minority groups with a language barrier differ from the majority on other outcomes such as social interactions (Cho, 2000) and cooperation with social workers (Chand, 2005). More importantly, an illustration of this difference is summarized by "3D occupations"—occupations that are "dirty," "dangerous," and "demeaning" or "difficult"—which are predominantly executed by ethnic minorities (Mucci et al., 2019; Sun, 2019). Furthermore, this group earns less (Barret & McCarthy, 2007), is less likely to own homes (Duffy, Gerald, & Kearney, 2005), and lives in housing with poorer conditions and more decay (Statistics Norway, 2009).

From a survey methodology perspective, ethnic migrant minorities are of particular interest because they often represent hidden populations that are hard to sample, identify, reach, and persuade and have a low propensity to participate in surveys (Bacher, Lemcke, Schmich, & Quatember, 2019; Tourangeau, Edwards, & Johnson, 2014; Willis, Smith, Shariff-Marco, & English, 2014). Consequently, research from this field focuses on methods to sample migrants and include them in the target population as an attempt to achieve better representativeness (Kappelhof & De Leeuw, 2019; Lohr, 2008). Given the rather low prevalence of migrants with a language barrier and their highly mobile nature (South, Crowder, & Chavez, 2006; Warfa et al., 2006), drawing samples from frames of national statistics offices proves insufficient, particularly when national registers frequently exclude such units. Alternatively, some of the frequently used but costly sampling techniques developed to date include snowballing or respondent-driven sampling (Shi, Cameron, & Heckathorn, 2019; Tyldum & Johnston, 2014), time-location sampling (Kalsbeek, 2003; Karon, 2005), name-based sampling (Ferguson, 2009; Schnell et al., 2013; Schnell, Trappmann, & Gramlich, 2014), random routes or random walk procedures (Agadjanian & Zotova, 2012), and other novel approaches (Raymond, Chen, & McFarland, 2019) or even a combination of techniques (Reichel & Morales, 2017).

If methods to sample and reach ethnic migrant minorities are available, the subsequent step is to encourage minorities' participation in the study. To encourage their participation, the research team needs to account for any potential language barriers faced during the survey process, including during the contact, recruiting, and interviewing stages. To cope with this challenge in a face-to-face survey, not only would the questionnaire need to be translated, but the interviewers also would need to speak the target language(s). However, translation is labor-intensive and time-consuming, and fieldwork agencies do not necessarily have a pool of interviewers who speak the needed language(s) at hand. This economic inefficiency usually leads to the exclusion of units with a language barrier from surveys altogether. Systematic exclusion, however, might have undesired critical implications for the generalizability of survey results. Despite the ongoing research and efforts from both survey scholars and practitioners to include eligible units in the population frame, the trade-off between methodological rigor and financial constraints still persists. Thus, this chapter explores whether the exclusion of migrants with a language barrier is sizable and whether they differ significantly from the rest of the population on various perceptible outcomes upon contact with a survey interviewer.

Methods

This research brief examines the excluded units facing a language barrier using data from the European Social Survey (ESS ERIC) round 8 fielded in 2016 (European Social Survey Round 8 Data, 2016), focusing on case studies of the three most populous European countries: Germany, France, and the United Kingdom. Data were obtained from publicly accessible contact information sheets that contain details about interviewers' contact process with potential respondents. Previous research shows that para-data stemming from contact sheets provide a fruitful source for understanding fieldwork and survey results but are as yet underused, despite promising results from some initial research (Kreuter, 2013). These sheets indicate that, apart from coding survey dispositions and refusal outcomes, interviewers gather information on the characteristics of the house and the immediate vicinity in which a unit lives and whether the interviewer faces any access impediments such as entry phones and locked gates or doors.

This research brief's objective is to use this data to determine how units with a language barrier differ with regard to their dwelling or area characteristics (e.g., type of house, overall physical condition of the building or house, amount of litter and rubbish, or vandalism and graffiti in the immediate vicinity, and access impediments) from all other units for which contact was attempted. The advantage of this approach lies in shifting the focus from participating units to nonrespondents who do not meet the survey eligibility requirements because of linguistic constraints. Thus, the analysis included comparisons of living conditions for units with and without a language barrier, and excluded units that could not be reached in any of the contact attempts or for whom contact sheets were unavailable. The unit of analysis is the household, so a unit with a language barrier refers to a household with at least one member facing a language barrier. To avoid small cell sizes, some of the variables of interest were recoded into binary or categorical variables with three levels of measurement. Using chi-squared tests, we assessed the independence between the dwelling or area characteristics and whether the unit faces a language barrier. Table 6-1 shows the cross-tabulated results and the corresponding chi-squared and p values.

Results

Of the 18,473 contacted units in the three countries under examination, 335 were identified as having a language barrier. The prevalence for this group is small and constitutes 2.0 percent of the observations in Germany (182 of 9,305 units), 1.9 percent in France (82 of 4,300 units), and 1.5 percent in the United Kingdom (71 of 4,868 units). On the whole, units with a language barrier seemed to be living in worse conditions than the remainder of the contacted respondents. To illustrate, across all three countries, a relative majority live in multi-unit buildings as opposed to single units (37 percent to 67 percent who have a language barrier vs. 17 percent to 40 percent who do not have a language barrier) that are in bad or very bad overall physical condition (13 percent to 16 percent who have a language barrier vs. 3 percent to 4 percent who do not have a language barrier); both results are significant at the $p < .001$ level. Likewise, a higher proportion of potential respondents who have a language barrier live in areas with a large or very large amount of litter and rubbish (12 percent to 20 percent vs. 1 percent to 4 percent) or vandalism and graffiti (4 percent to 11 percent vs. 1 percent to 2 percent) compared with those without a language barrier. The proportions of those with a language barrier are relatively large, especially in France. However, results are mixed for whether those with a language barrier live in dwellings with access impediments: although this is the case in France and the United Kingdom, findings from Germany suggest the opposite but are inconclusive as they do not reach statistical significance.

Discussion and Conclusions

The results presented in this chapter show a clear trend with minor country-specific differences. Overall, households with at least one person who has a

Table 6-1. Cross-tabulations of units with and without a language barrier and their dwelling or area characteristics

	Germany			France			United Kingdom		
	No barrier	Language barrier	Chi-squared test	No barrier	Language barrier	Chi-squared test	No barrier	Language barrier	Chi-squared test
Type of house respondent lives in									
Single unit	34%	14%	$\chi^2 = 62^{***}$	55%	30%	$\chi^2 = 25^{***}$	71%	58%	$\chi^2 = 21^{***}$
Multi-unit	37%	65%	$df = 2$	40%	67%	$df = 2$	17%	37%	$df = 2$
Other	28%	21%	$p < .001$	6%	2%	$p < .001$	13%	6%	$p < .001$
Entry phone or locked gate/door before reaching respondent's individual door									
Yes	75%	70%	$\chi^2 = 1.43$	46%	63%	$\chi^2 = 10^{**}$	16%	32%	$\chi^2 = 14^{***}$
No, neither of these	25%	30%	$df = 1$ $p = .233$	54%	37%	$df = 1$ $p = .001$	84%	68%	$df = 1$ $p < .001$
Overall physical condition of building or house									
Very good/good	73%	43%	$\chi^2 = 83^{***}$	83%	65%	$\chi^2 = 47^{***}$	66%	38%	$\chi^2 = 32^{***}$
Satisfactory	23%	44%	$df = 2$	14%	20%	$df = 2$	30%	49%	$df = 2$
Bad/very bad	4%	13%	$p < .001$	3%	16%	$p < .001$	4%	13%	$p < .001$
Amount of litter and rubbish in the immediate vicinity									
Very large/large	4%	12%	$\chi^2 = 21^{***}$	1%	20%	$\chi^2 = 158^{***}$	3%	12%	$\chi^2 = 22^{***}$
Small/none or almost none	96%	88%	$df = 1$ $p < .001$	99%	80%	$df = 1$ $p < .001$	97%	88%	$df = 1$ $p < .001$
Amount of vandalism and graffiti in the immediate vicinity									
Very large/large	2%	6%	$\chi^2 = 6^{*}$	1%	11%	$\chi^2 = 61^{***}$	1%	4%	$\chi^2 = 10^{**}$
Small/none or almost none	98%	94%	$df = 1$ $p = .012$	99%	89%	$df = 1$ $p < .001$	99%	96%	$df = 1$ $p = .002$

* $p < .05$; ** $p < .01$; *** $p < .001$.

language barrier tend to inhabit impoverished houses, buildings, or vicinities. They are likely to be found in multi-unit buildings in all countries under observation, more frequently so than those without any language barrier. This finding is in line with a large, long-standing body of literature focusing on ethnic minorities, which, among other findings, concludes that ethnic minorities tend to live in cities and towns where there are more multi-unit households than in rural areas, which typically have more single-unit dwellings (Duffy et al., 2005; Razum et al., 2008; Statistics Norway, 2009). A similar pattern prevails when looking at other indicators: households that have at least one person with a language barrier are located in neighborhoods with higher amounts of both litter and rubbish as well as vandalism and graffiti; these indicators clearly speak to the deprivation of these migrant communities. Again, these results align with previous research on ethnic minorities (Spallek, Zeeb, & Razum, 2010; Statistics Norway, 2009). With the exception of Germany, residents with a language barrier also seem harder to reach because they often dwell in buildings with access impediments such as entry phones and locked gates or doors. This finding is not surprising given that access impediments (e.g., intercoms or entry phones) often go along with multi-unit household buildings, which arguably indicate a lower socioeconomic status of the inhabitants in these countries. Therefore, it is reasonable to suggest that migrant units living in more precarious settings could also differ in their demographic composition, socioeconomic status, and worldview from those who live in less precarious settings. As a result, even though units with a language barrier compose a small proportion of the resident population, their exclusion is likely to be a source of bias and could affect the ESS estimates.

Although these findings offer a glimpse into the poor living conditions of sampling units with a language barrier, no discussion of substantial results for this group is possible because they were excluded from survey interview recruitment, and no additional information is available. Nevertheless, the added value of this study is that it uncovers the housing situation of this hidden segment in the three largest European countries. The analysis from the para-data can serve as a proxy for further interpretation given that unfavorable living conditions are likely to be correlated with the respondents' other demographic, attitudinal, or behavioral traits.

Upcoming surveys targeting either migrant or general populations need to be cautious in excluding resident units facing a language barrier. Based on their distinctive living conditions, these units might also differ on other substantial measures and, consequently, threaten the inference potential of the collected data. Suggestions for future research include taking more of the available ESS countries into account to explore cross-country differences and similarities, collecting other auxiliary data on excluded units via contact sheets or other para-data procedures to investigate this population in more detail, and ultimately assessing the feasibility of including this population in surveys.

References

Agadjanian, V., & Zotova, N. (2012). Sampling and surveying hard-to-reach populations for demographic research: A study of female labor migrants in Moscow, Russia. *Demographic Research, 26*, 131–150.

Bacher, J., Lemcke, J., Schmich, P., & Quatember, A. (2019). Probability and nonprobability sampling: Representative surveys of hard-to-reach and hard-to-ask populations. Current surveys between the poles of theory and practice. *Survey Methods: Insights from the Field.* Retrieved from https://surveyinsights.org/?p=12070

Barrett, A., & McCarthy, Y. (2007). The earnings of immigrants in Ireland: Results from the 2005 EU Survey of Income and Living Conditions. (IZA Discussion Paper, No. 2990). Bonn, Germany: IZA, Institute of Labor Economics.

Biemer, P. P. (2010). Total survey error: Design, implementation, and evaluation. *Public Opinion Quarterly, 74*(5), 817–848.

Biemer, P. P., De Leeuw, E., Eckman, S., Edwards, B., Kreuter, F., Lyberg, L. E., & West, B. T. (Eds.), (2017). *Total survey error in practice.* Hoboken, NJ: John Wiley & Sons.

Bousmah, M., Combes, J. B. S., & Abu-Zaineh, M. (2019). Health differentials between citizens and immigrants in Europe: A heterogeneous convergence. *Health Policy, 123*(2), 235–243.

Chand, A. (2005). Do you speak English? Language barriers in child protection social work with minority ethnic families. *British Journal of Social Work, 35*(6), 807–821.

Cho, G. (2000). The role of heritage language in social interactions and relationships: Reflections from a language minority group. *Bilingual Research Journal, 24*(4), 369–384.

Diamond, L., Izquierdo, K., Canfield, D., Matsoukas, K., & Gany, F. (2019). A systematic review of the impact of patient–physician non-English language concordance on quality of care and outcomes. *Journal of General Internal Medicine, 34*(8), 1591–1606. https://doi.org/10.1007/s11606-019-04847-5

Ding, H., & Hargraves, L. (2009). Stress-associated poor health among adult immigrants with a language barrier in the United States. *Journal of Immigrant and Minority Health, 11*(6), 446–452.

Duffy, D., Gerald, J. F., & Kearney, I. (2005). Rising house prices in an open labour market. *Economic and Social Review, 36*(3), 251–272.

European Social Survey. (2016). ESS8 – 2016 data download: Integrated file edition 2.1. London, United Kingdom: ESS ERIC. https://doi.org/10.21338/NSD-ESS8-2016

Ferguson, D. A. (2009). Name-based cluster sampling. *Sociological Methods & Research, 37*(4), 590–598.

Groves, R. M. (2004). *Survey errors and survey costs* (Vol. 536). Hoboken, NJ: John Wiley & Sons.

Groves, R. M., Fowler, F. J., Jr., Couper, M. P., Lepkowski, J. M., Singer, E., & Tourangeau, R. (2011). *Survey methodology* (Vol. 561). Hoboken, NJ: John Wiley & Sons.

Jaeger, F. N., Pellaud, N., Laville, B., & Klauser, P. (2019). The migration-related language barrier and professional interpreter use in primary health care in Switzerland. *BMC Health Services Research, 19*(1), 429.

Kalsbeek, W. D. (2003). Sampling minority groups in health surveys. *Statistics in Medicine, 22*(9), 1527–1549.

Kappelhof, J. W., & De Leeuw, E. D. (2019). Estimating the impact of measurement differences introduced by efforts to reach a balanced response among non-Western minorities. *Sociological Methods & Research, 48*(1), 116–155.

Karon, J. M. (2005, March). The analysis of time-location sampling study data. In *Proceeding of the Joint Statistical Meeting, Section on Survey Research Methods* (pp. 3180–3186). Minneapolis, MN: American Statistical Association.

Kreuter, F. (Ed.). (2013). *Improving surveys with paradata: Analytic uses of process information* (Vol. 581). Hoboken, NJ: John Wiley & Sons.

Lohr, S. L. (2008). Coverage and sampling. In *International handbook of survey methodology* (pp. 97–112). New York, NY: Taylor & Francis.

Mucci, N., Traversini, V., Giorgi, G., Garzaro, G., Fiz-Perez, J., Campagna, M., & Arcangeli, G. (2019). Migrant workers and physical health: An umbrella review. *Sustainability, 11*(1), 232.

Raymond, H. F., Chen, Y. H., & McFarland, W. (2019). "Starfish sampling": A novel, hybrid approach to recruiting hidden populations. *Journal of Urban Health, 96*(1), 55–62.

Razum, O., Zeeb, H., Meesmann, U., Schenk, L., Bredehorst, M., Brozska, P., & Saß, A. C. (2008). Schwerpunktbericht der gesundheitsberichterstattung des bundes. *Migration und gesundheit.* [*Federal focus report on health. Migration and health.*] Berlin, Germany: Robert-Koch-Institut.

Reichel, D., & Morales, L. (2017). Surveying immigrants without sampling frames—Evaluating the success of alternative field methods. *Comparative Migration Studies, 5*(1), 1.

Schnell, R., Gramlich, T., Bachteler, T., Reiher, J., Trappmann, M., Smid, M., & Becher, I. (2013). A new name-based sampling method for migrants using n-grams. German Record Linkage Center Working Paper Series. Retrieved from https://pdfs.semanticscholar.org/812f/18bfbf9695e2f93df742791770f82a482b0e.pdf

Schnell, R., Trappmann, M., & Gramlich, T. (2014). A study of assimilation bias in name-based sampling of migrants. *Journal of Official Statistics, 30*(2), 231–249.

Shi, Y., Cameron, C. J., & Heckathorn, D. D. (2019). Model-based and design-based inference: Reducing bias due to differential recruitment in respondent-driven sampling. *Sociological Methods & Research, 48*(1), 3–33.

South, S., Crowder, K., & Chavez, E. (2006). Geographical mobility and spatial assimilation among U.S. Latino immigrants. *International Migration Review, 39*(3), 577–607.

Spallek, J., Zeeb, H., & Razum, O. (2010). Prevention among immigrants: The example of Germany. *BMC Public Health, 10*(1), 92.

Statistics Norway. (2009). *Living conditions among immigrants in Norway 2005/2006*. Reports 2009/2. Oslo, Norway: Author.

Sun, L. (2019). Work-related injuries: Injured but not entitled for legal compensation. In *Rural urban migration and policy intervention in China* (pp. 137–151). Singapore: Palgrave Macmillan.

Tourangeau, R., Edwards, B., & Johnson, T. P. (Eds.), (2014). *Hard-to-survey populations*. Cambridge, UK: Cambridge University Press.

Tyldum, G., & Johnston, L. (2014). *Applying respondent driven sampling to migrant populations: Lessons from the field*. London, UK: Palgrave Macmillan UK.

Warfa, N., Bhui, K., Craig, T., Curtis, S., Mohamud, S., Stansfeld, S., … Thornicroft, G. (2006). Post-migration geographical mobility, mental health and health service utilisation among Somali refugees in the UK: A qualitative study. *Health & Place, 12*(4), 503–515.

Watson, H., Harrop, D., Walton, E., Young, A., & Soltani, H. (2019). A systematic review of ethnic minority women's experiences of perinatal mental health conditions and services in Europe. *PloS One, 14*(1), e0210587.

Willis, G. B., Smith, T. W., Shariff-Marco, S., & English, N. (2014). Overview of the special issue on surveying the hard-to-reach. *Journal of Official Statistics, 30*(2), 171–176.

PART II

Survey Questionnaire Development and Implementation

Pretesting Methods in Cross-Cultural Research

Eva Aizpurua

Introduction

In recent years, substantial advances have been made in the field of multinational, multiregional, and multicultural research (commonly referred to as 3MC survey research; Johnson, Pennell, Stoop, & Dorer, 2018). This research magnifies challenges associated with monocultural studies and poses unique ones at both the organizational and methodological levels. Because cross-cultural surveys seek to make comparative estimates across populations, the data must be valid and reliable for each specific group, as well as comparable across them. Even when questionnaires are carefully translated and adapted, groups may systematically differ in the way they interpret certain questions or respond to them, posing a threat to the validity of the comparisons. In this context, pretesting becomes particularly beneficial to identify potential problems in survey questions and to assess comparability (Willis, 2015).

This chapter introduces the concept and importance of pretesting in cross-cultural survey research. The most common methods used to pretest 3MC surveys are described, highlighting recent applications and developments, as well as current challenges. These methods include cross-cultural cognitive interviewing, online probing, vignettes, and behavior coding. Next, reference is made to the combination of multiple pretesting methods to assess and improve cross-cultural surveys. In the last section of this chapter, the main challenges and opportunities of pretesting in comparative contexts are discussed.

Pretesting Methods and Their Role in Cross-Cultural Research

Pretesting refers to a variety of methods designed to assess the adequacy of survey instruments and field procedures (Caspar et al., 2016). The potential of these methods to identify the existence and sources of problems makes pretesting an indispensable phase of the survey life cycle. In the context of cross-cultural research, pretesting offers valuable information about the role that language and culture play in the question response process, pointing to noncomparability bias, for example, by identifying questions or response options that are interpreted differently across cultural groups, leading to systematic measurement errors that may be attributed to translation issues, cultural connotations, or both. By detecting questions that function differently when translated or administered to different groups, and by providing information about sources of bias, pretesting allows for corrections prior to data collection.

Pretesting methods are often used once the survey materials have been developed and adapted. In these instances, testing all versions of the survey with the target populations is a crucial step to promote equivalence (Goerman & Caspar, 2010). As an iterative process, pretesting involves multiple rounds, in which changes to the instruments are followed by subsequent rounds of testing. Although less frequently observed, pretesting can be used at an earlier stage to inform the design of the questionnaire (e.g., by identifying terms and concepts used by the population of interest). Pretesting can also be used after data collection to facilitate the interpretation of the data. For example, pretesting methods may help interpret unexpected quantitative findings from one or more groups. In the context of repeated cross-sectional and longitudinal surveys, pretesting also informs future design decisions (e.g., modification of survey questions) (Fitzgerald & Zavala-Rojas, 2020).

To promote data quality, several methods have been developed for pretesting and improving questionnaires. These methods have traditionally been used in single-population studies and are gaining popularity in the context of cross-cultural research due to their potential to reduce measurement and comparison errors that restrict the quality of 3MC surveys. Nevertheless, there is a lack of consensus regarding the amount, type, and combination of pretesting that should be conducted (see the forthcoming report of the American Association for Public Opinion Research [AAPOR]/ World Association for Public Opinion Research [WAPOR] Task Force on Comparative Survey Quality). Further, the design and implementation of pretesting in cross-cultural research poses challenges in addition to those encountered in single-population studies. These challenges are the result of an increased number of parties involved, often located in different regions and speaking a variety of languages (Miller, 2018). Recruiting participants from multiple cultural and linguistic groups, designing protocols that are culturally appropriate and comparable, and adopting consistent methods to report results are some of the aspects resulting in increased logistical complexity of pretesting in 3MC surveys (Sha & Pan, 2013).

Several considerations guide the selection of pretesting methods, including the objectives of this process, the characteristics of the population, and the availability of resources. In the context of 3MC survey research, cultural appropriateness should also be taken into consideration because differences in communication styles and cultural norms may require adaptation of the protocols or implementation of different methods. In the next section, the most frequently used pretesting methods in cross-cultural studies will be discussed, emphasizing recent applications and challenges.

Pretesting Methods: Current Developments and Challenges

Cross-Cultural Cognitive Interviewing

Cross-cultural cognitive interviewing (CCCI) has become the most widely used method for pretesting and evaluating questionnaires in 3MC survey research. Cognitive interviewing refers to a range of techniques that provide information about the way in which respondents process and answer survey questions (Willis & Miller, 2011). To this end, two main strategies are used, alone or in conjunction: thinking aloud and verbal probes. Thinking aloud encourages participants to verbalize their thoughts as they answer survey questions. In contrast, probing requires interviewers to ask follow-up questions to obtain additional information about the response process. These probes can be designed in advance or be spontaneous and nonscripted, triggered by participants' behaviors. Probes administered immediately after tested survey questions are called concurrent probes, whereas probes administered at the end of the survey are referred to as retrospective probes.

Different types of probes serve different purposes (see Table 7-1), and their effectiveness may vary by cultural groups. For example, Martin et al. (2017) found paraphrasing, thinking aloud, and hypothetical probes to be difficult for women in Ethiopia and Kenya with low education levels. Other researchers have identified difficulties with paraphrasing, meaning-oriented probes, and thinking aloud tasks when used with non-English-speaking groups in the United States, regardless of their education levels (e.g., Goerman, 2006; Pan, 2004, 2008). Other multilingual studies have reported significant differences in the effectiveness of various types of probes in eliciting the desired information across linguistic groups, which may reflect

Table 7-1. Frequently used probes

Probe Type	Purpose	Example
Meaning oriented	Assesses respondent interpretation of terms, phrases, or questions	"What does the term 'property' mean to you here?"
Process oriented	Examines the process by which respondents select their answers	"How did you choose that answer?"
Paraphrase	Assesses respondent interpretation of questions	"What is this question asking in your own words?"
Elaborative	Gathers further information about the response process	"Could you explain your answer a little further?"
Hypothetical	Analyzes responses to hypothetical situations	"Please, report babies as age 0 when the child is less than 1 year old. If a person has a 4-month-old baby girl, what age should the respondent write here?"
Evaluative	Investigates the appropriateness of questions and response options	"Was it difficult for you to answer some of these questions here? Which ones?""Does the question here sound natural to you in <language>?"

Note: Examples taken from Park, Sha, and Willis (2016) and Park, Sha, and Pan (2013).

cultural norms and communication styles. The results from a multilingual cognitive project involving five languages indicated that evaluative and hypothetical probes were more effective for English, Russian, and Spanish respondents when compared with Chinese and Korean participants (Pan, Landreth, Park, Hinsdale-Schouse, & Schoua-Glusberg, 2010). Another study reported different outcomes for three types of probes used to assess the sensitivity of a series of translated questions in the Saudi context (Mneimneh et al., 2018). The findings show that proactive indirect probes asking whether "others" would find it uncomfortable to answer the questions resulted in more survey questions being identified as sensitive than direct probes asking about the respondents themselves and general probes asking respondents to elaborate on the questions in general. Further research is needed to better understand how different probes perform across cultural and linguistic groups and to understand the effects of education and culture in probe suitability.

In addition to the probes, the protocols for the interviews require adaptation to ensure that they comply with linguistic conventions and communication styles. Researchers have encountered difficulties in applying standard protocols developed from the perspective of English speakers to respondents from other cultural and linguistic groups that are less familiar with the interview task (Martin et al., 2017). Park, Goerman, and Sha (2017) compared the performance of different types of practice sessions to help Asian language speakers become more familiar with the cognitive interview process. They found that an action-based enhanced practice worked better than the traditional one translated from English. Interviewers indicated that participants in the enhanced practice felt more comfortable and better understood the purpose of the interview when compared with those presented with the traditional practice. Similarly, in an experimental project testing the American Community Survey (ACS) with Spanish speakers, protocols including additional rapport building and less structured interviews performed better than conventional protocols translated from English (Park & Goerman, 2018). However, more research is needed comparing different approaches to cognitive interview outcomes across languages and cultures.

The selection of participants and interviewers poses unique challenges in CCCI. Given the need to understand what the sources of error are, it is essential for interviewers to be fluent in the language of the pretest, as well as sensitive to cultural and linguistic nuances (Caspar et al., 2016). Although some flexibility in the conduct of the interviews has been advised, a common strategy to compensate for less skilled interviewers in applied settings has been the development of highly structured interviews (Lee, 2014; Miller et al., 2011). Despite the lack of guidelines regarding appropriate sample sizes in cognitive interviews generally (Blair & Conrad, 2011), it has been recommended that the number of interviewees be greater than that normally used in standard cognitive interviewing (Willis, 2015). The rationale behind this recommendation is to increase the likelihood of identifying problems that may arise or be more prevalent only among certain groups (Fitzgerald, Widdop, Gray, & Collins, 2011). Based on 132 interviews conducted in four countries (Bolivia, Fiji, New Zealand, and the United States), Hagaman and Wutich (2017) indicated that sample sizes of 12–16 may be sufficient for studies with homogeneous populations. However, they found that larger sample sizes are required to reach data saturation in heterogeneous and culturally diverse populations. As the literature suggests, several factors should be weighted when determining sample sizes, including participant characteristics, interviewer skills and experience, available economic resources, pretesting design (e.g., whether CCCI is going to be used alone or in combination with other methods), and anticipated problems (Blair & Conrad, 2011; Lee, 2014).

When testing translated questionnaires, participants may be restricted to monolingual non-English speakers or may include bilingual speakers. Although it was traditionally assumed that only monolingual speakers should be interviewed, recent studies suggest the value of evaluating translated questionnaires with both groups. Results from cognitive interviews of the Chinese and Korean translations of the ACS Language Assistance Guide indicated that the issues reported by monolingual and partially bilingual speakers were similar. When differences were found, they seemed to be driven by demographic differences (age, education, years living in the country) and not as much by language proficiency (Park et al., 2016). Results from cognitive interviews of the 2020 Decennial Census questionnaire with monolingual and bilingual Spanish speakers ratify the added value of including both groups. While bilingual participants identified most of the problems reported by monolinguals, there were a number of issues that were problematic for only one group. For example, the concept of "live or stay somewhere else" was only misunderstood by monolinguals, while the concept of "housemate or roommate" was more frequently misunderstood by bilinguals (Goerman, Meyers, Sha, Park, & Schoua-Glusberg, 2019).

CCCI has been mostly used to assess the cross-cultural equivalence of survey questions and to detect problems associated with translations. For example, a study conducted with participants in the Netherlands and Spain uncovered construct differences in the interpretation of "quality of life" (Benítez, Padilla, van de Vijver, & Cuevas, 2018). Although this term was mainly associated with relationships among Spaniards, it was more generic and linked to happiness for the Dutch. Similarly, findings from another CCCI project in six countries pointed to differences in the interpretation of the scope of "friends and acquaintances." In five of the six countries (Australia, Malaysia, Mexico, United States, and Uruguay), the term encompassed family members, but in Thailand it connoted only non-kin (Thrasher et al., 2011). These examples indicate that equivalent translations do not guarantee functional equivalence because connotations associated with context depend on social, cultural, and linguistic elements. CCCI has also shed light on systematic differences in the interpretation and use of response options. The study conducted by Benítez et al. (2018) showed that, when compared with the Dutch, Spanish respondents were more influenced by question order effects and showed less consistency across responses.

Despite the wide use of CCCI, there has been a lack of standards for analyzing and reporting on interview data (Ridolfo & Schoua-Glusberg, 2011). Drawing on sociolinguistic approaches, Pan and Fond (2014) developed a coding scheme to classify translation issues leading to measurement error in multilingual surveys. They identified five sources of errors: (1) linguistic rules (e.g., unnatural syntax), (2) cultural norms (e.g., address and naming conventions), (3) social practices (e.g., concepts that do not exist in a target language), (4) production errors (e.g., typographical errors), and (5) respondent errors (e.g., selecting multiple answers for questions when only one response should be selected). Other coding schemes have been developed in recent years, including the Cross-National Error Source Typology (CNEST), which emerged as part of the European Social Survey questionnaire design process (Fitzgerald et al., 2011). The Cross-National Error Source Typology defines three types of errors arising from different sources: source question problems, translation problems, and cultural portability. Source question problems arise when a questionnaire is designed in one language and then translated to another (or others). In these instances, problematic issues in the source questionnaire are likely to be replicated in the translated instruments (e.g., overly complex syntax, use of jargon). Translation problems refer to errors stemming from the translation process, ranging from typographical errors to using terms that are not equivalent in meaning, resulting in a loss of equivalence. Cultural portability problems occur when the concept of interest does not exist in all groups or when it manifests itself in different ways. For example, Pan and Fond (2014) reported difficulties with translations of certain concepts that appeared to be uniquely American, including "mobile homes" and "nursing homes," which were uncommon in the translated languages (Chinese, Korean, Russian, and Vietnamese).

In addition to preexisting tools for the analysis of qualitative data, Q-Notes, a specific software product for data entry and the structured analysis of cognitive interviews, has been developed by the US National Center for Health Statistics. Given its ability to centralize the process of data entry and its analytical flexibility, this software has been used in cross-cultural studies of various scales (Benítez & Padilla, 2014; Miller, 2018; Ridolfo & Schoua-Glusberg, 2011). Among its benefits for CCCI, Q-Notes can be used to analyze entire data sets, as well as examine the performance of questions across cultural or linguistic groups (Miller, 2018). In terms of reporting, Boeije and Willis (2013) proposed the Cognitive Interviewing Reporting Framework (CIRF) to guide the presentation of findings from this pretesting method in a comprehensive and systematic way. CIRF is a 10-category checklist that includes the following sections, allowing for flexibility in their ordering: (1) research objectives; (2) research design; (3) ethics; (4) participant selection; (5) data collection; (6) data analysis; (7) findings; (8) conclusions, implications, and discussion; (9) strengths and limitations of the study; and (10) report format. CIRF has been used to report cognitive interviewing studies in various countries, as well as mixed-method studies combining cognitive interviews with quantitative methods (Boeije & Willis, 2013; Padilla, Benítez, & Castillo, 2013).

Although CCCI has been mainly used to assess responses to survey questions, it has proven useful in testing multilingual advance materials, such as brochures and advance letters (Chan & Pan, 2011; Pan et al., 2010), and to refine scales measuring latent constructs (Reeve et al., 2011). Research conducted to date provides evidence of the utility of CCCI to identify issues and understand the sources of bias across cultural and linguistic groups (Benítez et al., 2018; Park et al., 2013). However, previous research also emphasizes the need to culturally adapt the protocols because interviewing techniques may not work equally well in all cultural groups.

Online Probing

In recent years, several studies have assessed the potential of online probing to uncover problems with survey questions and identify interpretation differences across countries (see Behr, Meitinger, Braun, & Kaczmirek, 2020, for a review of cross-cultural online probing). In online probing, after answering a survey question, respondents receive one or more probes to explore different aspects of the cognitive process they went through to answer the question. Among the probing techniques, mostly comprehension (e.g., "What does this term mean to you?") and category selection probes (e.g., "Please, explain why you selected this answer.") have been used to explore the country-specific interpretation of questions and assess item comparability (Behr et al., 2014). Despite using probes similar to in-person cognitive interviewing, several aspects vary between the two methods, including the mode, the appropriate sample size, and the level of interactivity (Meitinger & Behr, 2016). Unlike CCCI, online probing does not include interviewers, which removes potential interviewer effects but rigidifies the interview process. Responses provided by participants cannot be followed up through subsequent probes if the desired information has not been gathered. However, online probing allows for increased standardization and cost-effective recruitment of participants, particularly when they are dispersed across geographical areas (Neuert & Lenzner, 2019).

Meitinger, Braun, Bandilla, Kaczmirek, and Behr (2014) tested a composite scale measuring national pride across five countries in Europe (Germany, Great Britain, and Spain) and North America (United States and Mexico). Their results indicated that online probing was effective in identifying systematic variations across countries. For example, the question about pride in the Social Security system was interpreted differently in the United States and Spain. While respondents in the United States tended to equate the Social Security system with retirement benefits, in Spain most respondents associated "Seguridad Social" with the health care system. Another study exploring the cross-national comparability of a "civil disobedience" item across six countries (Canada, Denmark, Germany, Hungary, Spain, and the United States) pointed to substantial interpretation differences. In particular, respondents in Canada and the United States associated civil disobedience with violence and destruction more often than those in any of the other countries, leading to a lack of cross-national equivalence (Behr et al., 2014).

As part of the same project, Meitinger and Behr (2016) compared the findings from cognitive interviewing and online probing in Germany. They found that online probing resulted in higher nonresponse rates and shorter responses to the probes. Although participants in the standard cognitive interviews uncovered slightly more potential problems, the overlap between the two methods was high. Further research comparing cognitive interviewing and online probing in cross-cultural settings is needed to better understand their performance.

Previous studies suggest that when multiple probes follow a survey question, the sequence in which they are presented may affect the quality of the responses and the motivation of the participants, although the effects seem to vary across countries (Meitinger, Braun, & Behr, 2018). Given the scarcity of studies and the increased popularity of online probing, further research is needed comparing the performance of different combinations of online probes in a wider set of cultural contexts. In addition, more research is needed examining the impact of design features (e.g., probe placement, text box size) and number of probes on the responses to them. Given that most studies have used this pretesting technique with online panelists, who tend to be experienced survey respondents, future research would benefit from applying online probing to general population samples, furnishing the current evidence with greater validity (Neuert & Lenzner, 2019).

Vignettes

Vignettes are hypothetical situations that can be used to assess survey questions. When applied, participants are provided with one or more scenarios, in textual or visual form, and asked to answer a series of questions regarding the interpretation of terms and the process followed to answer the questions. This method has been often used in the context of cognitive interviews and focus groups; it offers several advantages including the ability to test multiple situations without the challenge of recruiting participants who would correspond to each specific situation. For example, multiple scenarios have been used to assess different categories of the relationship question used on the Census form (e.g., "housemate or roommate," "roomer or boarder," "stepson or stepdaughter," "unmarried partner"), because recruiting participants from each group would become very costly (Sha, 2016). In addition, vignettes can be particularly useful to test sensitive questions, because they shift the focus from participants to hypothetical cases (Goerman & Clifton, 2011). Vignettes have proven to be effective in examining comprehension issues with Spanish and Asian language translations (Goerman & Clifton, 2011; Sha, 2016).

Despite their potential, vignettes have several drawbacks, including that participants' responses to scenarios may differ from their own responses in real-life situations. In the context of cross-cultural research, particular attention should be paid to the cultural appropriateness of the vignettes, as scenarios developed for and tested with a group may not be appropriate in other contexts. For example, Sha (2016) reported some discomfort among Vietnamese participants presented with a scenario describing a couple living together without being married. Similarly, Goerman and Clifton (2011) found that a vignette depicting two women renting a room to an unrelated man was culturally inappropriate for some Spanish speakers.

Vignettes have often been used in combination with other pretesting methods, particularly cognitive interviews. A recent study comparing the performance of vignettes in focus groups and cognitive interviews in seven languages concluded that administering the vignettes in cognitive interviews was more effective for identifying problems with survey questions, particularly for Arabic and Spanish speakers (Meyers, García Trejo, & Lykke, 2017). Because studies comparing the performance of vignettes across pretesting methods are scarce, more research is needed in this area. In terms of vignette design, although some studies have used textual information only (Sha, 2016), others have combined vignettes with pictures or drawings (Goerman & Clifton, 2011). Considering the cognitive burden posed by vignettes, this latter approach could be particularly useful with participants whose education levels are low.

Behavior Coding

Behavior coding is a method by which behaviors displayed by interviewers and respondents during the question response process are systematically observed, coded, and analyzed (Johnson, Holbrook, et al., 2018). Originally developed to assess interviewer performance, behavior coding is increasingly used to evaluate survey questions and examine difficulties for both respondents and interviewers. The assumption on which this method relies is that deviations from the optimal survey process can help identify problematic questions. These deviations can be reflected in respondents' behavior (e.g., requests for repetition or clarification of questions, answers that do not use the options offered with the questions) or in interviewers' behavior (e.g., not reading the questions exactly as written). Table 7-2 shows examples of codes used in previous research to identify survey problems.

Although behavior coding provides systematic information that can be used to improve survey questions, little is known about the comparability of behavior codes across cultural and linguistic groups. To fill this gap, studies have begun investigating cultural variability in respondents' and interviewers' behaviors during survey interviews. Comparing behavior coding across cultural groups interviewed in English, Holbrook et al. (2006) reported greater comprehension difficulties among the three minority groups participating in their study (African Americans, Mexican Americans, and Puerto Ricans) when compared with non-Hispanic whites. They explained these differences indicating that "questions that are written from the perspective of the dominant cultural group seem to be difficult for members of minority cultural groups" (Holbrook et al., 2006, p. 587). Similarly, findings from a behavior coding study with African American, Latina, and non-Latina white women in the United States suggested cultural variability in comprehension and mapping difficulties. Specifically, Latinas expressed more comprehension difficulties than white respondents, and African Americans were more likely to report mapping difficulties compared to whites (Cho, Fuller, File, Holbrook, & Johnson, 2006).

Table 7-2. Examples of behavior codes

Respondent	
Clarification	Respondent indicates uncertainty about the meaning of a question
	Respondent indicates uncertainty about the time frame of the question
	Respondent indicates uncertainty about the meaning of the response options
	Respondent asks the interviewer to repeat part of or the entire question
Inadequate answer	Respondent provides an answer not using the response options offered with the question
Interviewer	
Incomplete reading	Interviewer does not read the question entirely, omitting parts of it
Poor reading	Interviewer does not read the question as written, by adding or changing one or more words

Note: Examples taken from Holbrook, Cho, and Johnson (2006) and Johnson, Holbrook, et al. (2018).

Differences across languages have also been found in previous research. Using behavioral coding, Pascale (2016) analyzed interviews conducted in English and Spanish to evaluate the ACS Content Test. Nonstandard interviewer behavior was more frequent when interviews were conducted in Spanish. Major changes to the questions, higher rates of skipping, and incorrectly verifying questions occurred more often in interviews conducted in Spanish than in English (54 percent versus 39 percent). More recently, Johnson, Holbrook, et al. (2018) conducted a study in which questions designed to produce difficulties were deliberately introduced (e.g., questions asking about nonexistent policies or objects, double-barreled questions, mismatches between the question stem and the response options). This study included respondents from different cultural backgrounds, who were interviewed in various languages (English, Korean, and Spanish). Their findings suggest that respondents across racial, ethnic, and linguistic groups generally reacted in a consistent way when confronted with questions designed to elicit problems. When compared with nonproblematic questions, they generated more problems, as expressed by behavioral codes. Although most groups reacted to the poorly designed questions in a similar manner, differences were found between Korean Americans and non-Hispanic whites interviewed in English. Specifically, Korean Americans reported fewer mapping difficulties when responding to the questions designed to elicit mapping problems than non-Hispanic whites. In addition to respondents' behavior, differences were found in interviewers' behavior, with non-English-speaking interviewers misreading questions more often than English-speaking interviewers.

A similar experimental study conducted in Korea raised questions about the effectiveness of behavior coding in identifying problematic survey questions (Park & Lee, 2018). In this experiment, respondents were randomly assigned to an intentionally problematic questionnaire (e.g., omitting response options that were likely to be selected, unusually wide reference periods making recall difficult) or to a control featuring existing questions that have been extensively pretested and fielded. Behaviors indicative of potential problems were found to be very limited. Despite finding a higher number of problematic behaviors among respondents when the flawed questionnaire was used, the differences between the groups were not significant. Moreover, the number of problematic behaviors displayed by interviewers was not higher in the group receiving the flawed questionnaire, with codes suggesting the opposite pattern (a higher number of interviewers' problematic behaviors in the control group).

Another study has pointed to potential differences in the effectiveness of behavior coding across countries, which may be attributed to communication norms and styles. Thrasher et al. (2011) assessed the equivalence of survey questions across six countries (Australia, Malaysia, Mexico, Thailand, Uruguay, and the United States), finding that behavioral coding was more successful identifying problems in the two English-speaking, Western countries (Australia and the United States). In Western countries, where directness and openness are the preferred communication styles, behavior coding may be more effective than in other countries with a preference for indirect styles (Pan et al., 2010; Park & Lee, 2018). Although behavior coding is a promising tool to identify problematic questions in 3MC surveys, further research is needed examining the comparability of behavior codes across cultural and linguistic groups. Because behavior coding is based on overt behaviors, important requirements for comparability include ensuring that members of various groups are equally likely to express problems during survey interviews and that the codes capture cultural variations of these behaviors.

Combining Pretesting Methods

Combining pretesting methods and triangulating their findings provides additional information that helps to make informed decisions. Despite this, few studies have used multiple methods to assess noncomparability bias across linguistic and cultural groups. Thrasher et al. (2011) combined behavioral coding and cognitive interviewing to identify issues in survey questions for adult smokers across six countries. Their findings suggest that both methods yield similar conclusions, although more potential errors were identified using cognitive interviews. Childs and Goerman (2010) highlighted the benefits of using a mixed-method approach to pretest the US Census Test Nonresponse Followup (NRFU) in Spanish and English. Whereas findings from cognitive interviews were very similar between the languages, behavior coding pointed to significantly more problems with the Spanish instrument. For example, questions in English were administered correctly (i.e., asking questions as worded and correctly verifying information) more often than those in Spanish.

In addition, some studies have combined quantitative and qualitative methods to assess the cross-cultural comparability of constructs. For example, the European Social Survey (Fitzgerald & Zavala-Rojas, 2020) and the European Health and Social Integration Survey (Wilmot, 2020) exemplify two large-scale projects in which a variety of pretesting methods have been used. On a smaller scale, Meitinger (2017) applied multigroup, confirmatory factor analysis and online probing in a mixed methods approach to examine the cross-national equivalence of patriotism and nationalism in five countries (Germany, Great Britain, Mexico, Spain, and the United States). Her findings suggest that online probing can help clarify quantitative results and better understand the reasons for the lack of cross-national equivalence. Similarly, Reeve et al. (2011) combined cognitive interviewing with psychometric methods to evaluate the performance of a scale measuring discrimination in a multiethnic population comprising African Americans, Asian Americans, and Latinos in the United States. Their findings reinforce the notion that qualitative and quantitative techniques complement each other by identifying distinct problems and providing different types of information on the same issues. However, the different focuses of qualitative and quantitative methods may result in situations in which these approaches lead to contradictory solutions. In this study, cognitive interviews suggested that a relatively short, 12-month reference period functioned best, while quantitative findings revealed that few individuals reported experiencing discrimination frequently, which called for a longer recall period to capture both usual and rare acts of discrimination. In these instances, the approach to be taken will depend on the goals of the study and the specific use of the scale.

Because different pretesting methods elicit different problems and may not work equally well across cultural groups, combining them maximizes their benefits, providing information to improve survey instruments in different ways. Of particular note are studies combining qualitative and quantitative techniques because they offer the value of the generalization afforded by quantitative methods with the in-depth information provided by qualitative techniques. Given the singularities of the different groups involved in cross-cultural research, combinations of pretesting methods may also vary across the groups (Caspar et al., 2016). In addition to the specific methods, the sequence in which these methods are used may have major consequences on the results, such that it requires careful consideration.

Concluding Remarks

Recent years have witnessed an increase in the number and scope of cross-cultural surveys. This trend has been accompanied by theoretical developments and innovations in all stages of the survey cycle, including pretesting methods and applications. These methods were originally developed for single-population studies and require adaptation to be used across a range of languages, regions, and cultures. Despite the increased use of pretesting methods in 3MC surveys, there remains no consensus regarding best practices for their design and implementation.

In this chapter, the current state of pretesting in cross-cultural surveys has been reviewed, focusing on recent applications and current challenges. Most of the studies investigating differences across linguistic and cultural groups have used a limited number of pretesting methods, primarily cognitive interviewing. Despite this, best practices for CCCI are underdeveloped, and more empirical evidence is needed to better understand the performance of different interviewing approaches and probe types across groups (Boeije & Willis, 2013; Lee, 2014). This field of study would also benefit from additional research examining appropriate sample sizes and numbers of iteration rounds in cross-cultural research with groups featuring various levels of homogeneity.

In contrast to CCCI, very little is known about the performance of other pretesting methods in the context of cross-cultural research. Of particular note is the scarcity of studies utilizing widely used pretesting methods in single-population studies, such as focus groups, expert reviews, and usability testing. Some exceptions include recent applications of focus groups (Sha, Hsieh, & Goerman, 2018) and expert reviews (Goerman, Meyers, & García

Trejo, 2019) to assess and refine questionnaires and other survey materials in multilingual projects. In addition, a few studies have assessed the usability of translated questionnaires and survey materials with non-English or limited English speakers (Leeman, Fond, & Ashenfelter, 2012; Sha et al., 2018; Wang, Sha, & Yuan, 2017), successfully identifying navigation problems. For example, a usability test of the online version of the Puerto Rico Community Survey found that respondents experienced difficulties entering their names into the single box provided. These difficulties were attributed to differences in naming conventions between the United States, with one family name, and Puerto Rico, where two last names (paternal and maternal) are common, requiring additional boxes to enter the information. The evaluation of these and other pretesting methods across different cultures and linguistic groups is an important area for future research. In addition to expanding the use and combination of pretesting methods, much can be learned by sharing the outcomes of tested questions in cross-cultural projects using repositories that researchers and organizations can consult (e.g., Q-Bank, developed by the US National Center for Health Statistics, SQP software; Saris & Gallhofer, 2014).

Acknowledgments

This chapter stems from the "Prisons: The Rule of Law, Accountability and Rights" project, with funding from the European Research Council under the European Union's Horizon 2020 research and innovation program (grant agreement 679362). The author would like to thank Sophie van der Valk for her insightful comments on a previous draft of this paper and Mandy Sha for her support and encouragement.

References

Behr, D., Braun, M., Kaczmirek, L., & Bandilla, W. (2014). Item comparability in cross-national surveys: Results from asking probing questions in cross-national web surveys about attitudes towards civil disobedience. *Quality & Quantity, 48*, 127–148. https://doi.org/10.1007/s11135-012-9754-8

Behr, D., Meitinger, K., Braun, M., & Kaczmirek, L. (2020). Cross-national web probing: An overview of its methodology and its use in cross-national studies. In P. C. Beatty, D. Collins, L. Kate, J. L. Padilla, G. B. Willis, & A. Wilmot (Eds.), *Advances in questionnaire design, development, evaluation and testing* (pp. 521–544). Hoboken, NJ: Wiley & Sons.

Benítez, I., & Padilla, J. (2014). Analysis of nonequivalent assessments across different linguistic groups using a mixed methods approach. *Journal of Mixed Methods Research, 8*(1), 52–68. https://doi.org/10.1177/1558689813488245

Benítez, I., Padilla, J. L., van de Vijver, F., & Cuevas, A. (2018). What cognitive interviews tell us about bias in cross-cultural research: An illustration using quality-of-life terms. *Field Methods, 30*(4), 277–294. https://doi.org/10.1177/1525822X18783961

Blair, J., & Conrad, F. G. (2011). Sample size for cognitive interview pretesting. *Public Opinion Quarterly, 75*(4), 636–658. https://doi.org/10.1093/poq/nfr035

Boeije, H., & Willis, G. (2013). The Cognitive Interviewing Reporting Framework (CIRF): Towards the harmonization of cognitive testing reports. *Methodology, 9*, 87–95. https://doi.org/10.1027/1614-2241/a000075

Caspar, R., Peytcheva, E., Yang, T., Lee, S., Liu, M., & Hu, M. (2016). Pretesting. *Cross-cultural survey guidelines*. Ann Arbor, MI: Survey Research Center, Institute for Social Research, University of Michigan. Retrieved from https://ccsg.isr.umich.edu/index.php/chapters/pretesting-chapter

Chan, A. Y., & Pan, Y. (2011). The use of cognitive interviewing to explore the effectiveness of advance supplemental materials among five language groups. *Field Methods, 23*(4), 342–361. https://doi.org/10.1177/1525822x11414836

Childs, J., & Goerman, P. (2010). Bilingual questionnaire evaluation and development through mixed pretesting methods: The case of the U.S. Census Nonresponse Followup instrument. *Journal of Official Statistics, 26*(3), 535–557.

Cho, Y. I., Fuller, A., File, T., Holbrook, A. L., & Johnson, T. P. (2006). *Culture and survey question answering: A behavior coding approach*. American Statistical Association 2006 Proceedings of the Section on Survey Research Methods. Washington, DC: American Statistical Association.

Fitzgerald, R., Widdop, S., Gray, M., & Collins, D. (2011). Identifying sources of error in cross-national questionnaires: Application of an error source typology to cognitive interview data. *Journal of Official Statistics, 27*(4), 569–599.

Fitzgerald, R., & Zavala-Rojas, D. (2020). A model for cross-national questionnaire design and pretesting. In P. C. Beatty, D. Collins, L. Kate, J. L. Padilla, G. B. Willis, & A. Wilmot (Eds.), *Advances in questionnaire design, development, evaluation and testing* (pp. 493–520). Hoboken, NJ: Wiley & Sons.

Goerman, P. L. (2006). *Adapting cognitive interview techniques for use in pretesting Spanish language survey instruments.* Washington, DC: US Census Bureau, Statistical Research Division.

Goerman, P. L., & Caspar, R. A. (2010). A preferred approach for the cognitive testing of translated materials: Testing the source version as a basis for comparison. *International Journal of Social Research Methodology, 13*(4), 303–316. https://doi.org/10.1080/13645570903251516

Goerman, P. L., & Clifton, M. (2011). The use of vignettes in cross-cultural cognitive testing of survey instruments. *Field Methods, 23*(4), 362–378. https://doi.org/10.1177/1525822X11416188

Goerman, P., Meyers, M., & García Trejo, Y. (2019). *The place of expert review in translation and questionnaire evaluation for hard-to-count populations in national surveys.* (Survey Methodology Working Paper Number 2019-02). Washington, DC: Research and Methodology Directorate, Center for Behavioral Science Methods Research Series, US Census Bureau.

Goerman, P. L., Meyers, M., Sha, M., Park, H., & Schoua-Glusberg, A. (2018). Working toward comparable meaning of different language versions of survey instruments: Do monolingual and bilingual cognitive testing respondents help to uncover the same issues? In T. P. Johnson, B. E. Pennell, I. A. L. Stoop, & B. Dorer (Eds.), *Advances in comparative survey methods: Multinational, multiregional, and multicultural contexts (3MC)* (pp. 251–269). Hoboken, NJ: Wiley & Sons.

Hagaman, A. K., & Wutich, A. (2017). How many interviews are enough to identify metathemes in multisited and cross-cultural research? Another perspective on Guest, Bunce, and Johnson's (2006) landmark study. *Field Methods, 29*(1), 23–41. https://doi.org/10.1177/1525822X16640447

Holbrook, A., Cho, Y. I., & Johnson, T. (2006). The impact of question and respondent characteristics on comprehension and mapping difficulties. *Public Opinion Quarterly, 70*(4), 565–595. https://doi.org/10.1093/poq/nfl027

Johnson, T. P., Holbrook, A., Cho, Y. I., Shavitt, S., Chavez, N., & Weiner, S. (2018). Examining the comparability of behavior coding across cultures. In T. P. Johnson, B.-E. Pennell, I. A. L. Stoop, & B. Dorer (Eds.), *Advances in comparative survey methods: Multinational, multiregional, and multicultural contexts (3MC)* (pp. 271–292). Hoboken, NJ: John Wiley & Sons.

Johnson, T. P., Pennell, B.-E., Stoop, I. A. L., & Dorer, B. (Eds.) (2018). *Advances in comparative survey methods: Multinational, multiregional, and multicultural contexts (3MC).* Hoboken, NJ: John Wiley & Sons.

Lee, J. (2014). Conducting cognitive interviews in cross-national settings. *Assessment, 21*(2), 227–240. https://doi.org/10.1177/1073191112436671

Leeman, J., Fond, M., & Ashenfelter, K. T. (2012). *Cognitive and usability pretesting of the online version of the Puerto Rico Community Survey in Spanish and English.* (SSM2012-09). Washington, DC: US Census Bureau.

Martin, S. L., Birhanu, Z., Omotayo, M. O., Kebede, Y., Pelto, G. H., Stoltzfus, R. J., & Dickin, K. L. (2017). "I can't answer what you're asking me. Let me go, please.": Cognitive interviewing to assess social support measures in Ethiopia and Kenya. *Field Methods, 29*(4), 317–332. https://doi.org/10.1177/1525822X17703393

Meitinger, K. (2017). Necessary but insufficient: Why measurement invariance tests need online probing as a complementary tool. *Public Opinion Quarterly, 81*(2), 447–472. https://doi.org/10.1093/poq/nfx009

Meitinger, K., & Behr, D. (2016). Comparing cognitive interviewing and online probing: Do they find similar results? *Field Methods, 28*(4), 363–380. https://doi.org/10.1177/1525822x15625866

Meitinger, K., Braun, M., Bandilla, W., Kaczmirek, L., & Behr, D. (2014, July). *Aspects of measuring national pride: Insights from online probing.* Paper presented at the XVIII ISA World Congress. Yokohama, Japan.

Meitinger, K., Braun, M., & Behr, D. (2018). Sequence matters in web probing: The impact of the order of probes on response quality, motivation of respondents, and answer content. *Survey Research Methods, 12*, 103–120. https://doi.org/10.18148/srm/2018.v12i2.7219

Meyers, M., García Trejo, Y. A., & Lykke, L. (2017). The performance of vignettes in focus groups and cognitive interviews in a cross-cultural context. *Survey Practice, 10*(3), 1–11.

Miller, K. (2018). Conducting cognitive interviewing studies to examine survey question comparability. In T. P. Johnson, B.-E. Pennell, I. A. L. Stoop, & B. Dorer (Eds.), *Advances in comparative survey methods: Multinational, multiregional, and multicultural contexts (3MC)* (pp. 203–225). Hoboken, NJ: John Wiley & Sons.

Miller, K., Mont, D., Maitland, A., Altman, B., & Madans, J. (2011). Results of a cross-national structured cognitive interviewing protocol to test measures of disability. *Quality & Quantity, 45*(4), 801–815. https://doi.org/10.1007/s11135-010-9370-4

Mneimneh, Z., Cibelli Hibben, K., Bilal, L., Hyder, S., Shahab, M., Binmuammar, A., & Altwaijri, Y. (2018). Probing for sensitivity in translated survey questions: Differences in respondent feedback across cognitive probe types. *Translation & Interpreting, 10*, 73–88.

Neuert, C., & Lenzner, T. (2019, August 13). Effects of the number of open-ended probing questions on response quality in cognitive online pretests. *Social Science Computer Review*, 1–13. https://doi.org/10.1177/0894439319866397

Padilla, J. L., Benítez, I., & Castillo, M. (2013). Obtaining validity evidence by cognitive interviewing to interpret psychometric results. *Methodology, 9*, 113–122. https://doi.org/10.1027/1614-2241/a000073

Pan, Y. (2004, May). *Cognitive interviews in languages other than English: Methodological and research issues.* Paper presented at the American Association for Public Opinion Research, Phoenix, AZ.

Pan, Y. (2008). Cross-cultural communication norms and survey interviews. In H. Sun & D. Kádár (Eds.), *It's the dragon's turn. Chinese institutional discourses (Linguistic Insights)* (1st ed., pp. 17–76). Bern, Switzerland: Peter Lang.

Pan, Y., & Fond, M. (2014). Evaluating multilingual questionnaires: A sociolinguistic perspective. *Survey Research Methods, 8*(3), 181–194. https://doi.org/10.18148/srm/2014.v8i3.5483

Pan, Y., Landreth, A., Park, H., Hinsdale-Schouse, M., & Schoua-Glusberg, A. (2010). Cognitive interviewing in non-English languages: A cross-cultural perspective. In J. A. Harkness, M. Braun, B. Edwards, T. P. Johnson, L. Lyberg, P. Ph. Mohler, B.-E. Pennell, & T. W. Smith (Eds.), *Survey methods in multinational, multiregional, and multicultural contexts* (pp. 91–113). Hoboken, NJ: Wiley.

Park, H., & Goerman, P. L. (2018). Setting up the cognitive interview task for non-English-speaking participants in the United States. In T. P. Johnson, B.-E. Pennell, I. A. L. Stoop, & B. Dorer (Eds.), *Advances in comparative survey methods: Multinational, multiregional, and multicultural contexts (3MC)* (pp. 227–249). Hoboken, NJ: John Wiley & Sons.

Park, H., Goerman, P., & Sha, M. (2017). Exploring the effects of pre-interview practice in Asian language cognitive interviews. *Survey Practice, 10*, 1–11. https://doi.org/10.29115/sp-2017-0019

Park, H., & Lee, J. (2018). Exploring the validity of behavior coding. *Field Methods, 30*(3), 225–240. https://doi.org/10.1177/1525822x18781881

Park, H., Sha, M. M., & Pan, Y. (2013). Investigating validity and effectiveness of cognitive interviewing as a pretesting method for non-English questionnaires: Findings from Korean cognitive interviews. *International Journal of Social Research Methodology, 17*(6), 643–658. https://doi.org/10.1080/13645579.2013.823002

Park, H., Sha, M. M., & Willis, G. (2016). Influence of English-language proficiency on the cognitive processing of survey questions. *Field Methods, 28*(4), 415–430. https://doi.org/10.1177/1525822X16630262

Pascale, J. (2016). Behavior coding using computer assisted audio recording: Findings from a pilot test. *Survey Practice, 9*, 1–11. https://doi.org/10.29115/sp-2016-0012

Reeve, B. B., Willis, G., Shariff-Marco, S. N., Breen, N., Williams, D. R., Gee, G. C., … Levin, K. Y. (2011). Comparing cognitive interviewing and psychometric methods to evaluate a racial/ethnic discrimination scale. *Field Methods, 23*(4), 397–419. https://doi.org/10.1177/1525822X11416564

Ridolfo, H., & Schoua-Glusberg, A. (2011). Analyzing cognitive interview data using the constant comparative method of analysis to understand cross-cultural patterns in survey data. *Field Methods, 23*(4), 420–438. https://doi.org/10.1177/1525822X11414835

Saris, W. E., & Gallhofer, I. (2014). *Design, evaluation, and analysis of questionnaires for survey research* (2nd ed.). Hoboken, NJ: Wiley & Sons.

Sha, M. (2016). The use of vignettes in evaluating Asian language questionnaire items. *Survey Practice, 9*, 1–8. https://doi.org/10.29115/sp-2016-0013

Sha, M., Hsieh, Y. P., & Goerman, P. (2018). Translation and visual cues: Towards creating a road map for limited English speakers to access translated Internet surveys in the United States. *The International Journal for Translation & Interpreting Research, 10*(2), 142–158.

Sha, M., & Pan, Y. (2013). Adapting and improving methods to manage cognitive pretesting of multilingual survey instruments. *Survey Practice, 6*(4), 1–8. https://doi.org/10.29115/SP-2013-0024

Sha, M., Son, J., Pan, Y., Park, H., Schoua-Glusberg, A., Tasfaye, C., ... Clark, A. (2018). *Multilingual research for interviewer doorstep messages, final report.* (Survey Methodology RSM2018-08). Washington, DC: Research and Methodology Directorate, Center for Behavioral Science Methods Research Series, US Census Bureau.

Thrasher, J. F., Quah, A. C., Dominick, G., Borland, R., Driezen, P., Awang, R., ... Boado, M. (2011). Using cognitive interviewing and behavioral coding to determine measurement equivalence across linguistic and cultural groups: An example from the International Tobacco Control Policy Evaluation Project. *Field Methods, 23*(4), 439–460. https://doi.org/10.1177/1525822X11418176

Wang, L., Sha, M., & Yuan, M. (2017). Cultural fitness in the usability of U.S. Census internet survey in the Chinese language. *Survey Practice, 10*(3), 1-8. https://doi.org/10.29115/SP-2017-0018

Willis, G. B. (2015). The practice of cross-cultural cognitive interviewing. *Public Opinion Quarterly, 79*(S1), 359–395. https://doi.org/10.1093/poq/nfu092

Willis, G., & Miller, K. (2011). Cross-cultural cognitive interviewing: Seeking comparability and enhancing understanding. *Field Methods, 23*(4), 331–341. https://doi.org/10.1177/1525822X11416092

Wilmot, A. (2020). Measuring disability equality in Europe: Design and development of the European Health and Social Integration Survey Questionnaire. In P. C. Beatty, D. Collins, L. Kate, J. L. Padilla, G. B. Willis, & A. Wilmot (Eds.), *Advances in questionnaire design, development, evaluation and testing* (pp. 545–570). Hoboken, NJ: Wiley & Sons.

Cross-Cultural Comparison of Focus Groups as a Research Method

Mandy Sha, Hyunjoo Park, Yuling Pan,[1] and Jennifer Kim[2]

[1]Mandy Sha, Hyunjoo Park, and Yuling Pan contributed equally to this chapter.

Introduction

The validity of inferences drawn from focus groups rests on the verbal interaction between the focus group moderator and participants. When the focus group method is applied to research studies conducted in languages other than English, researchers need to make cultural and linguistic adaptations appropriate for the target population to maximize the effectiveness of the focus groups. However, there is a scarcity of research literature examining how focus groups perform in non-English languages, especially in Asian languages.

Prior studies on the use of focus groups in cross-cultural research have centered on cultural sensitivity issues, procedures, planning, practicalities, and logistics (e.g., Colucci, 2008). As Clarke (1999) pointed out, the assumption underpinning the focus group method is that individuals are valuable sources of information and can express their own feelings and behaviors. It follows that focus group participants must verbally express their thoughts and behaviors; thus, the use of language plays a central role in focus group discussions. Although the research includes extensive discussion of methodological issues related to applying focus groups in non-English speaking cultures (Halcomb, Gholizadeh, DiGiacomo, Phillips, & Davidson, 2007), it lacks a systematic investigation to compare how speakers of different languages express their views and opinions in focus groups using those languages. Because focus groups use guided group discussions to gain insight into a specific topic, it is critical to examine the extent to which focus group participants engage in the discussion through verbal expression.

---

[2] Disclaimer: Any views expressed are those of the author(s) and not necessarily those of the US Census Bureau.

Our purpose in this chapter is to conduct a systematic analysis of the linguistic behavior of speakers of five different languages to compare how active they are in focus group discussions. This chapter has two objectives: (1) to examine the conversational style of focus group participants across languages and (2) to outline the interaction patterns between focus group moderators and participants as well as among participants. The ultimate goal is to provide a general picture of differences and similarities across language and cultural groups in terms of participatory patterns.

More specifically, we used a coding scheme, based on sociolinguistic theory, to compare and contrast how speakers of five languages (English, Chinese, Korean, Spanish, and Vietnamese) participated in focus groups. Four to six focus groups were conducted in each of the five languages to evaluate the data collection materials planned for the 2020 US Census. Our findings will contribute to ongoing research on the effective use of focus groups as a method of studying the public opinions of culturally and linguistically diverse populations in the United States.

Background and Cross-Cultural Concerns in Conducting Focus Groups

Use of Focus Groups in Social Science Research and Cross-Cultural Concerns

The purpose of a focus group is to generate group discussion to gather qualitative information about the group's beliefs, attitudes, and behaviors relating to an issue, product, or service. Use of focus groups increased among social scientists in the 1980s, and several textbooks on the subject appeared in the 1990s (e.g., Krueger, 1998; Morgan, 1997). Focus groups are now commonly used by market researchers, academics, nonprofit organizations, government agencies, and community organizations (Krueger & Casey, 2000). Survey designers have also used focus groups to help conceptualize, contextualize, and frame questions; identify appropriate terminology for respondents; and evaluate questions (e.g., Campanelli, 2008; Fuller, Edwards, Vorakitphokatorn, & Sermsri, 1993; Kaplowitz, Lupi, & Hoehn, 2004). Notably, nearly all of this research drew participants from the same language group.

Conducting research in languages that respondents prefer presents new challenges for focus groups. The basic assumption of the focus group method is that focus group participants are expected to verbalize their thoughts and express their opinions. In addition, they are encouraged to interact with one another and are not limited to answering the moderator's questions only.

Because of the high amount of language use in focus group discussions, differences in communication styles across language groups inevitably affect the level of interaction among participants.

Communication styles refer to the ways in which speakers of a language or members of a cultural group use language to interact with one another. Sociolinguistics scholars have long pointed out that systematic and observable differences in communication norms across different languages exist (e.g., Gumperz, 1982, 2001; Tannen, 1984). For example, when comparing Peninsular Spanish and British English in debates broadcast on television, Ardila (2004) found that Spanish speakers tended to be uncomfortable with silence. Thus, Spanish speakers often interrupted to express agreement and took advantage of a pause to take the floor. Félix-Brasdefer's (2003) study compared directness in declining an invitation among three groups: Latin American speakers of Spanish (native), Americans speaking Spanish (nonnative), and Americans speaking English (native). Controlling for gender, education, age, and Spanish dialects, researchers noticed that the Americans speaking English were more direct than the Latin Americans speaking Spanish, while the Americans speaking Spanish exhibited an intermediate frequency of directness.

In addition, language and cultural scholars have concluded that Confucian-based collectivist cultures (e.g., China, Korea, Vietnam) place a high emphasis on face (such as honor, respect, and social status); therefore, it is important to use the appropriate terms of address and polite expressions or lexicons that enhance the other's face (Kádár & Mills, 2011). Observational studies show that the Korean language uses a highly developed system of address terms that have many honorifics. Using a wrong term of address in speaking is a social taboo (Kim, 2011). The Vietnamese language is similar—honorific and kinship terms as politeness markers are considered important features in conversation (Chew, 2011).

This concern for politeness often leads speakers of Asian languages to habitually use vague expressions or short answers in question–answer settings. Some evidence in survey research shows that there are differences between Western- and Asian-language speakers when responding to questions in a survey research interview. Chan's (2013) study showed that, compared with English speakers, a higher proportion of Chinese speakers provided indirect responses when asked research interview questions and when asked to participate in a survey. Pan's studies (2008, 2012, 2013) also demonstrated remarkable differences between English and Chinese speakers in cognitive interview settings. English speakers were expressive during the English-language interviews. Their answers were characterized by detailed comments on the issues being discussed and elaboration on their individual opinions and feedback. In contrast, Chinese speakers in the Chinese-language interviews tended to provide brief, vague, and ambiguous answers; sometimes the answers were unrelated to the topics being discussed. They also used a community-based argumentation style (a we-based versus an I-based style) and answered "yes" freely to every question.

Researchers have documented the challenges of using focus groups in non-Western languages and cultures. Halcomb et al. (2007) conducted an extensive literature review of focus groups in culturally diverse settings and provided some key considerations for researchers. One consideration is that the concept of power relationships differs in non-Western cultures. For example, they note that in some non-Western cultures "it is considered rude for younger persons to even suggest they have different opinions from those of an older person or one who is considered more 'senior' or 'important'" (Halcomb et al., 2007 p. 1003).

Various aspects of culture may affect the degree and nature of interaction among focus group members as well. Huer and Saenz (2003) reported that cultural mistrust may negatively affect participants' willingness to disclose information. Extensive knowledge of the participants' cultures is considered essential for conducting focus groups successfully. For example, they note that some Vietnamese Americans experienced government persecution in Vietnam and, as such, may be unwilling to participate in research studies. Also, cultural mistrust may arise because of concerns about how members of the target population believe they are perceived by the larger society. Huer and Saenz (2003) noted that in focus groups on attitudes toward disabilities, many Vietnamese Americans qualified their answers because they wished to avoid negative stereotyping.

However, comparative studies examining focus groups across languages are limited. One notable study is that of Lee and Lee (2009), which reported comparisons between focus groups conducted in the Netherlands and South Korea. They drew on differences in communication styles between high-context cultures (e.g., China, South Korea) and low-context cultures (e.g., the Netherlands, the United States). They hypothesized that members of low-context, individualist cultures have different attitudes toward discussion and conflict than members of high-context, collectivist cultures. For example, particularly in focus groups conducted in South Korea compared with the Netherlands, they found lower levels of interaction among focus group members.

We contribute to this line of scientific inquiry with a comparative study that examined cross-cultural differences in conversational styles and interaction patterns among participants drawn from different language groups.

Research Questions

Based on the literature on cross-cultural differences in communication styles between speakers of Western and Asian languages, we predicted that a similar pattern can be observed in their focus group participation. We took the approach of treating a focus group as a communicative event (Saville-Troike, 1989). A focus group, like any other communicative events, has its general purpose of communication, topics of discussion, participants, language variety, tone, and rules for interaction in the discussion. When participants enter into a communicative event, they draw on background knowledge acquired through past communicative experience to infer what was intended and to act based on their cultural norms of communication (Scollon & Scollon, 2001). This background knowledge includes their familiar way of talking and the communication style that is preferred in the situation. Communication style can be investigated through a systematic analysis of linguistic features that constitute what Tannen (1984) calls "conversational style." According to Tannen (1984), conversational style results from habitual use of linguistic devices motivated by the overall strategies of Rules of Politeness (Lakoff, 1973; Lakoff's Rules of Politeness are [1] don't impose [distance], [2] give options [deference], and [3] be friendly [camaraderie]), which serve basic human needs in interaction, that is, the need for rapport (high involvement) and need for distance (considerateness). The involvement–considerateness dimension in conversation has shed light on research in cross-cultural communication (e.g., Gumperz, 1982; Tannen, 1980) because conversational style can be placed on a continuum of high involvement to high considerateness, which enables researchers to easily identify linguistic features that show a pattern of interaction (see Tannen, 1984, pp. 30–31, for a list of linguistic features of high-involvement style).

We borrowed Tannen's term *high involvement* in this study to refer to active participation in focus group discussion, such as volunteering answers, giving elaborate comments, and actively interacting with other focus group participants. We used the term *low involvement* in this study in contrast to high involvement. A low-involvement style is characterized by a lack of interaction among focus group participants or short or brief answers, silences, or pauses in discussion.

In our study, we used this tool of linguistic analysis of conversational style to answer three specific research questions that correspond to the study objectives:

- Do speakers of the five languages show the same or different interaction patterns in focus group discussions?
- Are Western-language speakers (i.e., English, Spanish) more likely to use a high-involvement style in focus groups?
- Are Asian-language speakers (i.e., Chinese, Korean, Vietnamese) more likely to use a low-involvement style in focus groups?

Data and Methods

This section documents the data and methods we used, the decisions and assumptions we made in the data collection and analysis process, and ways we mitigated the limitations. This transparent documentation approach was guided by the quality standards for qualitative research described in Lavrakas (2013) and Roller and Lavrakas (2015).

Data for the Study

Data for this study were drawn from focus group discussions that were part of a research study conducted by the US Census Bureau. The objective of the overarching study was to develop and pretest census data collection materials in multiple languages to ensure that they were linguistically and culturally appropriate. The materials and moderator's guide were developed in English first and then translated using a team-based translation approach (Harkness, 2013; Pan, Sha, & Park, 2019) by language experts who worked directly and iteratively with protocol designers and subject matter experts. Experienced focus group moderators used a semistructured protocol to conduct 22 focus groups with 205 participants. Six focus groups were conducted in Spanish, and four each were conducted in Korean, Chinese, Vietnamese, and English. Each group had 8–10 participants. For each language, half of the focus groups discussed data collection materials associated with an Internet self-response instrument, and half discussed materials designed for use on the in-person census interviewer visits. The focus groups took place between June and September 2015, and the 2-hour discussions were audio- and video-recorded with the consent of the participants.

Moderators and Participants

The study used six moderators: one each for Korean, Chinese, and Vietnamese and three for Spanish and English. Each moderator was experienced in conducting focus groups in the assigned language and was familiar with the census materials because they had worked on developing the non-English versions. Although they may have differed in their moderating styles and group dynamics were not predictable, we minimized inconsistency across the groups by having moderators use the same moderator's guide to ask questions, follow the topic sequence, and manage the allotted discussion time. All moderators completed up to 3 hours of formal, study-specific training, except the Korean moderator and one of the Spanish moderators who were part of the team that designed the study protocol. To build rapport with the participants before the start of the focus group discussion, the moderator engaged them in an icebreaker exercise about their shared experiences living in the United States.

The participants received $75 as a token of appreciation for participating in the 2-hour discussion. The majority of the focus groups were conducted in dedicated facilities in California, Illinois, Maryland, and Florida, while three focus groups were conducted in a professional conference room in North Carolina (one English and two Spanish). To be eligible for the non-English-language focus groups, a participant had to speak Spanish, Korean, Chinese, or Vietnamese as their native language and also speak limited English. This homogeneity gave them the same frame of reference when thinking about translations and the US Census. The participants in the English-language focus groups had to speak English as their native or near-native language, and they discussed English-language materials.

The participants were recruited via word of mouth, or they saw advertisements about the study and contacted the recruiters. To achieve a wide range of opinions in the discussion, we recruited participants based on characteristics such as education, age, sex, and, if applicable, the year they came to live in the United States. These characteristics represent a cross-section of the Spanish and Asian language speakers in the United States and reflect the authors' years of experience conducting research with these populations. For example, Koreans tend to have higher education, so recruitment of people based on educational attainment focused on high school and college graduates for the Korean focus groups. For the Spanish and Chinese focus groups, we also recruited participants from different origins to enrich the discussion about translations. For example, while there is a degree of universality in Spanish and in Chinese, there are differences in word use among people of various Spanish and Chinese origins. We did not intend to use these demographic and respondent characteristics as units of analysis because recruitment for qualitative research does not render a high enough number of cases to enable analysis by specific characteristics. Table 8-1 summarizes the composition of the specific groups.

Transcription Process and Verification

The focus group discussions were recorded and transcribed in the languages in which the focus groups were conducted. To ensure a level of consistency across the transcriptions, the transcribers were trained to type all utterances from the video recordings. They also followed a set of 15 transcription rules designed by the authors to indicate the speech pattern, such as stress (grammar), intonation (falling, rising, and continuing), pause, and laughter and nonverbal behaviors. The transcription was read by the moderator or a lead researcher to verify its accuracy.

Coding Scheme

We developed a coding scheme using the basic principles in linguistic analysis of conversational style (Tannen, 1984). We considered the interactions that take place in a focus group discussion (e.g., moderator-to-participant and participant-to-participant interaction) and the setup of such interactions (e.g., question–answer format and group setting). More specifically, we coded five distinct linguistic features to identify focus group participants' interaction patterns: participants' responses to moderators' questions, interaction direction, overlapping speech, and types of answers to the questions. Altogether, the four features have eight codes: interactions were labeled as voluntary, involuntary, participant oriented, moderator oriented, or overlapping, and each utterance from an interaction was coded as brief, elaborated, or back channeling. Table 8-2 shows the coding scheme with a description of the codes, their definitions, and objectives. After we developed the draft coding scheme, we piloted it on a small sample of focus group transcripts. The results suggested that the coders needed more specific instructions and examples, so we provided individual coaching.

Table 8-1. Focus group composition

Demographics	English	Spanish	Korean	Chinese	Vietnamese
Sex					
Female	19	31	25	18	18
Male	19	27	13	17	18
Education					
Less than high school	4	15	0	9	4
High school graduate or GED	12	31	15	14	18
College or beyond	22	12	23	12	14
Year came to US to live					
1990s or earlier	NA	11	14	12	16
2000s	NA	21	14	8	14
Since 2010	NA	26[a]	10	15	6
Age range					
18–44	20	26	19	11	15
45 or older	18	32	19	24	21
Number of groups	4	6	4	4	4
Number of participants	38	58	38	35	36

Language	Additional group-specific details
English	Participants included non-Hispanic whites ($n = 14$), African Americans ($n = 10$); US-born Hispanics ($n = 9$); and participants with origins in Jamaica, India, Laos, Korea, and Taiwan ($n = 5$).
Spanish	The participants represented origins from Mexico ($n = 12$), Central and South America ($n = 18$), and the Caribbean ($n = 9$), and two of the six focus groups were conducted with Puerto Ricans who lived stateside ($n = 19$).
Korean	Participants were grouped by age to minimize the seniority effect in the Korean culture that would affect group dynamics: two "younger" groups 18–44 years old ($n = 19$) and two "older" groups 45 years or older ($n = 19$).
Chinese	The written materials were in simplified Chinese, and the moderator and participants used Mandarin. Participants represented the major dialects of Mandarin, Cantonese, and Shanghainese and Chinese-speaking regions including China ($n = 22$), Taiwan ($n = 5$), and Hong Kong ($n = 8$).
Vietnamese	No additional specific characteristics were recruited.

[a]Nineteen of the 26 participants were Puerto Ricans who had lived stateside since 2010 because of the Census Bureau's research needs.

Table 8-2. Coding scheme definitions and objectives

1. Response to the moderator's question: Voluntary vs. involuntary (codes: V, I)	
Definition:	Voluntary = offer answers
	Involuntary = being called on to answer a question
Objective:	To identify how actively participants take part in the discussion
2. Interaction direction: Moderator oriented vs. participant oriented (codes: M, P)	
Definition:	Moderator oriented = interaction is between moderator and participant
	Participant oriented = interaction is between participant and participant
Objective:	To identify interaction directions (e.g., if mostly moderator oriented, it is a low-involvement style)
3. Overlapping speech: (code: O)	
Definition:	Two speakers speak at the same time, or one speaker starts to talk while the other one is still talking
Objective:	To identify how often or how much one participant overlaps another in speech to determine the involvement style of the group
4. Type of answers: Brief vs. elaborated vs. back channeling (codes: B, E, C)	
Definition:	Brief = short answer, usually yes or no, or repetition of part of the question
	Elaborated = with details and reasoning
	Back channeling = Empty words or sounds that a speaker produces in the another speaker's speech to indicate active listening. It does not produce an interruption to the other speaker's speech.
Objective:	To identify how elaborate participants are in expressing their opinions. To identify how often or how much one participant shows involvement or encouragement to other participants.

Each linguistic feature signaled a certain characteristic on a high- vs. low-involvement dimension. A high-involvement style is characterized by the participant's voluntary participation in the discussion, elaborated answers to probing questions, and multidirectional interactions (moderator to participant, participant to moderator, and participant to participant). A low-involvement style is characterized by the participant's involuntary participation (being called on), brief responses to probing questions, and single-directional interactions (moderator to participant). By examining these linguistic features, we compared and contrasted the conversational styles and interaction patterns across groups.

The unit for coding is a speaking turn taken by a speaker. A speaking turn is defined as the speech that a speaker produces without interruption from other speakers. A speaking turn can be as short as one word (e.g., "yes," "okay") or as long as several lines. Table 8-3 gives an example for each code

Table 8-3. Coding scheme examples

Codes	Example
Response to moderator's question: Voluntary (V) vs. involuntary (I)	Example of voluntary response Moderator: (to the group) Before we go into what you highlighted, I have a few questions. First of all, what do you think the purpose of the brochure is? Participant 2: To inform people as to why the census is taking place, and make it as simple as possible, I think. (coded as V) Example of involuntary response Moderator: Participant 9, you have something there? Participant 9: It's missing the last statement here, the toll-free, to provide the census information here over the phone? (coded as I)
Interaction direction: Moderator oriented (M) vs. participant oriented (P)	Example of moderator-oriented interaction Moderator: Do you think there are any sentences that some people might find confusing or difficult to understand? Other than what P3 brought up? Participant 6: Why is it, why would it be more costly for taxpayers to do this one? (coded as M) Example of participant-oriented interaction Participant 6: Well I'm just curious. I don't think I would go out my way to find out and call and say, you know, but just curious. Participant 4: Well that's the same kind of thing that I think of when I read this. Getting your "fair share" of federal funding, it's like, "okay, what is your fair share [of] federal funding?" (coded as P)
Overlapping speech (O)	Example of overlapping speech Moderator: So that's the kind of question that comes to mind for you? Why it wouldn't ... Participant 6: Yeah, I was just wondering how, or why it would make it less costly if you respond. (coded as O)
Type of answers: Brief (B) vs. elaborated (E) vs. Back channeling (C)	Example of brief answer Moderator: Let's go to the fourth and final paragraph saying "you are required by US law..." So what do you think this paragraph is trying to say? Other than what we already covered. Participant 1: Motivation. (coded as B) Example of elaborated answer Moderator: Yeah, more likely this is the real statement because we have to have it all fit. Participant 3: But like Participant 1 said, once we get that message, it makes it sound like this is mandatory. But even though this is just a test that you don't have to do it. It's not the census, but it's actually, you get through this like, you have to do this. And that's what it's making it sound like. And when in reality you don't. (coded as E) Example of back channeling Participant 2: This is just a test. Participant 8: Right. (coded as C)

from the data to further illustrate how the coding scheme works. Each speaking turn has at least three codes (up to four codes including "overlapping").

Coding Process and Verification

We selected one segment from each transcript for coding. For the transcripts from focus groups that reviewed self-response data collection materials, we selected the segment that discussed a multilingual trifold brochure that was printed in color. For the transcripts about the materials associated with in-person census interviewer visits, we selected the segment that discussed a video clip showing an interaction between the interviewer and the respondent. These segments were both at the beginning of the group discussions. We selected them rather than coding the entire transcript to better manage and monitor the accuracy of the coding across the five languages. We decided not to select later segments because there might be potential bias in the interactions about recurring translation issues (i.e., identical translation issues that appear more than once): the participants may not state their opinions again (or may shorten them), and the moderator was not trained to probe on recurring translation issues because it would be repetitive.

For each language in the transcripts, two coders completed the coding. They were part of the language expert panels assembled for the study that developed the materials for the focus group discussions but did not moderate the focus groups. The coders received 4 hours of training, including 2 hours of group training about the research objective, the coding scheme, and the procedure for documenting appropriate codes at each utterance, followed by instructions on using an Excel program for tallying. They also completed 2 hours of coding exercises at home and received feedback from the lead researchers.

The coding steps were as follows: (1) Using the same focus group transcript, both coders coded the same sections and then compared the codes. One of the coders was responsible for indicating discrepancies, making notes, and compiling results. (2) Coders consulted with lead researchers on the intent of specific codes and clarification of coding rules if there were discrepancies. (3) Coders for each language subsequently met in one or more meetings to reconcile any discrepancies.

After the first two coding steps, the Spanish and Vietnamese language coding did not reach 90 percent agreement, while the English, Chinese, and Korean language coding did. For all languages, the coders met once or more to reconcile the discrepancies and reach 100 percent agreement. For Spanish and Vietnamese, the reconciliation meeting revealed that the discrepancies

Table 8-4. Percentage agreement between coders in each language

Focus Group Language	English	Spanish	Chinese	Korean	Vietnamese
Total number of codes (utterances)	(N = 399)	(N = 467)	(N = 336)	(N = 355)	(N = 267)
Agreement after coding Steps 1 and 2	91.5%	82.0%	93.2%	92.4%	86.5%
Agreement after reconciliation meetings	100%	100%	100%	100%	100%

were primarily due to the process: (1) the Spanish language coders' inconsistent handling of the transcripts (e.g., unsure where overlapping comments started and ended) and (2) confusion about specific coding rules. The reconciliation meeting between coders of each language ultimately resolved the discrepancies, and the coders reached an agreement on all codes. Table 8-4 documents the agreement by language before and after the reconciliation meetings.

For this study, we did not use complex statistics to evaluate coder agreement because the coders facilitated intercoder agreement by reconciling coding discrepancies through discussions. The coders were also quite knowledgeable about the subject matter, which reduced the likelihood that their coding agreement occurred by chance rather than as a result of actual agreement between the coders.

In summary, the focus groups were conducted in five languages, and many variables could not be controlled (e.g., unpredictable group dynamics). We attempted to mitigate them by using a consistent approach: experienced moderators used the same protocols and had a common understanding of the research objectives through training or roles as the protocol designers. The transcribers and coders followed a set of standardized procedures and verifications. In addition, the participants were homogeneous in terms of shared native language and limited English-language proficiency. All groups reviewed the same content of materials and videos and, in general, did not differ greatly in demographic characteristics. Because the strength of the focus group method lies in its qualitative, explorative nature, the flexibility and focus on context in the group discussions make it difficult to render the data absolutely accurate or inaccurate like in structured quantitative data collection. By fully disclosing the group compositions and our consistent data collection and analysis process, we hope the reader is enabled to reach decision that the comparisons across groups in this study are valid.

Findings

To explore the conversational styles of focus group participants in the five language groups, we took two steps in our analysis. First, we examined the frequency of occurrences of each linguistic feature in each language group to get an overall interaction pattern. We then compared and contrasted the interaction patterns among the five language groups to identify similarities and differences in those patterns. Second, we conducted a qualitative analysis to explore salient points identified in the overall pattern and to provide context for the main departure from the communication norms found in the analysis. Our findings address interaction patterns (Research Question 1) and involvement styles (participatory patterns) of Western and Asian speakers (Research Questions 2 and 3).

Quantitative Analysis

To address the research questions, we examined the frequencies of utterances by each code. There were 1,824 utterances and 22 groups in the analyses. Because group dynamics were not identical and inaudible utterances in the transcripts were coded as missing, the number of utterances in each analysis was different.

As shown in Figure 8-1, English focus group participants had the highest percentages of voluntary responses, with 99 percent of the responses being

Figure 8-1. Percentages of linguistic features across the languages: Interaction direction and speech

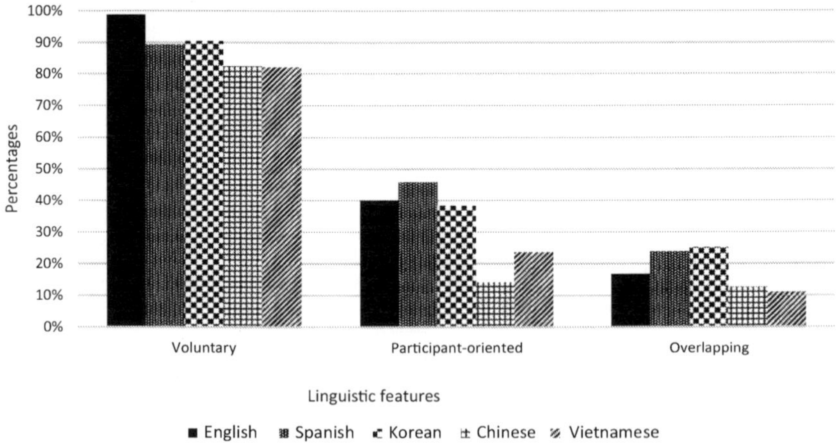

voluntary, followed by Korean (90 percent), Spanish (89 percent), Chinese (82 percent), and Vietnamese (82 percent). In other words, Chinese and Vietnamese focus group participants showed the highest level of involuntary responses at 18 percent. This finding suggests a strong participatory pattern for the English, Korean, and Spanish groups and a weaker participatory pattern for the Chinese and Vietnamese groups.

When we analyzed participants' utterances by interaction direction (moderator vs. participant orientation), we found that Spanish-speaking participants showed the highest level of participant-oriented interaction (46 percent), followed by English (40 percent), Korean (38 percent), Vietnamese (24 percent), and Chinese (14 percent) (see Figure 8-1). According to the coding scheme (see Table 8-2), participant-oriented interaction is mutually exclusive to moderator-oriented interaction. This means that Chinese and Vietnamese focus group participants showed the highest level of moderator-oriented interaction rather than responding to other focus group participants' comments. Again, the result shows a strong participatory pattern for the English, Korean, and Spanish groups. The Chinese and Vietnamese groups had a weaker participatory pattern.

Overlapping speech can also reveal the interaction patterns of the participants. As indicated by Figure 8-1, among the five language groups, the Korean focus group participants had the highest level of overlapping speech (25 percent), followed by Spanish (24 percent), English (17 percent), Chinese (13 percent), and Vietnamese (11 percent). These findings indicate that the Korean, Spanish, and English groups tended to be more involved by overlapping speech, which is also a sign of a stronger participatory pattern.

Figure 8-2 illustrates that, in terms of types of answers, the Korean focus groups had the highest level of brief answers (47 percent), followed by Chinese (40 percent), Spanish (25 percent), English (22 percent), and Vietnamese (16 percent). Vietnamese focus groups had the highest level of elaborated answers (81 percent), followed by Spanish (73 percent), English (72 percent), Chinese (52 percent), and Korean (50 percent). Chinese and English focus groups back channeled on a similar level, at 8 percent and 6 percent, respectively. Korean, Vietnamese, and Spanish focus groups back channeled similarly between 2 percent and 3 percent. Figure 8-2 illustrates a strong participatory pattern for the English and Spanish focus groups because of their elaboration and back channeling. Although Chinese and English groups back channeled at a similar rate, Chinese groups did not provide elaborated answers and therefore had a weaker participatory pattern in this analysis, along with Korean groups.

Figure 8-2. Percentages of linguistic features across the languages: Types of answers and back channeling

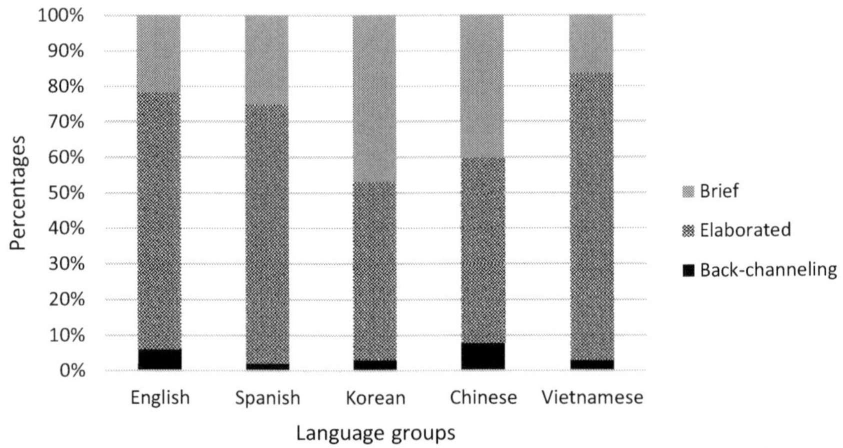

Vietnamese groups exhibited a strong participatory pattern that was driven by being elaborate in expressing opinions but maintained a weak participatory pattern in prior analyses.

Next, we conducted further analyses to investigate how each language differs from one another in terms of their linguistic features. The results in Table 8-5 indicate that for every linguistic feature, the differences between each language are statistically significant at the .05 level. The use of statistical tests to interpret coded qualitative data collected in focus group discussions does not differ in spirit from how researchers quantify recorded human communications in content analysis (Krippendorff, 2013, pp. 194–199).

As shown in Table 8-5, English focus groups were significantly different at the .05 level from the other four language groups in terms of voluntary responses made. Looking at the percentages, the Chinese and Vietnamese focus groups provided voluntary responses less frequently than any other languages, and these two groups were also significantly different from the Korean and Spanish focus groups in the pairwise comparisons of voluntary responses.

The Chinese and Vietnamese focus group participants were also less frequently engaged in participant-oriented interaction, and they were significantly different from the Spanish, English, and Korean focus group participants who demonstrated participant-oriented interaction more frequently.

Table 8-5. Pairwise differences across the five languages and linguistic features

	ANOVA			Pairwise Comparison (Difference Between Means)									
Linguistic Features	*F*	*df*	*p*	EN-SP	EN-KR	EN-CH	EN-VT	SP-KR	SP-CH	SP-VT	KR-CH	KR-VT	CH-VT
Voluntary	17.82	4	<.0001	.09*	.08*	.16*	.17*	—	.07*	.07*	.08*	.08*	—
Participant initiated	29.47	4	<.0001	—	—	.26*	.17*	—	.32*	.22*	.24*	.15*	—
Overlapping	9.67	4	<.0001	—	−08*	—	—	—	.11*	.13*	.13*	.14*	—
Elaborated	29.67	4	<.0001	—	.22*	.20*	—	.23*	.21*	—	—	−31*	−29*
Brief	28.45	4	<.0001	—	−25*	−19*	—	−22*	−15*	—	—	.31*	.24*
Back channeling	5.19	4	.0004	.04*	—	—	—	—	−06*	—	−05*	—	.05*

ANOVA = analysis of variance; EN = English; SP = Spanish; KR = Korean; CH = Chinese; VT = Vietnamese.

* The pairwise comparisons are reported when there are statistically significant differences between the languages. Comparison is significant at the .05 level.

In terms of overlapping speech, Chinese and Vietnamese focus group participants overlapped less frequently than Korean and Spanish focus group participants, and the differences were significant. However, the Spanish focus groups were not significantly different from the English focus groups on overlapping speech.

For the level of elaborated answers, the Vietnamese focus groups were significantly different from the Korean and Chinese focus groups. Vietnamese focus groups were not significantly different from the English and the Spanish focus groups, which provided elaborated answers more frequently than the Korean and Chinese groups. The Korean and Chinese groups were not significantly different from each other, but they were different from the other language focus groups and provided elaborated answers less frequently. Lastly, the English and Chinese focus groups were not significantly different in back channeling. These two groups back channeled more frequently, and they were significantly different from the Spanish focus groups that back channeled less frequently. Although the Korean and Vietnamese focus groups were significantly different from the Chinese focus groups, they were not significantly different from the English focus groups.

Qualitative Analysis

The qualitative analysis supports the quantitative findings that the English and Spanish focus groups had similar interaction patterns of a high-involvement style. They were characterized by more voluntary responses to the moderator's questions, more interaction among participants, and more elaborated answers in the discussion compared with the Chinese and Vietnamese focus groups (except Vietnamese for elaborated answers). Table 8-6 from an English focus group exemplifies the participants' active participation in the discussion. In this segment of the discussion, the moderator requested the group's reaction to a multilingual brochure that asked respondents to participate in a census test. The moderator showed the group the multilingual brochure and asked for their impressions regarding the placement of multiple languages in the brochure. As shown in Table 8-6, the first noticeable feature was the high level of overlapping speech. For example, when the moderator commented on the layout of the brochure (lines 502–504), Participant P9 started talking before the moderator finished his comment and gave an elaborated answer (lines 506–508). Second, multiple participants took part in the discussion (P3, P6, and P9), and there was

Table 8-6. English-language focus group interaction

502 M:	That's interesting to know. I think the intention was when you open it, you get the
503	most common languages. But, when you open it further, yeah, then it becomes the
504	last. I think they're to be {intending to be this ...
505	
506 P9:	{But it contradicts with the way that the languages are ordered on
507	the front and on the back. In the front and the back they're kept consistent, it's once you open the
508	back when you lose that consistency. (V, E, M, O)
509	
510 M:	So in your case you'd rather see the Spanish to be the second one here?
511	
512 P9:	Yes, on the second page. (V, B, M)
513	
514 P3:	So that's the reality of normally that's {what you... (V, B, P, O)
515	
516 P9:	{Yeah. (V, B, P, O)
517	
518 M:	Yeah.
519	
520 P3:	Normally that's what you ultimately would see anyways. (V, E, M)
521	
522 P6:	That's how I opened it. I didn't open it like this [demonstrates]. (V, E, P)
523	
524 P3:	Yeah that's when you open it all the way. (V, E, P)
525	
526 Group:	??? [unintelligible]
527	
528 P6:	So it depends on the person I think, and how they open it, yeah. I think it's kind of a
529	negative ... but one thing that I did want to mention was that, French? It's very
530	common language, I can understand that they can't put all 5,000 languages on the
531	card, same as they can't put all 5,000 languages on instructions for a product that
532	you purchase, but I've always seen French. And I speak French and you know I
533	think it's just as common as Spanish. (V, E, P)

M = moderator; P = participant; Codes: V = voluntary; E = elaborated; M = moderator oriented; O = overlapping; B = brief; P = participant oriented.

Note: The number preceding each line is the identifying line number in the transcript.

overlapping speech between P9 and P3 and the moderator and P9. Participants' responses were all voluntary and were elaborated in most instances. Finally, the discussion was multidirectional, with interactions between the moderator and participants and among participants.
The interaction pattern of the Spanish focus group is similar to that of the English group. (Due to space limitations, we only look at an English example here because the Spanish example had similar results.)

Compared with the English and Spanish focus groups, the Chinese and Vietnamese groups showed a low-involvement style or weak participatory patterns, which are characterized by more involuntary responses to the moderator's questions, more interactions between the moderator and participants (than between participants), and briefer answers. (Chinese and Vietnamese groups shared similar interaction patterns except for one feature—elaborated answers.) Table 8-7 shows that in the Chinese focus group discussion, the moderator had to call on participants to provide feedback, and the participants' responses were brief. The number of involuntary responses was in sharp contrast to the English-language interactions. For example, in lines 552–553, the moderator tried to ask for a volunteer to respond. When no one volunteered, he urged the group to hurry up and speak and then called on P9. In this short segment, the moderator called on four participants (P9 in line 553, P4 in line 557, P8 in line 565, and P7 in line 571). In addition, the interaction was between the moderator and participants only. There was no interaction among the participants; they simply answered the moderator's questions and did not make comments on one another's responses. Most of their responses were brief. All these features suggest a weak participatory tendency for the Chinese-language focus groups.

The Vietnamese-language focus group differed from the Chinese group in one feature: types of answers. While the Chinese focus groups had the second lowest percentages of elaborated answers shown in Figure 8-2, the Vietnamese interactions identified the highest frequency of elaborated answers. As shown in Table 8-8, the moderator asked a simple yes or no question, but P11 volunteered an elaborate answer, stating why the material under review was easy to understand. This participant was a younger, more recent immigrant. Other instances of elaborated answers in the Vietnamese focus groups were also made by younger, more recent immigrants.

Among the three Asian-language focus groups, the Korean-language interactions showed the highest involvement and were the liveliest. The Korean focus group members voluntarily participated in the discussion at a much

Table 8-7. Chinese-language focus group interaction (Chinese transcript followed by its meaning in English)

552 M:	OK。这个不画啊，不画。看过以后告诉我这一段啊。它是那个手册上八月二十四号
553	一段哈。它又表达了什么意思。还有谁，抓紧哈。九号说。
	(OK. No need to underline this. After you have read, please tell me what this section is about. That is the section on the brochure dated August 24th. What is it trying to say? Anybody would like to speak? Please hurry. P9, please speak.)
554	
555 P9:	省纳税人的钱。(I, B, M) (To save taxpayers' money)
556	
557 M:	好这是一个。省纳税人的钱。他要说的。四号呢?
	(OK. This is one. To save taxpayers' money. That is what it is trying to say. How about P4?)
558	
559 P4:	这次人口普查哦...是有更新更简易的方法 。还有它有很多的优点。(I, E, M)
	(This census ... there is a newer and easier method. It also has many advantages.)
560	
561 M:	嗯 OK 讲到它有很多的优点。还有吗？有没有讲简易的方法。什么方法呢？这个地方?
	(Oh, OK. It talks about many advantages. Anything else? Did it talk about the easier methods? What methods? Here?)
562	
563 P4:	没有…没有。(I, B, M) (No ... No.)
564	
565 M:	没有哦，是吧？其他有补充吗？八号。(No, is that right? Other comments? P8.)
567	
568 P8:	就是...就是...它就是...在讲一个这个人口普查它的功能就是要给帮助这个整个社区。
569	后给不一样的住户公平的那些...代表性。(I, E, M)
	(That is ... that is ... it says ... it says this census's function is to help the entire community then to provide equal representation to all kinds of households.)
570	
571 M:	代表性哦。好。七号。它想，它想，哦...这一段落要表达的是什么的?
	(Representation, OK. P7. What, what is this paragraph trying to convey?)
572	
573 P7:	就…我就感觉它是人口普查。(I, B, M) (Just ... I just think it's about census.)
574	
575 M:	就说人口普查。(It's about the census.)
576	
577 P7:	对。(I, B, M) (Right.)

M = moderator; P = participant; V = voluntary; E = elaborated; M = moderator oriented; I = involuntary; B = brief.

Note: The number preceding each line is the identifying line number in the transcript.

Table 8-8. Vietnamese-language focus group discussion (Vietnamese transcript followed by its meaning in English)

717 M:	Có từ nào khó hiểu hay dễ hiểu không ạ? (Is there any word that is easy or hard to understand?)
718 P11:	Em thấy cũng rất là dễ hiểu chị. Tại vì người ta cũng đã để rất rõ ràng là để biết thêm
719	thông tin về quy cách chúng tôi bảo mật của quý vị thì xin vui lòng truy cập trang mạng,
720	ví dụ thì thấy cái đó cũng rất là dễ hiểu. (V, E, M) (I think it's easy to understand because it indicated very clearly that to get more information about how we protect your information please visit the website. For example, I see that is easy to understand.) (V, E, M)

M = moderator; P = participant; V = voluntary; E = elaborated; M = moderator oriented.

Note: The number preceding each line is the identifying line number in the transcript.

higher rate than the Chinese and Vietnamese focus group participants in terms of their frequency of voluntary responses, participant-oriented interactions, and overlapping speech. The Korean groups also resembled English and Spanish groups when making voluntary and participant-oriented responses and had the highest overlapping rate of any language. Table 8-9 from a Korean focus group discussion demonstrates the group's higher involvement. In this excerpt, P10 voluntarily initiated a comment about the design of the multilingual brochure without being called on (lines 704–705). While P10 was still speaking, P6 indicated her agreement and added more points (line 707), also without the moderator's prompting. Another participant (P11) pointed out an observation that the other participants did not mention (line 711), and the moderator gave her feedback in line 713. The interactions continued when P11 clarified the point in line 715. Then, P3 (line 719) asked P11 a question, and finally, P9 wrapped up the whole conversation with a concluding remark in lines 723–724. In this short excerpt, we can see that the conversation was lively and included six people (five participants and the moderator).

The finding that the Korean focus group discussions showed higher involvement and livelier participation is unexpected because it does not conform to the typical communication pattern of Asian languages as discussed in research literature (Lee & Lee, 2009). We attribute this unexpected finding to two factors. First, all the Korean focus groups were moderated by one of the lead researchers who designed the study protocol. She readily clarified points of confusion and flexibly guided the flow of the conversation. In comparison, the moderators of the other Asian-language focus groups followed the moderator's guide more closely. They were similarly

Table 8-9. Korean-language focus group interaction (Korean transcript followed by its meaning in English)

704 P10:	예 여기 자동차. 이거... 인구 조사를 하는데, {자동차 보다는. 사람들... 에 그 사진을
705	여기에다가 집어 넣는 게 낫지 않을까요? [V, P, E, O]
	(Yes, for this vehicles.... this is regarding a population survey {rather than cars, would it be better to include some pictures of people?
706	
707 P6:	{그러니까. 자동차가 왜 들어가 있냐고.
708	스쿨 버스는 왜 있고. 사람들이 도보를 건너가는.. 모습이라던지, 사는, 그 삶을 바로
709	느낄 수 있는 그런 사진이 있으면 참 좋겠어요. [V, P, E, O]
	{Exactly, why a picture of cars is here. I don't understand why school bus are here. Like a people crossing the road, I'd like to have a picture that I can feel how people live and their life.
710	
711 P11:	제 생각에는 여기 센서스 로고가 빠진 것 같은데. 그걸 집어 넣으면 더.. [V, P, E, O]
	(I think the census logo is omitted here. If the census logo is inserted here, then ...)
712	
713 M:	여기, 제일 밑에 있는건데.. 눈에 잘 안 띄나요? (Here it is at the bottom. It is not eye-catching?)
714	
715 P11:	그거 말고 또 있는데 똥그랗게 생긴 거? [I, M, B]
	(I meant the round shape one, not that one ...?)
716	
717 M:	아 그래요? 어.. (Oh, is it?)
718	
719 P3:	글씨 말고 로고로 되어 있는 거가 있어요? [V, P, B]
	(It's not made of letters, but a picture?)
720	
721 P11:	아 동그란 그림으로 그 만들어진 {상무분가? 거기.. [V, P, B, O]
	(It is something made of a round shape picture {Perhaps a logo of Department of Commerce?
722	
723 P9:	{센서스를 글씨만 하지 말고, 거기에 어떤사람 같은
724	로고. 뭐 그런 것이 있으면 딱 보기만 해도 아! 이거 인구 조사구나. 하고. [V, P, E, O]
	{Not just showing the letters, but a person—like 724. If that sort is shown, people would see Oh! It is a census at the first glance.

M = moderator; P = participant; V = voluntary; P = participant oriented; E = elaborated; O = overlapping; I = involuntary; M = moderator oriented; B = brief.

Note: The number preceding each line is the identifying line number in the transcript.

experienced in focus group moderation and familiar with the census materials, but they did not have the advanced knowledge of the study objectives like the Korean focus group moderator. Second, the Korean focus groups were divided into two groups—a younger group (aged 18–44) and an older group (aged 45 or older). This methodological consideration reflected the Korean cultural orientation on emphasizing varying expressions of politeness according to social hierarchy and respect for elders (Kim, 2011). The combination of subject matter expertise and culturally appropriate group composition likely fostered rapport among the participants and between the moderator and the participants. As a result, the discussion was livelier than it might have been otherwise.

Discussion

We conducted both quantitative and qualitative analyses to illustrate focus group participants' linguistic behaviors. The systematic analyses indicate that Western languages (English and Spanish) demonstrated similar interaction patterns. Asian languages (Korean, Chinese, and Vietnamese) shared patterns in many interactions, but the moderator's subject matter expertise and a culturally appropriate group composition could change that pattern (as was the case in the Korean group). In general, Western language speakers were more likely to use high-involvement styles and strong participatory patterns in focus groups than Asian-language speakers.

Our study also demonstrates that each language has specific cultural dynamics and notable differences in focus group interactions. These interactions ranged from somewhat different to very different, and focus groups using the same language did not always exhibit very similar conversational styles. These findings reflect the dynamic nature of focus group data collection (which is also a strength that researchers rely on to interpret dynamic human interactions). Focus groups can still be an effective method for conducting research across cultural and linguistic groups when inherent sources of variability are mitigated by using a consistent data collection and analysis process and fully disclosing the details (see Data and Methods section).

In our experience, the efficacy of focus groups increases when the researcher develops strategies to address the factors that may affect group dynamics. For example, we recommend designing open-ended focus group probes (e.g., questions starting with "why," "when," and "what") to encourage more voluntary and elaborated answers and taking advantage of nonverbal cues (e.g., raising hands to show agreement) to facilitate group discussions. This way, there is sufficient information from a variety of participants to assess or inform the design of the data collection materials that are being discussed. In addition, an experienced and charismatic moderator with in-depth knowledge about the discussion topic and materials can encourage discussion while attending to cultural barriers and language nuances in conducting the focus group. Further research should be done to evaluate the efficacy of these strategies across language groups.

This study raised some important methodological considerations for conducting focus groups in non-English languages. The Korean interaction pattern in this study shows that with careful attention to group dynamics and methodological design (including moderator selection and training), researchers can obtain the desired participatory pattern in a non-Western language focus group discussion. Researchers also need to consider the factors of sex, age, group size, and possibly year of emigration to the United States to achieve the ideal group dynamics. For example, in the Vietnamese focus groups, younger, more recent immigrants tended to elaborate on comments when they spoke (while still having low involvement in terms of other linguistic features). The Vietnamese population in the United States has a different history than the Chinese and Korean populations. The earlier Vietnamese arrivals were refugees of the Vietnam War, but the more recent immigrants mainly consist of immigrants reuniting with relatives already residing in the United States (Rumbaut, 2007). Grouping the Vietnamese participants by the year they moved to the United States could have possibly created more homogeneity in the group and encouraged higher involvement in their interactions.

Conclusion

Focus group discussion is a communicative event governed by cultural norms of communication. The observable patterns of interaction across different language groups might affect the effectiveness of focus groups in gathering in-depth information from participants. However, the differences in interaction patterns can be minimized if researchers are aware of these differences and the interrelatedness of cultural norms of communication and interaction patterns. This study is an attempt to offer some insights into these differences and potential barriers in conducting focus groups in languages other than English. We propose two ideas for future research: (1) examine whether these differences affect the quality of data collected from focus groups and (2) explore ways of designing focus groups to address these differences across languages and cultures.

This study has several limitations. First, the focus group data were based on a purposive sample limited to the speakers of the five languages in several US geographic areas. It may be difficult to generalize the findings to the home cultures of the non-English-language groups. Second, the specific group characteristics may have contributed to the observed differences. In our design, we were not able to randomly allocate participants to language groups. We also did not use sophisticated statistical analyses to tease out issues related to speaking turns. Although our intention was to not force a qualitative study into a quantitative model, future research could explore the use of appropriate statistical modeling to interpret coded focus group data to study public opinion (e.g., similar to content analysis research). Doing so might enable deeper comparisons of the outcome of the discussions, such as whether groups that provide longer responses in fewer speaking turns (e.g., Vietnamese) offer insights about data collection materials the same way as language groups that have more speaking turns but keep their responses brief.

Acknowledgments

The authors acknowledge the US Census Bureau's research team in the Decennial Census Management Division and the Language and Cross-Cultural Research Group in the Center for Behavioral Science Methods. Their vision and commitment to cross-cultural and multilingual research made this study possible. We also thank RTI International's team of Korean-, Chinese-, Vietnamese-, Spanish-, and English-language coders who made invaluable contributions to the research. We are grateful to reviewers from the Census Bureau, RTI International Journal Club supported by the RTI Fellows Program and the Survey Research Division, and Eric Plutzer and three anonymous reviewers for their constructive comments and suggestions for improving an earlier version of the paper.

References

Ardila, J. G. (2004). Transition relevance places and overlapping in (Spanish-English) conversational etiquette. *Modern Language Review, 99*(3), 635–650.

Campanelli, P. (2008). Testing survey questions. In E. D. de Leeuw, J. J. Hox, & D. A. Dillman (Eds.), *International handbook of survey methodology* (pp. 176–200). New York, NY: Erlbaum/Taylor & Francis.

Chan, A. Y. (2013). Discourse analysis of Chinese speakers' indirect and contrary-to-face-value responses to survey interview questions. In Y. Pan & D. Kádár (Eds.), *Chinese discourse and interaction: Theory and practice* (pp. 175–199). London, England: Equinox.

Chew, G. C. L. (2011). Politeness in Vietnam. In D. Kádár & S. Mills (Eds.), *Politeness in East Asia* (pp. 208–225). Cambridge, UK: Cambridge University Press.

Clarke, A. (1999). Focus group interviews in health-care research. *Professional Nurse (London, England), 14*(6), 395–397.

Colucci, E. (2008). On the use of focus groups in cross-cultural research. In P. Liamputtong (Ed.), *Doing cross-cultural research* (pp. 233–252). Netherlands: Springer.

Félix-Brasdefer, C. J. (2003). Declining an invitation: A cross-cultural study of pragmatic strategies in American English and Latin American Spanish. *Multilingua, 22*, 225–255.

Fuller, T. D., Edwards, J. N., Vorakitphokatorn, S., & Sermsri, S. (1993). Using focus groups to adapt survey instruments to new populations. In D. L. Morgan (Ed.), *Successful focus groups: Advancing the state of the art* (pp. 89–104). Newbury Park, CA: SAGE.

Gumperz, J. J. (1982). *Discourse strategies*. Cambridge, UK: Cambridge University Press.

Gumperz, J. J. (2001). Interactional sociolinguistics: A personal perspective. In D. Schiffrin, D. Tannen, & H. E. Hamilton (Eds.), *The handbook of discourse analysis* (pp. 215–228). Malden, MA: Blackwell Publishing.

Halcomb, E. J., Gholizadeh, L., DiGiacomo, M., Phillips, J., & Davidson, P. M. (2007). Literature review: Considerations in undertaking focus group research with culturally and linguistically diverse groups. *Journal of Clinical Nursing, 16*(6), 1000–1011.

Harkness, J. (2003). Questionnaire translation. In J. Harkness, F. J. R. Van de Vijver, & P. Ph. Mohler (Eds.), *Cross-cultural survey methods* (pp. 37–39). Hoboken, NJ: Wiley-Interscience.

Huer, M. B., & Saenz, T. I. (2003). Challenges and strategies for conducting survey and focus group research with culturally diverse groups. *American Journal of Speech-Language Pathology, 12*(2), 209–220.

Kádár, D., & Mills, S. (2011). Introduction. In D. Kádár & S. Mills (Eds.), *Politeness in East Asia* (pp. 1–15). Cambridge, UK: Cambridge University Press.

Kaplowitz, M. D., Lupi, F., & Hoehn, J. P. (2004). Multiple methods for developing and evaluating a stated-choice questionnaire to value wetlands. In S. Presser, J. M. Rothgeb, M. P. Couper, J. T. Lessler, E. Martin, J. Martin, & E. Singer (Eds.), *Methods for testing and evaluating survey questionnaires* (pp. 503–524). New York, NY: John Wiley and Sons.

Kim, A. H. (2011). Politeness in Korea. In D. Kádár & S. Mills (Eds.), *Politeness in East Asia* (pp. 176–207). Cambridge, UK: Cambridge University Press.

Krippendorff, K. (2013). *Content analysis: An introduction to its methodology* (3rd ed.). Thousand Oaks, CA: SAGE.

Krueger, R. A. (1998). *Developing questions for focus groups.* Thousand Oaks, CA: SAGE.

Krueger, R. A., & Casey, M. A. (2000). *Focus groups: A practical guide for applied research* (2nd ed.). Thousand Oaks, CA: SAGE.

Lakoff, R. (1973). The logic of politeness: Or, minding your p's and q's. In C. Corum, T. Cedric Smith-Stark, & A. Weiser (Eds.), *Papers from the 9th Regional Meeting of the Chicago Linguistic Society* (pp. 292–305). Chicago, IL: Chicago Linguistic Society.

Lavrakas, P. J. (2013). Presidential address. Applying a total error perspective for improving research quality in the social, behavioral, and marketing sciences. *Public Opinion Quarterly, 77*(3), 831–850.

Lee, J. J., & Lee, K. P. (2009). Facilitating dynamics of focus group interviews in East Asia: Evidence and tools by cross-cultural study. *International Journal of Design, 3*(1), 17–28.

Morgan, D. L. (1997). *Focus groups as qualitative research.* SAGE Focus Editions (Vol. 16). Thousand Oaks, CA: SAGE.

Pan, Y. (2008). Cross-cultural communication norms and survey interviews. In H. Sun & D. Kádár (Eds.), *It's the dragon's turn—Chinese institutional discourse(s)* (pp. 17–76). Bern, Switzerland: Peter Lang.

Pan, Y. (2012). Facework in refusal in Chinese survey interviews. *Journal of Politeness Research, 8*, 53–74.

Pan, Y. (2013). What are Chinese respondents responding to? A close examination of question-answer sequences in survey interviews. In Y. Pan & D. Kádár (Eds.), *Chinese discourse and interaction: Theory and practice* (pp. 152–175). London, UK: Equinox.

Pan, Y., Sha, M. & Park, H. (2019). *The sociolinguistics of survey translation.* New York, NY: Routledge.

Roller, M., & Lavrakas, P. J. (2015). *Applied qualitative research design: A total quality framework approach.* New York, NY: Guilford Publications.

Rumbaut, R. (2007). Vietnam. In M. C. Waters, R. Ueda, & H. B. Marrow (Eds.), *The new Americans: A handbook to immigration since 1965* (pp. 652–673). Cambridge, MA: Harvard University Press.

Saville-Troike, M. (1989). *The ethnography of communication.* Cambridge, MA: Basil Blackwell.

Scollon, R., & Scollon, S. W. (2001). *Intercultural communication.* Malden, MA: Blackwell Publishing.

Tannen, D. (1980). Implications of the oral/literate continuum for cross-cultural communication. In J. E. Alatis (Ed.), *Georgetown University round table on languages and linguistics 1980: Current issues in bilingual education* (pp. 326–347). Washington, DC: Georgetown University Press.

Tannen, D. (1984). *Conversational style: Analyzing talk among friends* (1st ed.). Norwood, NJ: Ablex Publishing.

Hmong and Chinese Qualitative Research Interview Questions: Assumptions and Implications of Applying the Survey Back Translation Method

Maichou Lor and Chenchen Gao

Introduction

More than 7,000 languages are currently spoken around the world (Eberhard, Simons, & Charles, 2019). Although researchers are not currently working with all 7,099 languages, cross-cultural research and international collaborations involving researchers and participants from all over the world are increasing. Often, such collaborations are conducted in English, despite the involvement of multilingual speakers, while the research is conducted in non-English-speaking communities. Consequently, translation is necessary for researchers to work with one another.

Translation is used for surveys, standardized interviews, and qualitative interviews. Translation, in general, involves converting one language (the source language—e.g., English) into another (the target language—e.g., Chinese; Bassnett, 2014). Translation can occur at many stages in the research process, including (1) prior to data collection, as the researchers develop interview guides or question items (Epstein, Santo, & Guillemin, 2015); (2) during data preparation, when interviews are translated into transcripts (Chen & Boore, 2010); (3) during data analysis, when codes and themes are translated (Santos, Black, & Sandelowski, 2015); and (4) during the dissemination of findings, including translating quotations (Al-Amer, Ramjan, Glew, Darwish, & Salamonson, 2015).

Back translation is the most commonly used translation approach in research across disciplines (Chen & Boore, 2010; Maneesriwongul & Dixon, 2004; Willgerodt, Kataoka-Yahiro, Kim, & Ceria, 2005) and has been considered the gold standard for decades. Recently, however, back translation has been viewed as a less than ideal method for assessing translation quality in survey research because of its literal translation procedures (Behr & Shishido, 2016; Swaine-Verdier, Doward, Hagell, Thorsen, & McKenna, 2004; Van Widenfelt, Treffers, De Beurs, Siebelink, & Koudijs, 2005). Nevertheless, we are not aware of prior research that has identified and discussed the inherent assumptions and implications of back translation for qualitative research. Qualitative studies are critical to the development of effective survey items for survey research.

This chapter discusses, for the first time, assumptions and implications related to back translation in qualitative research with the aim of enhancing the survey process. Specifically, the purpose of this chapter is to discuss the challenges that researchers encounter during translation prior to data collection in qualitative studies, using two different study examples of back translation (Brislin, 1970). We discuss translation challenges in designing and implementing qualitative interviews based on the back translation method (Brislin, 1970), and we also identify and discuss this method's inherent assumptions and implications for data analysis and quality. The commonly accepted assumptions underlying back translation are as follows: (1) equivalent words and concepts exist in the source and target languages, (2) grammatical forms of the source language are the same in the target language, and (3) concepts are understood in the same way in both languages. With these assumptions in mind, this chapter makes use of examples from two qualitative studies with Hmong and Chinese samples to identify the challenges of finding equivalent words and concepts; cultural conventions in the target language that require more structured interview questions; and variations in perceived meaning that exist between each translator and between the translators and study participants because of differences in class, age, education level, and gender. We focus on qualitative research for several reasons. First, qualitative research is designed to assist survey researchers in testing their survey items with participants. Second, in qualitative studies, each interview must be translated without the opportunity to question the participants about meanings, and participants' responses in the source language are likely to contain language for which conceptual equivalents in the target language are difficult to identify. Third, it is important to focus on translating interviews prior to data collection because the quality of the data depends on the quality of the translated interview questions.

Back Translation

Back translation involves two bilingual translators working separately, without collaboration, in a process whereby one individual translates from the source to the target language and the other translates "blindly back" (i.e., this standard method is followed, regardless of whether the second translator is aware of the first translation) from the target to the source language (Brislin, 1970). Both translated documents are then compared against the source text to ensure accuracy. Inaccuracy is identified by translation errors and instances in which the two documents are not equivalent in words. In other words, the errors are discrepancies that occur when the source language forms (i.e., the source, target, and back translated texts) are not identical (see Figure 9-1). The researcher discusses discrepancies in the documents with the translators through an iterative process until the meaning of the translated documents is mutually agreed upon. For instance, Brislin suggests that, "if the two source language forms are not identical, [the researcher] can confer with the two bilinguals, clearing up errors" (Brislin, 1970, p. 2). With regard to changes in the vocabulary or concept, he advises that the researcher "will have to revise the original English to be sure of eventual identical items in the foreign and back translation versions" (Brislin, 1970, p. 2). Furthermore, Brislin (1970) states that "[t]he bilingual translating from the source to the target may retain many of the grammatical forms of the source" (p. 2).

The process of back translation described by Brislin assumes that words, concepts, and grammatical forms are equivalent and understood between

Figure 9-1. Back translation process

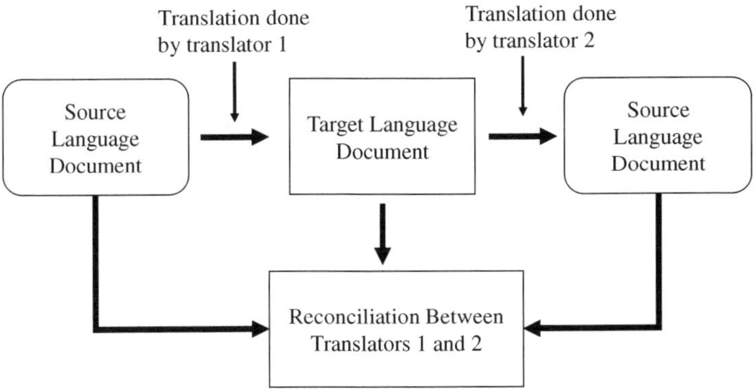

languages and that the skills of the bilingual translators are adequate in both the source and target languages. However, researchers have not addressed how these assumptions affect qualitative research, specifically during the development of interview questions and in terms of the quality or accuracy of data.

Challenges in Qualitative Studies Using Back Translation

Challenges in the accuracy of back translation in qualitative research have been acknowledged by various researchers (Kirkpatrick & van Teijlingen, 2009; Squires, 2009). Translation challenges in qualitative research occur when there is a lack of conceptual (meaning) equivalence across languages and cultures, when there is no comparable concept, and when context changes the significance of the concept (Chen & Boore, 2010; Lopez, Figueroa, Connor, & Maliski, 2008; van Nes, Abma, Jonsson, & Deeg, 2010). In addition, translation problems can arise as a result of differences in the skill levels of the translators, including a lack of familiarity with the culture of Western countries or that of the target language, which may include generational issues, subtle regional differences, and language proficiencies that are not necessarily recognized in one's own cultural context (e.g., different names for colors; Lor, 2018a; Lor, Xiong, Park, Schwei, & Jacobs, 2016; Squires, 2009; Wallin & Ahlström, 2006). Furthermore, there can be differences in the type or degree of challenge associated with translating different types of interview questions (Fontana & Frey, 2000). For instance, questions in highly structured interviews have been found to be more difficult to translate than those in loosely structured or unstructured interviews because highly structured questions allow less room to address differences between the source and target languages (Fontana & Frey, 2000). However, such differences do not mean that these questions have less of an effect on the translations, particularly if the researcher is unaware of these differences. Despite the acknowledged translation challenges in qualitative interviews, researchers have not focused on how the characteristics of back translation influence such challenges.

Medrano et al. (2010) reviewed 100 studies (39 interviews and 67 surveys) using translated data for analysis and reported that 68 percent of interview studies and 53 percent of the studies that used surveys failed to provide information regarding their translation processes, challenges, and decisions. Despite this gap in information related to translation processes, researchers have not addressed how back translation of interview questions affects the data quality of qualitative interviews. Therefore, this chapter reports on the inherent assumptions of back translation and discusses the implications of this form of translation for the analysis and data quality of qualitative interviews. We illustrate our points with examples from two qualitative studies: (1) a Hmong cancer disparity study conducted in the United States and (2) a Chinese diabetes self-management study conducted in China. These samples were selected because we have the most experience with these language groups. Our findings have implications for improving the design of interview questions for both surveys and qualitative interviews.

Background: Culture and Language

To understand how concepts, grammatical forms, and translators' skills influence back translation in qualitative studies, it is critical to understand the cultural context of the population(s) of study (i.e., Hmong and Chinese populations). Cultural contexts such as health beliefs and practices are examples of how cultural differences influence translation. Hence, it is important to understand a study population's health beliefs and practices as well as its grammatical structures, because high-quality translation depends on the researcher's or translator's fluency in both the source language and target language and on knowledge of both cultures (Chen & Boore, 2010).

Culture and Concepts

Culture is critical to individuals' experiences of health, well-being, and the provision of health care. Culture can be conceptualized as a set of practices and behaviors (e.g., customs, habits, language, and geography) that groups of individuals share (Triandis, 1994). For example, Eastern countries (e.g., East Asian countries such as China and India) are considered to be collectivist societies, whereas Western countries (e.g., the United States and the United Kingdom) are considered individualistic societies (Hofstede, 1984; Triandis, 1995). Research has suggested that these different societies have different values and behaviors, including the way in which individuals express themselves (Triandis, 2001; Triandis, 1995; Tsai, Knutson, & Fung, 2006).

Although the concepts of individualism and collectivism have been addressed in survey studies, they have not been addressed in qualitative studies. Survey studies have documented that the aforementioned cultural traits affect survey responses. For example, persons from nations with individualistic cultures seek clarity in their explicit verbal statements (Triandis, 1995), indicating that extreme response styles may be more common among persons from individualistic countries (e.g., Johnson, Kulesa, Cho, & Shavitt, 2005; Johnson, O'Rourke, Burris, & Owens, 2002; Johnson & Van de Vijver, 2003). Conversely, collectivist cultures are associated with greater emphasis on interpersonal harmony and less on individual opinions (Chen, Lee, & Stevenson, 1995; Johnson et al., 2005). Thus, researchers may misreport socially desirable responses as an overstatement of positive qualities or behavior among persons from collectivistic countries (Johnson, Shavitt, & Holbrook, 2011). These findings have implications for any research, including qualitative studies, in which researchers work with individuals from different cultures and societies. In particular, there are implications for collecting health information from culturally diverse populations. Understanding these cultural traits of individualism and collectivism helps researchers determine how these traits affect the experiences of health and illness in culturally diverse populations.

The Hmong Versus Chinese

The Hmong are an ethnic group who originate from a collectivist culture. Many Hmong emigrated from Southeast Asia to the United States in the 1970s (Duffy, 2007). There are over 260,000 Hmong people living in the United States (Pfeifer, Sullivan, Yang, & Yang, 2012). Although some Hmong have converted from their traditional beliefs to other religions (e.g., Christianity), the majority of the Hmong in the United States still engage in traditional healing practices, including animistic folk healing, and believe in the healing power of shamans (Culhane-Pera, Vawter, & Xiong, 2003). The Hmong believe that their health can be altered by spiritual causes, including the loss of a soul or a frightened soul (Culhane-Pera et al., 2003; Lor et al., 2016). It is well documented that the Hmong have a limited understanding of Western medical terminology (Lee & Vang, 2010; Lor, 2018b). Historical knowledge, traditions, and skills are passed orally from generation to generation (Duffy, 2007; Duffy, Harmon, Thao, & Yang, 2004; Lor & Bowers, 2014; Park, 2002). Understanding that the Hmong have an oral tradition is critical to qualitative research and translation involving this population because translators need to ensure the conversation during the interview is conveyed so that it is consistent with the Hmong culture; that is, the translation should not be verbatim or direct.

There are 1.39 billion Chinese people living in mainland China (National Bureau Statistics of China, 2018). Chinese people practice a range of religions and traditional approaches, including Confucianism, Buddhism, and Taoism

(Chen, 2001). Chinese people believe that traditional Chinese medicine (TCM) can mobilize and activate the body's natural resources, such as a vital energy, "qi," and rebalance Yin and Yang to restore health (Xu, Towers, Li, & Collet, 2006) and treat chronic diseases. In the theory of Yin and Yang, Yin represents femaleness, darkness, passivity, absorption, and cold, while Yang represents maleness, light, activity, penetration, and warmth (Kaptchuk, 1983). It is critical for individuals to have a harmonious balance of Yin and Yang throughout their bodies to ensure optimal health. TCM treatment, including dietary manipulation, herbal therapy, and other modalities (e.g., acupuncture), provides solutions to restore an individual's overall balance of Yin and Yang. For example, Yang conditions (e.g., hypertension, infection, stomach upset, and venereal disease) can be treated with Yin herbs and cold foods (here, "cold" relates to the quiet energy and passivity associated with certain foods and does not refer to the literal temperature of a food). For instance, when someone has an ulcer (a Yang condition), they will eat grapefruit or drink green bean soup to restore the Yin–Yang balance (Hwu, Coates, & Boore, 2001). In contrast, Yin conditions (e.g., cancer, menstruation, pregnancy, and the postpartum period) can be treated with Yang herbs and hot foods. TCM is also used as a disease prevention method, which is consistent with the philosophy of Zhi-Wei-Bing. The philosophy of Zhi-Wei-Bing includes disease prevention, treatment, and rehabilitation and is a unique part of traditional Chinese culture (Fen et al., 2018).

Grammatical Structure

The Hmong people have an oral tradition (Duffy, 2007). The Hmong language is commonly spoken using ideophones or "expressive language," which involves feelings, emotions, and images (Williams, 2013). For example, Hmong ideophones are used to describe concepts such as rain falling (*plij plooj*) or a fish writhing on a hook (*nplhib nplhob*). Expressions in the Hmong language are derived from the listener's interpretation of the interplay of pattern, tone, and consonant and vowel choice across the two syllables (Williams, 2013). There are two different Hmong dialects: White and Green. The White dialect is the most commonly spoken language. There are seven major tones in White Hmong. The basic sentence structure of the Hmong language is similar to English: subject-verb-object (Williams, 2013). However, unlike English, the Hmong language lacks all affixes that can indicate a word's grammatical function, such as tense, case, and gender. Because Hmong lacks all affixes, Hmong listeners rely heavily on the exact sentence structure and the context of the phrase being spoken to derive meaning. Specifically, word order and conversational context in Hmong are critical in determining the grammatical function of a word. For example, consider the following instance of how the time element (aspect) of the verb is inferred by the situational context, even though there is no verb conjugation to indicate tense in Hmong. Assume that you are leaving a friend's house when the friend asks, "Where are you going?" You respond as follows, with the first line being the sentence in Hmong, the second line being a literal translation of each word into English, and the third line being the sentence in colloquial English:

Kuv mus tsev.
I go home.
"I am going home."

By considering the context of this conversation, it is evident that your friend has asked you this question because he has seen you preparing to leave the house. Because you are in the process of "going," you understand the verb to be the present continuous "going" rather than the past tense "gone" or "went."

Written Hmong only recently developed when two Christian missionaries established the Romanized Popular Alphabet for the Hmong language in the 1950s (Duffy, 2007). As such, written Hmong is unfamiliar to most older Hmong individuals, who can neither read nor write this newly developed language (Duffy, 2007).

In contrast, the Chinese have a written language that was established as early as 1500 BC. Chinese (the examples used in this chapter are in standard Chinese/Mandarin [普通话]) has the same sentence constituents as English. As with the majority of English phrases, the basic phrase structure in Chinese is of the subject-verb-object type. However, the basic phrase structure is written and spoken differently than in English. For example, "What is it?" in English is literally "It is what?" (它是什么?) in Chinese. In addition, if a time and place are indicated, the time and location expressions generally precede the verb. The use of these preposed particles in a series varies considerably. The subject-object-verb structure is used more often in Archaic Chinese and in the bǎ-construction. For example, the first line that follows is a sentence in standard Chinese/Mandarin (普通话); the second line is the transcription system—pinyin zimu; and the third line is the sentence in English:

我把他打了。
Wǒ bǎ tā dǎ le
"I hit him."

Bǎ ("把") in the sentence functions as an objective case marker, and the object "他" (him) preposes the verb "打" (hit).

The official Chinese transcription system, like the phonetic spelling shown earlier, is pinyin zimu. The pinyin system was invented to help people pronounce the sound of the Chinese characters. The characters themselves are often composed of parts that may represent physical objects, abstract notions (Wieger, 1915), or pronunciation (DeFrancis, 1986). The primary language spoken in China is Mandarin (Lin, 2001), which is officially defined as the standard Chinese language.

Back Translation: Assumptions, Examples, and Implications

In this next section, we present how the assumptions of back translation affected two qualitative studies with Hmong and Chinese samples. The Hmong sample of participants had a median age of 55 (age range: 34–70 years) and had been residing in the United States for an average of 20 years (residency range: 8–33 years). All Hmong participants had limited English proficiency; that is, they could speak and read English less than well. The Chinese sample consisted of patients with type II diabetes, with an average age of 55 (age range: 34–78 years). The participants were mostly male and had a literacy level ranging from illiterate to undergraduate level. They had diabetes for an average of 7 years (range: 0.5–22 years), and nearly half of them lived in rural communities.

Assumption: Equivalence of Concepts in Source and Target Languages

Back translation assumes that there are words that represent equivalent concepts in both the source and target languages. However, this is not always the case, and the absence of such equivalence or the cultural context of the concepts could change their meaning in translation.

Absence of Equivalent Concepts

There are some words in the source language (i.e., English) that do not exist in the target language. For example, the word "prostate" does not exist in the Hmong language. Consequently, researchers and translators must find an alternative way to ask questions involving this word. The original English interview question in the Hmong study was "Have you ever done a prostate cancer screening?" Acknowledging that the Hmong come from an oral tradition and the prostate exists as neither a word nor a concept in their language, the interviewer provided a visual that displayed the anatomy and an oral description of the body part. The interviewer explained,

> This is called the "prostate" [said in English]. It is located below your bladder. It is this thing [interviewer points to the diagram]. People call it a prostate and, most of the time, they check it by drawing your blood to see if you have cancer in your prostate. Have you done something like this?

When the researchers asked this question, one male participant responded: "if it's below your bladder then for us Hmong people, we called it urinary tract infection" (*peb hais tias mob txeeb zis no os*). Another male participant shared: "I don't know." In the first response, the participant associated the prostate with another body part with which he was familiar (i.e., the urinary tract). Therefore, the question about prostate cancer screening could not be translated verbally in a way that participants would understand. In addition, this example illustrates that translation, including back translation, could not be used in this case because there is no word for "prostate" in Hmong, regardless of its delivery format (i.e., visual or verbal).

Cultural Context Changes Meaning

The translation from the source language to the target language may not fit within the cultural context of the participants. In other words, asking questions in certain ways could ultimately change the meaning of the original concept. For example, the question "Where do you have pain?" can have multiple meanings if it is not carefully translated. A common translation of such a question is "*Koj mob qhov twg*?" This translation in Hmong has two meanings: "Where do you have pain?" or "What health condition or illness do you have?" When asked this question, one participant shared, "I have diabetes and high blood pressure," whereas another participant responded, "My left hand hurts." In these examples, the first participant understood the interviewer to be asking about her specific medical conditions, while the second participant understood the interviewer to be asking her to identify where she felt pain. As illustrated here, the word "*mob*" in the Hmong language has multiple meanings, including pain or hurt and illness or health condition.

To specify that the question referred to pain, we revised it to "Tell me where you hurt on your body. For example, does it hurt on your head, shoulder, hands, chest, stomach, and so forth?" Providing examples of locations prompted Hmong participants to think of the location of the pain instead of their illness or health condition. Hence, Hmong participants were able to indicate their pain location. One participant shared: "The hurting started with my nose, then [moved] to my throat. The doctor said that I had cancer from my nose to my throat."

Implications

If there is no comparable word or a concept does not exist in the participants' culture, researchers must ask themselves how to convey this information. Are there visual, auditory, or sensory examples that can be used to convey the word or concept? Is providing examples of the concept in a question appropriate in the culture? If it is appropriate, how would such an approach affect the quality of the data?

Assumption: The Grammatical Form of the Source Language Is the Same as That of the Target Language

When using back translation, translators also assume that the grammatical form of the source language is the same as that of the target language. However, this assumption does not take into account that there are often cultural conventions in the target language that require more structure than Western participants might be comfortable with if asked in English. For example, a typical question that is asked in qualitative interviews and used across qualitative methodologies is "What is it like for you to have … [the phenomenon or health condition]?" This question may seem understandable to English-speaking participants, but it may not be understandable to non-English-speaking participants from a different culture after it has been translated. For instance, participants from Western cultures may understand this question as an invitation to describe their experiences with the phenomenon. However, other cultures may interpret this differently. In the Chinese study, this phrase was difficult to translate into Mandarin because it is not consistent with the Chinese language structure (i.e., the grammatical style). Hence, we changed the word order in the question to be consistent with the Chinese grammatical style: "Having diabetes is like what?" (得了糖尿病是怎么样的?). When we asked this question, one participant responded, "I don't know. You mean symptoms? Feelings? Which aspects do you want me to share?" This response illustrated that the word "what" is a broad concept, which made it difficult for the participant to understand what the interviewer wanted him to address. In addition, the phrasing of the question does not fit within the Chinese language, as evidenced by the participant's request to clarify a specific domain of experience (e.g., feelings, symptoms).

However, when the interviewer specified the "what" and added a noun to the sentence, this elicited a different response to the initial question of "Having diabetes is like what?" For example, the interviewer replaced "what" with "feelings," which resulted in the following question: "What is your feeling about having diabetes?" (你患了糖尿病有什么感受？). The additional noun elicited a different understanding of the revised question than that of the initial question. To illustrate, after the noun was added, one participant responded: "I often feel sleepy and can't get accustomed to the controlled diet. Besides, it is not convenient to inject insulin in public places sometimes." The participant's response illustrated that he understood the interview question. However, this revision narrowed the scope of the item to focus on the participant's psychological experience; it limited the participant's answer to feelings about having diabetes and thus altered the question, undermining the equivalence of the interview questions and limiting comparison across languages.

Consequently, we used one strategy to address the initial interview question without changing it. To maintain consistency in the meanings of the question, we rephrased it to specify the context. For example, in the Chinese study, rephrasing the question from "Having diabetes is like what?" to "Can you tell me about your *experience* with diabetes?" (您能和我说说患糖尿病的经历/体验吗?) elicited responses that were different from the aforementioned example about feeling. For instance, one participant responded,

> Having diabetes is ... I feel a little bit of suffering ... As for eating, I feel hungrier compared to before I had diabetes, even when I have normal meals. The main thing is to control my mouth. It is difficult to control my mouth because I don't feel full ... After you have diabetes, the most important thing is to control your mouth, but it's difficult.

Another participant responded as follows:

> I didn't feel anything. I had a physical examination and a blood test, the blood sugar showed 16 mmol/L. The doctor told me that I have diabetes. I still had a job at that time. I did business. Well, I drank alcohol every day and kept the routine as usual ... Almost 2 years later, I had ketosis. And I was sent to the hospital.

From the responses provided by both participants, it appears that rephrasing the question helped researchers get closer to the intended goal of the original question: "What is it like for you to have diabetes?"

Implications

Despite the alternative solution from the previous example, researchers should consider the following questions: When one uses another word, what is the effect of that word? Does the new word still have the same meaning? How should that new word be described or reported? How does that word affect the responses of the participants? Does the new word indicate a wider possible range of responses from the participants? How will this affect interpretation of responses and the ultimate findings of the study? What claims can be made about the findings?

Assumption: Concepts Are Understood in the Same Way in Both Languages

Back translation also assumes that each bilingual translator interprets words or concepts as their study participants do, disregarding differences in translation based on class, age, education, and gender between each translator and between the translators and study participants (Lor, Xiong, Schwei, Bowers, & Jacobs, 2016; Schatzman & Strauss, 1955). Specifically, translators are often more aware of interlanguage variations in their native language than they are of those in another language, and they sometimes have limited awareness of interlanguage variations. Brislin's concept of equivalence assumes that two translators have the same understanding of the interview questions and also understand the questions in the same way as the participants (Lor, Xiong, Schwei, et al., 2016). Thus, equivalent words would not necessarily convey the researcher's intended meaning because there are subtle differences in some words.

It has long been established that social status conventions influence how people talk to one another (Schatzman & Strauss, 1955). We illustrate this point by comparing how age differences between interviewers influenced their translation of the question "Can you tell me about your experience with menopause?" A young female Hmong translator who was fluent in both Hmong and English (born in Thailand, raised and attended school in the United States) and an older female Hmong translator (born in Laos, raised in Thailand) translated the same question but phrased it in different ways and, therefore, elicited different responses. The young translator posed it thusly: "Tell me about your experience when *your vagina stops bleeding*" (Qhia kuv nws zoo li cas rau koj thaum koj *lub pim tsis los ntshav*). In response to this question from the younger translator, a participant answered with anger: "I don't know how to respond to that. What did you just say?" In this example, when the interviewer directly translated the meaning of the word "menopause" without knowing the actual word in the participant's language, it created a negative experience for the participant. Specifically, the direct translation of "vagina stops bleeding" created an offensive phrase for the participant because of the lack of cultural sensitivity in the translation. In addition, the translation in the target language was not socially acceptable in the Hmong culture. Such an experience could negatively affect the development of rapport and trust between the interviewer and the participant.

In contrast, when the older Hmong translator, who was born in Laos and raised in Thailand, phrased the same question as "Tell me about your experience with *not menstruating*" (Qhia kuv nws zoo li cas rau koj thaum koj *tsis coj khaubncaws*), the participant said, "My body no longer feels like it is a woman because I don't menstruate anymore. I feel like a man." The participant's response illustrated that the translation of the older interviewer was more culturally sensitive, and the participant was more comfortable with the phrasing used (i.e., *tsis coj khaubncaws*). This example confirms that direct translation can cause participants discomfort, especially when mentioning body parts. Hence, the older Hmong interviewer was able to elicit a more useful response.

Implications

It is clear from our examples that bilingual translators may interpret words and concepts differently from the study participants because of variations in translation related to differences in class, age, education level, and gender between translators and between the translators and study participants. Hence, it is critical for researchers to consider the following implications when they use back translation: How do two bilingual translators agree on a word or phrase that may differ based on attributes such as their class, age, gender, and so forth? Should researchers consider including a representative from the intended study participants in the translation process? Which personal attributes influence meanings and create translation challenges? How many and what type of bilingual translators are needed to achieve content equivalence between the source and target languages? How should translators address interlanguage variations? Are two bilingual translators ever adequate, and how would a researcher determine whether they are?

Discussion

In this chapter, we addressed the assumptions that translators make when performing back translation and provided real-life examples with implications for researchers to consider when using back translation for qualitative research. As shown in the examples presented in this chapter, certain factors influence the quality of back translation, including language, culture, and the translator. For instance, we provided examples of how different cultures have different concepts; hence, words and concepts in the source and target languages are not always equivalent. These examples of differences in concepts have implications for researchers who are developing and designing cross-cultural questionnaires with regard to the need to understand how participants are communicating their responses and how they might qualify their answers in response to questions asking for the exact qualities of the response.

Furthermore, in survey research, the development of a questionnaire requires a robust process of development and testing that involves using qualitative approaches. For instance, questionnaire design is a multistage process that requires attention to detail, including translation of questionnaires. We illustrated two examples of how the quality or accuracy of translations can be altered if researchers fail to acknowledge that translations are likely to differ according to the class, age, education, and gender of the translators and study participants (Schatzman & Strauss, 1955). Specifically, if the sociodemographic characteristics of the study population or the translator are not considered, the data gathered from the translator could be poor, ultimately leading to a less rigorous qualitative research study that will affect the quality of a questionnaire. This finding highlights the need to consider translators' sociodemographic characteristics when selecting translators to assist in survey translation and when conducting survey interviews.

Our observations of the drawbacks of the back translation method in qualitative interviews are consistent with those of other scholars and researchers who have studied survey translation (Harkness, 2008; Harkness, Pennell, & Schoua-Glusberg, 2004; Harkness, Van de Vijver, & Mohler, 2003). For instance, some have argued that back translation does not allow researchers to detect whether the translation is simple and clear enough for its intended target participants to understand (Harkness, 2008; Harkness et al., 2004; Harkness et al., 2003). Furthermore, some scholars have argued that back translation is not an appropriate assessment tool because translation is not a process of adapting the instrument from the source language directly into a target language (equivalence), but rather a process of adapting the instrument into a target language and culture to measure the same construct in the hope of achieving functional equivalence (Behr & Shishido, 2016;

Harkness, Dorer, & Mohler, 2010; Pan & de La Puente, 2005; Przepiórkowska, 2016). In contrast, others have argued that back translation could be a useful tool for documentation of "good" and "bad" translations (Son, 2018).

Consequently, the dissatisfaction with back translation has led survey researchers to depart from it. Although no translation method has been standardized, we recommend that scholars, students, and researchers consider other translation methods beyond back translation, given the limitations we have illustrated, including its inability to allow translators to find similar or comparable concepts. One translation method that has recently been acknowledged to be the best practice in survey research is called the translation, review, adjudication, pretesting, and documentation (TRAPD) model (Harkness, 2003). The TRAPD model is a team translation approach that involves five steps: (1) translation, which involves the production of two or more independent drafts of translations; (2) review, which involves the translators and a reviewer comparing the draft translations and deciding on the final translation (note that this step is sometimes referred to as expert review, depending on the context); (3) adjudication, which involves an adjudicator (often the reviewer) comparing the reviewed translation with the master questionnaire and approving the translation for the pretest or for fieldwork; (4) pretesting, which involves testing the adjudicated questionnaire in a small-scale study and amending the translation based on the test results; and (5) documentation, which involves documenting the entire process (i.e., draft translations; the exchange of comments between the translators, the reviewer, and the adjudicator; feedback from the pretest; and final translation). Although the TRAPD method has been recommended as the best practice for survey translation, more research is needed to understand how TRAPD can be used in qualitative studies to inform the development and testing of surveys.

Conclusion

We have highlighted assumptions of back translation and provided some real-life examples. In addition, we have raised questions for researchers to consider as they use back translation when working with culturally and linguistically diverse populations and in determining how this approach may affect the quality of their data. The challenges in the examples that we have presented are common among research studies. Thus, it is critical that international scholars, students, and researchers understand the implications of their choice of translation methodology and the effect of this choice on modifying interview questions in the source language.

References

Al-Amer, R., Ramjan, L., Glew, P., Darwish, M., & Salamonson, Y. (2015). Translation of interviews from a source language to a target language: Examining issues in cross-cultural health care research. *Journal of Clinical Nursing, 24*(9–10), 1151–1162.

Bassnett, S. (2014). *Translation studies* (4th ed.). London, England: Routledge.

Behr, D., & Shishido, K. (2016). The translation of measurement instruments for cross cultural surveys. In C. Wolf, D. Joye, T. W. Smith, & Y. C. Fu (Eds)., *The SAGE handbook of survey methodology* (pp. 269–287). London, England: SAGE.

Brislin, R. W. (1970). Back-translation for cross-cultural research. *Journal of Cross-Cultural Psychology, 1*(3), 185–216.

Chen, C., Lee, S.-Y., & Stevenson, H. W. (1995). Response style and cross-cultural comparisons of rating scales among East Asian and North American students. *Psychological Science, 6*(3), 170–175.

Chen, H.-Y., & Boore, J. R. (2010). Translation and back-translation in qualitative nursing research: Methodological review. *Journal of Clinical Nursing, 19*(1–2), 234–239.

Chen, Y. (2001). Chinese values, health and nursing. *Journal of Advanced Nursing, 36*(2), 270–273.

Culhane-Pera, K. A., Vawter, D. E., & Xiong, P. (2003). *Healing by heart: Clinical and ethical case stories of Hmong families and Western providers.* Nashville, TN: Vanderbilt University Press.

DeFrancis, J. (1986). *The Chinese language: Fact and fantasy.* Honolulu, HI: University of Hawaii Press.

Duffy, J. (2007). *Writing from these roots: Literacy in a Hmong-American community.* Honolulu, HI: University of Hawaii Press.

Duffy J., Harmon, R., Thao, B., & Yang, K. (2004). *The Hmong: An introduction to their history and culture.* Washington, DC: Center for Applied Linguistics.

Eberhard, D., M., Simons, G. F., & Charles, F. D. (2019). *Ethnologue: Languages of the world*. Retrieved from https://www.ethnologue.com/guides/how-many-languages

Epstein, J., Santo, R. M., & Guillemin, F. (2015). A review of guidelines for cross-cultural adaptation of questionnaires could not bring out a consensus. *Journal of Clinical Epidemiology, 68*(4), 435–441.

Fen, X., Meng, F., Wang, D., Guo, Q., Ji, Z., Yang, L., & Ogihara, A. (2018). Perception of traditional Chinese medicine for chronic disease care and prevention: A cross-sectional study of Chinese hospital-based health care professionals. *BMC Complement Alternative Medicine, 18*(1), 209–219.

Fontana, A., & Frey, J. (2000). The interview: From structured questions to negotiated text. *Collecting and Interpreting Qualitative Materials, 2*(6), 61–106.

Harkness, J. A. (2003). Questionnaire translation. In J. A. Harkness, F. J. Van de Vijver, P. Ph. Mohler (Eds.), *Cross-cultural survey methods* (pp. 35–56). Hoboken, NJ: Wiley-Interscience.

Harkness, J. A. (2008). Comparative survey research: Goals and challenges. In E. D. de Leeuw, J. J. Hox, & D. A. Dillman (Eds.), *International handbook of survey methodology* (pp. 56–77). New York, NY: Lawrence Erlbaum Associates.

Harkness, J., Dorer, B., & Mohler, P. (2010). Translation: Assessment. In *Guidelines for best practice in cross-cultural surveys*. Ann Arbor, MI: Survey Research Center, Institute for Social Research, University of Michigan. Retrieved from http://www.ccsg.isr.umich.edu

Harkness, J., Pennell, B.-E., & Schoua-Glusberg, A. (2004). Survey questionnaire translation and assessment. In S. Presser, J. M. Rothgeb, M. P. Couper, J. T. Lessler, E. Martin, J. Martin, & E. Singer (Eds.), *Methods for testing and evaluating survey questionnaires* (pp. 453–473). Retrieved from http://onlinelibrary.wiley.com/doi/10.1002/0471654728.ch22/summary

Harkness, J., Van de Vijver, F. J. R., & Mohler, P. Ph. (Eds.), (2003). *Cross-cultural survey methods*. Hoboken, NJ: Wiley-Interscience.

Hofstede, G. (1984). *Culture's consequences: International differences in work-related values*. Thousand Oaks, CA: SAGE.

Hwu, Y. J., Coates, V. E., & Boore J. R. (2001). The health behaviours of Chinese people with chronic illness. *International Journal of Nursing Studies, 38*(6), 629–641.

Johnson, T., Kulesa, P., Cho, Y. I., & Shavitt, S. (2005). The relation between culture and response styles: Evidence from 19 countries. *Journal of Cross-Cultural Psychology, 36*(2), 264–277. https://doi.org/10.1177/0022022104272905

Johnson, T. P., O'Rourke, D., Burris, J., & Owens, L. (2002). Culture and survey nonresponse. In R. M. Groves, D. A. Dillman, & J. L. Eltinge (Eds.), *Survey nonresponse* (pp. 55–70), New York, NY: John Wiley.

Johnson, T. P., Shavitt, S., & Holbrook, A. L. (2011). Survey response styles across cultures. In D. Matsumoto & F. J. R. Van de Vijver (Eds.), *Cross-cultural research methods in psychology* (pp. 130–175), New York, NY: Cambridge University Press.

Johnson, T. P., & Van de Vijver, F. J. (2003). Social desirability in cross-cultural research. In J. A. Harkness, F. J. Van de Vijver, & P. Ph. Mohler (Eds.), *Cross-cultural survey methods* (pp. 193–202). Hoboken, NJ: Wiley-Interscience.

Kaptchuk, T. J. (1983). *The web that has no weaver: Understanding Chinese medicine*. New York, NY: McGraw-Hill.

Kirkpatrick, P., & van Teijlingen, E. (2009). Lost in translation: Reflecting on a model to reduce translation and interpretation bias. *The Open Nursing Journal*, *3*, 25–32.

Lee, H. Y., & Vang, S. (2010). Barriers to cancer screening in Hmong Americans: The influence of health care accessibility, culture, and cancer literacy. *Journal of Community Health*, *35*(3), 302–314. https://doi.org/10.1007/s10900-010-9228-7

Lin, H. (2001). *A grammar of Mandarin Chinese* (Vol. 344). München, Germany: Lincom Europa.

Lopez, G. I., Figueroa, M., Connor, S. E., & Maliski, S. L. (2008). Translation barriers in conducting qualitative research with Spanish speakers. *Qualitative Health Research, 18*(12), 1729–1737. https://doi.org/10.1177/1049732308325857

Lor, M. (2018a). Color-encoding visualizations as a tool to assist a nonliterate population in completing health survey responses. *Informatics for Health & Social Care, 16*, 1–12. https://doi.org/10.1080/17538157.2018.1540422

Lor, M. (2018b). Systematic review: Health promotion and disease prevention among Hmong adults in the USA. *Journal of Racial and Ethnic Health Disparities*, *5*(3), 638–661. https://doi.org/10.1007/s40615-017-0410-9

Lor, M., & Bowers, B. (2014). Evaluating teaching techniques in the Hmong breast and cervical cancer health awareness project. *Journal of Cancer Education*, *29*(2), 358–365. https://doi.org/10.1007/s13187-014-0615-0

Lor, M., Xiong, P., Park, L., Schwei, R. J., & Jacobs, E. A. (2016). Western or traditional healers? Understanding decision making in the Hmong population. *Western Journal of Nursing Research*, *39*(3), 400–415. https://doi.org/10.1177/0193945916636484

Lor, M., Xiong, P., Schwei, R. J., Bowers, B. J., & Jacobs, E. A. (2016). Limited English proficient Hmong- and Spanish-speaking patients' perceptions of the quality of interpreter services. *International Journal of Nursing Studies*, *54*, 75–83. https://doi.org/10.1016/j.ijnurstu.2015.03.019

Maneesriwongul, W., & Dixon, J. K. (2004). Instrument translation process: A methods review. *Journal of Advanced Nursing*, *48*(2), 175–186. https://doi.org/10.1111/j.1365-2648.2004.03185.x

Medrano, M. A., DeVoe, P. H., Padilla, A., Arevalo, L., Grant, J. W., & Aldape, A. (2010). A targeted review to examine reporting of translation methodology in Hispanic health studies. *Hispanic Health Care International*, *8*(3), 145–153.

National Bureau Statistics of China. (2018). *China statistical yearbook 2018*. Retrieved from http://www.stats.gov.cn/tjsj/ndsj/2018/indexeh.htm

Pan, Y., & de La Puente, M. (2005). *Census Bureau guideline for the translation of data collection instruments and supporting materials: Documentation on how the guideline was developed* (Research Report Series: Survey Methodology #2005-06). 1–38. Retrieved from https://www.census.gov/srd/papers/pdf/rsm2005-06.pdf

Park, C. C. (2002). Crosscultural differences in learning styles of secondary English learners. *Bilingual Research Journal*, *26*(2), 443–459.

Pfeifer, M. E., Sullivan, J., Yang, K., & Yang, W. (2012). Hmong population and demographic trends in the 2010 Census and 2010 American Community Survey. *Hmong Studies Journal*, *13*(2), 1–31.

Przepiórkowska, D. (2016). Translation of questionnaires in cross-national social surveys: A niche with its own theoretical framework and methodology. *Między Oryginałem a Przekładem*, *31*, 121–135.

Santos, H. P. O., Black, A. M., & Sandelowski, M. (2015). Timing of translation in cross-language qualitative research. *Qualitative Health Research*, *25*(1), 134–144. https://doi.org/10.1177/1049732314549603

Schatzman, L., & Strauss, A. (1955). Social class and modes of communication. *American Journal of Sociology, 60*(4), 329–338. https://doi.org/10.1086/221564

Son, J. (2018). Back translation as a documentation tool. *Translation & Interpreting, 10*(2), 89–100.

Squires, A. (2009). Methodological challenges in cross-language qualitative research: A research review. *International Journal of Nursing Studies, 46*(2), 277–287. https://doi.org/10.1016/j.ijnurstu.2008.08.006

Sullivan, J., Yang, K., & Yang, W. (2012). Hmong population and demographic trends in the 2010 Census and 2010 American Community Survey. *Hmong Studies Journal, 13*(2), 1.

Swaine-Verdier, A., Doward, L. C., Hagell, P., Thorsen, H., & McKenna, S. P. (2004). Adapting quality of life instruments. *Value in Health, 7*(1), S27–S30.

Triandis, H. C. (1994). *Culture and social behavior.* New York, NY: McGraw-Hill.

Triandis, H. C. (1995). *Individualism & collectivism.* Boulder, CO: Westview Press.

Triandis, H. C. (2001). Individualism-collectivism and personality. *Journal of Personality, 69*(6), 907–924. https://doi.org/10.1111/1467-6494.696169

Tsai, J. L., Knutson, B., & Fung, H. H. (2006). Cultural variation in affect valuation. *Journal of Personality and Social Psychology, 90*(2), 288–307. https://doi.org/10.1037/0022-3514.90.2.288

van Nes, F., Abma, T., Jonsson, H., & Deeg, D. (2010). Language differences in qualitative research: Is meaning lost in translation? *European Journal of Ageing, 7*(4), 313–316. https://doi.org/10.1007/s10433-010-0168-y

Van Widenfelt, B. M., Treffers, P. D., De Beurs, E., Siebelink, B. M., & Koudijs, E. (2005). Translation and cross-cultural adaptation of assessment instruments used in psychological research with children and families. *Clinical Child and Family Psychology Review, 8*(2), 135–147.

Wallin, A.-M., & Ahlström, G. (2006). Cross-cultural interview studies using interpreters: Systematic literature review. *Journal of Advanced Nursing, 55*(6), 723–735. https://doi.org/10.1111/j.1365-2648.2006.03963.x

Wieger, L. (1915). *Chinese characters.* New York, NY: Paragon Book Reprint Corp/Dover Publications.

Willgerodt, M. A., Kataoka-Yahiro, M., Kim, E., & Ceria, C. (2005). Issues of instrument translation in research on Asian immigrant populations. *Journal of Professional Nursing, 21*(4), 231–239. https://doi.org/10.1016/j.profnurs.2005.05.004

Williams, J. P. (2013). *The aesthetics of grammar: Sound and meaning in the languages of Mainland Southeast Asia.* Cambridge, UK: Cambridge University Press.

Xu, W., Towers, A. D., Li, P., & Collet, J.-P. (2006). Traditional Chinese medicine in cancer care: Perspectives and experiences of patients and professionals in China. *European Journal of Cancer Care, 15*(4), 397–403. https://doi.org/10.1111/j.1365-2354.2006.00685.x

Sociocultural Issues in Adapting Spanish Health Survey Translation: The Case of the Quality of Well-Being Scale (QWB-SA)

Nereida Congost-Maestre and Maichou Lor

Introduction

Health-related quality-of-life (HRQoL) instruments have been used to assess and monitor health outcomes as well as inform national health priorities, including those in the United States (Centers for Disease Control and Prevention [CDC], 2018). For instance, the US CDC used HRQoL instruments to inform its national priorities for the Healthy People 2020 initiative to develop quality of life goals and initiatives to reduce health disparities (CDC, 2018). HRQoL is a multidimensional concept that has four domains: (1) physical, (2) mental, (3) emotional, and (4) social functioning. To measure HRQoL, a number of instruments have been developed in the United States and the United Kingdom including the Quality of Well-Being Scale (QWB) (Kaplan, Sieber, & Ganiats, 1997). QWB has gone through multiple iterations and has become a self-administered instrument, the QWB Self-Administered (SA). QWB-SA assesses an individual's symptoms and has been translated into seven languages, including Spanish (University of California, San Diego, n.d.).

Although QWB-SA has been used internationally by many researchers, little research has assessed the applicability of the translated QWB-SA instruments in the countries in which they are used. Therefore, the purpose of this chapter is to evaluate the degree to which the Spanish QWB-SA is applicable in Spain. To evaluate its applicability, we focus on identifying problems of translation in the Spanish QWB-SA and offer possible solutions. We focus on the Spanish QWB-SA because we could not locate any studies that have examined its applicability in Spain. In particular, this chapter addresses the following research questions: (1) Is the existing Spanish translation linguistically and pragmatically appropriate for Spain? (2) What recommendations can be given regarding the adaptation of the Spanish translation for Spain?

Translation of Health and Quality-of-Life Questionnaires

Recent literature related to research instrument translation suggests that adaptation is crucial when the same instrument is used in a different culture or country (Harkness, 2003; Valderas, Ferrer, & Alonso, 2005; van Widenfelt, Treffers, De Beurs, Siebelink, & Koudijs, 2005; Wagner et al., 1998; Wild et al., 2009). The translation is adapted to account for cultural differences in the source text and ultimately to achieve pragmatic equivalence or cultural viability. On the other hand, when a translation is to be used in different countries or cultures that share the same language, as in the study presented here, harmonization steps aim to reduce translation focused on only one community and foster consideration of cultural and linguistic differences. This process is called shared language harmonization (Harkness, Dorer, & Mohler, 2016; Harkness, Pennell, & Schoua-Glusberg, 2004).

Although an increasing number of publications are focused on translated instruments, most publications do not describe the actual translation process (Maneesriwongul & Dixon, 2004; Squires, 2009). Nevertheless, the most frequently used technique to produce and review a translation in the health sciences field (especially in medicine and health psychology) is translation and back translation in a multistep approach (Acquadro, 2003; Anderson, Aaronson, Bullinger, & McBee, 1996; Bullinger, Anderson, Cella, & Aaronson, 1993; Guillemin, Bombardier, & Beaton, 1993; Squires, 2009). This method was first used in international comparative studies in the 1960s. Proponents included Robert Edward Mitchell in 1965, quoted by Deutscher (1973) and Werner and Campbell (1970) in intercultural research.

Brislin (1973) also applied back translation to assess the quality of translated texts from English to Navajo, Vietnamese, or Chamorro; the same method was used for assessing the quality of translations from English to Tagalog and Urdu (Sechrest, Fay, & Zaidi, 1972). However, there are opposing views on back translation. Some argue that back translation is useful because the question developers can compare the two versions in a language they understand. The drawback, however, is that one can obtain the same or a similar back translation from a poor translation or from an appropriate one (Harkness, 2008). More recent criticism has centered on the idea that the target language text itself should be the object of interest, which means that revision processes should concentrate on the target language version rather than on the original version. Furthermore, Harkness, a linguist and cross-cultural survey methodologist, proposed eliminating the back-translation step altogether and introduced the translation, review, adjudication, pretesting, and documentation (TRAPD) model (Harkness, 2008). TRAPD is considered to be current best practice in survey translation (Przepiórkowska, 2016). However, some authors (Acquadro, Conway, Hareendran, Aaronson, & European Regulatory Issues Quality of Life Assessment Group, 2008; Angel, 2013; Kuliś, Arnott, Greimel, Bottomley, & Koller, 2011) argue that there is no clear evidence that one approach is superior to the other.

What is clear, however, is that back translation is not an ideal method to assess translation quality because it entails a literal translation of the actual translation back into the source language; therefore, it does not address translation quality in a comprehensive manner (Behr & Shishido, 2016; Coulthard, 2013; Hambleton, 1996; Swaine-Verdier, Doward, Hagell, Thorsen, & McKenna, 2004; van Widenfelt et al., 2005). Translating the actual translation literally—word for word—back into the source language and comparing the two source language versions is a simple way to achieve a high degree of agreement and obtain mere linguistic equivalence. However, back translation does not guarantee that the actual translation is linguistically and culturally appropriate (i.e., pragmatically equivalent) as well as comprehensible in the target culture. In addition, back translation is expensive and time consuming (Grunwald & Goldfarb, 2006).

Because of the lack of consensus on an appropriate translation method for health and quality-of-life instruments, multiple groups gathered at different times to create guidelines for translation. The first group consisted of members from various countries who participated in a project known as The International Quality of Life Assessment (Aaronson et al., 1992). The countries involved were Australia, Belgium, Canada, Denmark, France, Germany, Italy, Japan, the Netherlands, Norway, Spain, the United Kingdom, and the United States. The guidelines created were informed by the translation and back-translation model. Later, in 2001, the International Society for Pharmacoeconomic and Outcomes Research convened a group known as Translation and Cultural Adaptation (TCA) to carry out an extensive study of the then-current translation practices. The TCA group examined 12 major sets of guidelines available for translation and cultural adaptation. Subsequently, the TCA group published the International Society for Pharmacoeconomic and Outcomes Research Principles of Good Practice: The Cross-Cultural Adaptation Process for Patient-Reported Outcomes Measures, which recommended 10 steps to produce measurement instruments that take into consideration of how the instruments will be perceived by respondents (Wild et al., 2005). Although these guidelines were prepared for international use, a similar project was carried out by the European Regulatory Issues on Quality of Life Assessment (ERIQA) group with reference to HRQoL instruments (Acquadro, 2003). We believe that the recommendations from the TCA and ERIQA are very similar. We summarize the 10 steps recommended by Wild et al. (2005): (1) preparation: initial preparation work; (2) forward translation: translating the text from the source language into the target language; (3) reconciliation: comparing and merging more than one forward translation into a single forward translation; (4) back translation: retranslating the target language translation back to the source language; (5) back translation review: comparing the back translation with the source language version; (6) harmonization: comparing all new translations with each other and the source version; (7) pretesting and cognitive debriefing: pilot testing the translated instruments with actual users; (8) review of cognitive debriefing results and finalization: comparing the users' feedback with the source language version to identify issues and then change the translation; (9) proofreading: minimizing spelling, grammar, and style errors; and (10) final report: documenting the translation process. In addition to guidelines by Wild et al. (2005) on translation, there are more detailed guidelines on implementing the international harmonization step in instruments—one that involves cultural adaptation of the instruments for different settings (Beaton et al., 2000; Guillemin et al., 1993).

Notwithstanding the guidelines on international harmonization, there is a lack of consensus on how best to achieve it (Wild et al., 2005). Some groups advocate achieving harmonization in a separate step in which different translations are compared with each other and with the original. Others propose making these comparisons throughout the translation development process and argue that it is a cost-saving measure because translators from different countries are working collaboratively and simultaneously on the same project. In particular, for harmonizing different regional varieties of a shared language across countries, researchers are still investigating ways of improving implementation of the harmonization step (e.g., Harkness et al.,

2016). Regardless of the translation context, it is critical that researchers document the translation process; as most published literature demonstrates, there is little documentation on actual translation procedures (Maneesriwongul & Dixon, 2004; Squires, 2009). Furthermore, documentation should record whether the instrument was adapted before it was administered in a different culture or region.

Methods

The Spanish Translation of the QWB-SA

The QWB (Kaplan et al., 1997) was developed—in American English—by researchers at the University of California, San Diego in the mid-1990s to evaluate a patient's quality of life in relation to his or her state of health and also to determine the degree of efficacy of treatments, compare costs, and examine outcomes (Drummond, O'Brien, Stoddart, & Torrance, 2001). A later version (QWB-SA) was designed to be self-administered by the patient and consists of five sections with a total of 78 multiple-choice items and questions (see the QWB-SA website for the English and Spanish versions: https://hoap.ucsd.edu/qwb-info/). Each section refers to a particular topic, all measured over the previous 3 days: (1) symptoms and problems, (2) self-care, (3) mobility, (4) physical activity, and (5) usual everyday activity,. According to the developers of the QWB (personal communication with J. Harvey on behalf of the developers, University of California, San Diego, August 23, 2007; September 26, 2007), multiple translations into Spanish and back translations into English were carried out by a panel of bilingual translators of mainly Mexican origin. The QWB-SA Spanish translation process followed an approach in which a questionnaire was translated from an original source language into another language with no further harmonization step following the translation (Anderson, Aaronson, Bullinger, & McBee., 1996; Bullinger et al., 1993; van Widenfelt et al., 2005). The Spanish QWB-SA exists in a single Spanish version that is intended for use in Spain, in Latin America, and among Spanish-speakers residing in the United States.

Evaluation of the QWB-SA Spanish Translation

To evaluate the Spanish translation of the QWB-SA in the context of Spain, the lead author compared the official Spanish translation to the source questionnaire in English. The first author is fluent in both Spanish and

English and is trained in linguistics and questionnaire translation. A panel of reviewers was not used for this evaluation because of cost constraints. However, the evaluation was discussed with the chapter's coauthor to reduce the risk of subjectivity in the identification of translation issues. The Spanish translation and the English source text were compared using a contrastive-analysis model of parallel texts based on Nord's functional approach (Nord, 1991, 1997, 2009). According to Nord, the contrastive-analysis model should apply a functional approach to translation, which focuses on producing a translation that is adapted to the local culture of interest. This approach is firmly rooted in a sociocultural perspective, according to which a translation is a form of intercultural communication (Nord, 1991, 1997, 2009). In particular, the bilingual reviewer (the lead author) compared the Spanish translation with the original English QWB-SA and evaluated the appropriateness of the Spanish translation to the linguistic and cultural context of Spain.

Results

Translation Issues in the Spanish QWB-SA

Many translation issues were identified in the QWB-SA (Congost-Maestre, 2010); however, due to the space limitations of this chapter, we only present five major issues, with a limited number of examples for each. In addition, we provide recommendations on how to improve the translation to adapt it to the Spanish context. The five translation issues were:

- Literal translations (e.g., "shortness of breath" vs. *respiración corta*);
- Mistranslation of polysemic items (e.g., "discharge" vs. *flujo*);
- False friends (and lexical anglicisms), such as *severo* for "severe";
- US-specific concepts or terms, such as "Tylenol," race and ethnicity categories, or educational level (e.g., "8th grade"); and
- Regional (mostly Mexican) lexical choices (e.g., *manejar*).

Linguistic Level

Translations, Words, or Expressions That Are Too Literal

Multiple words or expressions used in the Spanish QWB-SA translation are not appropriate for the linguistic and cultural context in Spain. Specifically,

Table 10-1. Example 1

Language	Survey Instructions[a]
Source (American English):	Please do not use "check marks" or "felt tip pens."
QWB Spanish translation:	Por favor no use marcas de chequear o bolígrafos de felpa.
Adapted Spanish translation for Spain:	Por favor, no ponga la *marca de visto* [✓] ni utilice *rotuladores*.

QWB = Quality of Well-Being Scale.

[a]Keywords are in quotation marks (English) or in italics (Spanish) to clarify the issue described here.

there are many literal, word-for-word translations from English into Spanish (see Table 10–1, Example 1, and Table 10–2, Example 2).

In Table 10–1, Example 1 shows an incorrect literal translation of "check marks" and "felt tip pens." The Spanish term *chequear* derives from the English word "check," and it means to subject something or someone to a kind of control, examination, or verification. The expression *marcas de chequear* does not exist in the Spanish language as used in Spain. Whereas a "pen" can sometimes be *bolígrafo* and "felt" is certainly *felpa*, a "felt tip pen" is not a *bolígrafo de felpa* (plush pen) in Spain. Based on our analysis, the following would be an appropriate translation for Spain:

- A "check mark" would be correctly translated as a *señal o marca de visto* (sign or mark of having seen, tick), *marca de comprobación* (mark of check), *marca de verificación* (mark of verification), or even *tic* (tick), to convey the meaning of "Yes, this is the correct answer."
- A "felt tip pen" is called a *rotulador* in Spain and a *marcador* (marker) in Latin America.

In Table 10-2, Example 2 contains an incorrect literal translation of the expression "shortness of breath," which was translated as *respiración corta* (short breathing), an expression which does not exist in Spanish. Word

Table 10-2. Example 2

Language	Survey Question 2, Item k[a]
Source (American English):	Did you have "shortness of breath" or difficulty breathing?
QWB Spanish translation:	¿Tuvo Ud. *respiración corta* o dificultad al respirar?
Adapted Spanish translation for Spain:	¿Tuvo *sensación de ahogo* o dificultad para respirar?

QWB = Quality of Well-Being Scale.

[a]Keywords are in quotation marks (English) or in italics (Spanish) to clarify the issue described here.

combinations such as "shortness of breath" can rarely be translated word for word but need to be translated as lexical elements in their own right. "Shortness of breath" should be translated as *falta de aire o sensación de ahogo* (lack of air or feeling of breathlessness) in the Spanish language for Spain.

Mistranslation of Polysemic Words

Another issue identified in the Spanish QWB-SA translation was the mistranslation of polysemic words, that is, incorrect translation of words that have multiple meanings in a language. Tables 10–3 and 10–4 illustrate this issue.

In Table 10–3, Example 3 shows the wrong choice of meaning for "cramp." According to the Navarro (2006) English–Spanish medical dictionary, "cramp" is a polysemic word whose meaning and eventual translation depend on its linguistic environment or the overall context (e.g., *espasmo* [spasm], *calambre muscular* [muscle cramp], *cólico* [colic], or *tener la menstruación* [to get the cramps]). The concept "pelvic cramping" in Example 3 was translated as *calambre en el área pélvica* (cramp in the pelvic area). These phrases do not describe the same condition because *calambre* refers to "muscle pain," which is completely different from menstrual pain. The appropriate translation requires a Spanish phrase indicating "unusually severe menstrual pain, sometimes occurring outside the actual period of menstruation": *dolores de tipo menstrual más fuertes de lo normal o fuera del periodo de la menstruación*. In this particular example, there are also changes in the lexical register and changes from singular to plural, among others, which we do not examine further.

Table 10-3. Example 3

Language	Survey Question 2, Item q[a]
Source (American English):	Did you have genital pain, itching, burning, or abnormal discharge, or "pelvic cramping" or abnormal bleeding? (does not include normal menstruation)
QWB Spanish translation:	¿Tuvo Ud. dolor en los órganos sexuales, comezón, ardor o flujo anormal o *calambre en el área pélvica* o sangrado anormal?
Adapted Spanish translation for Spain:	¿Tuvo picor o escozor genital, flujos o sangrados anormales, o dolores de tipo menstrual más fuertes de lo normal o fuera del periodo de la menstruación?

QWB = Quality of Well-Being Scale.

[a]Keywords are in quotation marks (English) or in italics (Spanish) to clarify the issue described here.

Table 10-4. Example 4 and Example 5

Example 4	
Language	Survey Question 2, Item b[a]
Source (American English):	Did you have any eye pain, irritation, "discharge," or excessive sensitivity to light?
QWB Spanish translation:	¿Tuvo Ud. algún dolor en los ojos, irritación, *flujo* o sensibilidad excesiva a la luz?
Adapted Spanish translation for Spain:	¿Tuvo algún dolor, irritación o *secreción* de los ojos, o sensibilidad excesiva a la luz?
Example 5	
Language	Survey Question 2, Item e[a]
Source (American English):	Did you have difficulty hearing, or "discharge," or bleeding from an ear?
QWB Spanish translation:	¿Tuvo Ud. dificultad para oír, *flujo* o sangrar de un oído?
Adapted Spanish translation for Spain:	¿Tuvo dificultad para oír, o el oído le *supuró* o le sangró?

QWB = Quality of Well-Being Scale.

[a]Keywords are in quotation marks (English) or in italics (Spanish) to clarify the issue described here.

In Table 10–4, Examples 4 and 5, the word "discharge," despite its polysemic nature, has in both cases been translated as *flujo*, similar to Item q in Example 3. This reveals a lack of comprehension of the original English word in different contexts. It would be more appropriate to translate "discharge" as *secreción* (secretion from the eye) in Example 4 and as *supuración* (suppuration from the ear) in Example 5 to better match the context.

False Friends (and Lexical Anglicisms)

The Spanish QWB-SA does not adequately take into consideration of words that sound similar (in English and Spanish) but differ significantly in meaning. Table 10–5 uses Example 6 to illustrate this point. For instance, Example 6 includes the adjective "severe" and the adverb "severely." One must be wary of such words when translating them, since "severe"/*severo* and "severely"/*severamente* are known in linguistics as false friends: apparently close or even formally identical but not really so. *Severo* is also a lexical anglicism (an unmodified borrowing from English), which is now used in Spain with increasing frequency as a synonym for the Spanish word *grave*, but it is not accepted as correct. *Severo* means *serio* (serious) or *riguroso* (rigorous,

Table 10-5. Example 6

Language	Survey Question 1, Items a & d[a]
Source (American English):	Do you have... 1a. blindness or "severely" impaired vision in both eyes? 1d. any deformity of the face, fingers, hand or arm, foot or leg, or back (e.g., "severe scoliosis")?
QWB Spanish translation:	¿Tiene Ud... 1a. Pérdida completa de la vista o problemas *severos* en ambos ojos? 1d. Alguna deformidad de la cara, dedos, mano o brazo, pie o pierna, o espalda (por ejemplo, *escoliosis severo*)?
Adapted Spanish translation for Spain:	1a. ¿Tiene ceguera o problemas *graves* de la vista en los dos ojos? 1d. ¿Tiene alguna deformación en la cara, dedos, mano, brazo, pie, pierna o espalda (por ejemplo, *escoliosis grave*)?

QWB = Quality of Well-Being Scale.

[a]Keywords are in quotation marks (English) or in italics (Spanish) to clarify the issue described here.

strict, severe) and can only be used to refer to a person's character. Severe should therefore be translated as *grave* in this context (Navarro, 2006).

Sociocultural Level

US-Specific Concepts or Terms

The Spanish QWB-SA uses many US-specific concepts and terms; however, such concepts or terms may not be appropriate for the cultural context in Spain, as demonstrated in Table 10-6, Example 7. The term "Tylenol," a brand name registered in the United States, has *Termalgin* as the corresponding brand name for Spain. Because the brand names are different, using the generic name of the ingredients (analgesic paracetamol in this case) would,

Table 10-6. Example 7

Language	Survey Question 3, Item l[a]
Source (American English):	Have you had to take any medication including over-the-counter remedies (aspirin/"Tylenol," allergy medications, insulin, hormones, estrogen, or thyroid, "Prednisone")?
QWB Spanish translation:	¿Ha tenido Ud. que tomar algún medicamento incluyendo medicinas no recetadas (aspirina/*tylenol*, medicinas para alergias, insulina, hormonas, estrógeno, tiroides y *prednisone*)?
Adapted Spanish translation for Spain:	¿Ha tenido que tomar medicamentos? Por favor, incluya los que se pueden comprar sin receta (por ejemplo, aspirina, *paracetamol*, *prednisona*, insulina, hormonas, estrógenos, medicinas para la tiroides o para las alergias).

QWB = Quality of Well-Being Scale.

[a]Keywords are in quotation marks (English) or in italics (Spanish) to clarify the issue described here.

therefore, be more appropriate than a brand name. Only worldwide knowledge on the part of the translator can avoid such cultural confusions.

Another issue with the Spanish QWB-SA is that it does not adequately take into consideration of regional lexical variation. Table 10-7, Example 8, exemplifies this, where the expression "walk off the curb" is translated as *caminar fuera de la banqueta* (walk off the footstool), a translation based on Mexican Spanish; consequently, it is incomprehensible to other populations of Spanish-speakers, including those in Spain. The word "curb" (or "kerb") refers to the *bordillo de la acera* (the edge of a pavement or sidewalk), and there are many variants used throughout Latin America (e.g., *banqueta* in Mexico and Guatemala; *cordon* in Argentina, Bolivia, Chile, Costa Rica, Paraguay, and Uruguay; *sardinel* in Colombia and Peru; and *vereda* in other parts of Latin America). This diversity reveals the challenge encountered in attempting to achieve a valid translation for all speakers of the Spanish language.

Furthermore, throughout the Spanish QWB-SA, there are many questions that use words that are specific to Latin American linguistic communities (Mexico in particular) and are therefore not applicable to Spain (see the QWB-SA website for the overall questionnaire context). The Spanish term *ardor* (burning) in Item 1k should be *escozor* (burning) in Spain; *escozor* would be a more regionally appropriate rendering of this term. *Ardor* is used in Spain as *ardor de estómago* (heartburn produced by stomach acid). Another example is *comezón* (itching; Item 1k), which should be *picor* (itching) in Spain. When using *comezón* in Spain, it usually mean "moral discomfort". *Salpullido* (rash; Item 1k) should be *sarpullido o erupción cutánea* (rash) in Spain; *anteojos* (glasses; Item 1d) should be *gafas* (glasses) in Spain; *relumbrón* (flash, burst of light; Item 2a) should be *destello* (flash, burst

Table 10-7. Example 8

Language	Survey Question 7, Item a[a]
Source (American English):	Did you have trouble climbing stairs or inclines or "walking off the curb"?
QWB Spanish translation:	¿Tuvo Ud. dificultad al subir escaleras, usar rampas o *caminar fuera de la banqueta*?
Adapted Spanish translation for Spain:	¿Tuvo dificultad para subir escaleras o cuestas, o *para bajar de la acera*?

QWB = Quality of Well-Being Scale.

[a]Keywords are in quotation marks (English) or in italics (Spanish) to clarify the issue described here.

of light) in Spain; *quijada* (jaw; Item 2h) should be *mandíbula* (jaw) in Spain; *coyuntura* (joint, articulation; Item 2u) should be *articulación* (joint, articulation) in Spain (when using the word *coyuntura* in Spain, we usually mean "situation" or "opportunity"); *cruda* (hangover; Item 3h) should be *resaca* (hangover) in Spain; *manejar* (drive; Item 6c) should be *conducir* (drive) in Spain; and *banqueta* (curb; Item 7a) should be *acera* (curb) in Spain (when using *banqueta* in Spain, it means "footstool," as previously mentioned). These examples show that many lexical choices in the translation are either uncommon in Spain or have a different meaning. The questionnaire should have taken into account lexical differences between Spanish and the various Latin American (sub-) cultures and consequently should have proposed different adaptations with alternative terms for each linguistic community. In the example of "walking off the curb," the translation for Spain should read *bajar de la acera*. A potential solution could also be to try to find a broader Spanish word that would be well understood by most Spanish-speakers, but this is not always possible.

Discussion

We evaluated the Spanish QWB-SA translation and identified multiple translation issues that may make a successful implementation of the instrument in Spain difficult. These translation issues included literal translations, mistranslations of polysemic words, false friends, use of US-specific concepts instead of culturally appropriate or more universally understood concepts, and regional lexical choices. Interestingly, although the Spanish QWB-SA was translated using a common international protocol based on a translation and back translation multistep method and with a broad Spanish-speaking audience in mind (at least in theory), we discovered these translation issues. The translation issues highlight the need for shared language harmonization and improvements in the translation review process in general. For instance, deficiencies in lexical register differentiation stem from a lack of shared language harmonization between Spanish and Latin American cultures. The application of a questionnaire in different countries speaking the same language requires appropriate translation and cultural adaptation (Beaton, Bombardier, Guillemin, & Ferraz, 2000; Guillemin et al., 1993; Wild et al., 2005). This particular instrument, initially developed in the United States and translated principally into Mexican Spanish, will not necessarily be immediately applicable to any other Spanish-speaking country.

Because we were unable to find detailed documentation of how the Spanish translation was done in the United States, it was difficult to understand how much piloting or pretesting was done to ensure that the Spanish QWB-SA was truly applicable to all relevant Spanish-language target groups. From our evaluation, it appears that the Spanish QWB-SA was not translated and not assessed to be universally understood in Spanish-language countries, including Spain.

Although the original Spanish QWB-SA used back translation, the back translation did not identify (Spain-specific) translation issues, such as literal translation, polysemy, false friends, or anglicisms, among other possible issues. A possible explanation for the translation issues identified could be a lack of using bilingual or monolingual resources, such as including Spanish speakers from different Spanish-speaking countries during the translation process or using dictionaries from different countries to assist with the translation. However, we acknowledge that the translation procedures might have been deliberately chosen to accommodate cost and access to translators. Perhaps it was more cost effective to use translators who were Spanish-speaking but of Mexican descent because researchers simply had access to them. This highlights the need for researchers to weigh the cost of translation. Specifically, what do researchers need to consider in terms of costs to obtain high-quality translations that can be used in multiple Spanish-speaking countries?

With regard to the sociocultural issues at the lexical-semantic level, the deficiencies that have been revealed are due to the concepts not having been adapted to the target culture, in this case, Spain. It is essential, as we have seen, to bear in mind the sociocultural context and language usage in each country where the instrument is to be administered and to overcome the linguistic and cultural differences. Translators are not always acquainted with the situational and cultural context(s) to which the instrument belongs. They need to be equipped not only with a sound knowledge of the two languages, but also with a considerable wealth of world knowledge and cultural experience. Another option would, of course, be to use a more diverse translation team.

There are some limitations to this chapter. Because of space constraints, only certain lexical deficiencies, including linguistic and pragmatic cultural issues, were examined in this study. Further studies could examine more examples of both types of issue, as well as the impact of visual design (e.g., layout, format, and typographical variables that motivate the user to complete the questionnaire) on response bias of the Spanish QWB-SA. Another limitation is that only one reviewer examined the translation issues, although a second assessor was later involved in the discussion of these issues. The reviewer may have missed issues or had idiosyncratic interpretations. Future studies could use a panel of reviewers to conduct the analysis. In addition, testing the translation with respondents could be another solution to assess the quality of the translation—which is also one of the steps recommended by Wild et al. (2005).

Conclusions

The findings of this study highlight the need for the Spanish QWB-SA to be revised and adapted for use in Spain, and probably for its originally intended context as well. Further, understanding of which translation guidelines were followed requires documentation of the translation process. Finally, urgent measures are needed to improve research on the translation of health science and health psychology questionnaires, an area of study that is largely ignored in most departments of translation at the university level. Improvement in the quality of such translations can benefit the health of diverse populations.

Acknowledgments

The authors would like to thank Mandy Sha and Dorothée Behr for making significant contributions to an early version of the manuscript and encouraging collaboration between scholars.

References

Aaronson, N. K., Acquadro, C., Alonso, J., Apolone, G., Bucquet, D., Bullinger, M., . . . Keller, S. (1992). International Quality of Life Assessment (IQOLA) project. *Quality of Life Research, 1*(5), 349–351.

Acquadro, C. (2003, November). *ERIQA recommendations for translation and cultural adaptation of HRQL measures.* Paper presented at the ISPOR 6th Annual European Congress, Barcelona, Spain.

Acquadro, C., Conway, K., Hareendran, A., Aaronson, N., & European Regulatory Issues Quality of Life Assessment Group. (2008). Literature review of methods to translate health-related quality of life questionnaires for use in multinational clinical trials. *Value in Health, 11*(3), 509–521. https://doi.org/10.1111/j.1524-4733.2007.00292.x

Anderson, R. T., Aaronson, N. K., Bullinger, M., & McBee, W. L. (1996). A review of the progress towards developing health-related quality-of-life instruments for international clinical studies and outcomes research. *Pharmacoeconomics, 10*(4), 336–355. https://doi.org/10.2165/00019053-199610040-00004

Angel, R. J. (2013). After Babel: Language and the fundamental challenges of comparative aging research. *Journal of Cross-Cultural Gerontology, 28*(3), 223-238. https://doi.org/10.1007/s10823-013-9197-2

Beaton, D. E., Bombardier, C., Guillemin, F., & Ferraz, M. B. (2000). Guidelines for the process of cross-cultural adaptation of self-report measures. *Spine (Phila Pa 1976), 25*(24), 3186–3191. https://doi.org/10.1097/00007632-200012150-00014

Behr, D., & Shishido, K. (2016). The translation of measurement instruments for cross-cultural surveys. In C. Wolf, D. Joye, T. W. Smith, & Y. Fu (Eds.), *The SAGE handbook of survey methodology* (pp. 269–287). London, England: SAGE.

Brislin, R. W. (1973). Questionnaire wording and translation. In R. W. Brislin, W. J. Lonner, & R. M. Thorndike (Eds.), *Cross-cultural research methods* (pp. 32–58). New York: John Wiley & Sons

Bullinger, M., Anderson, R., Cella, D., & Aaronson, N. (1993). Developing and evaluating cross-cultural instruments from minimum requirements to optimal models. *Quality of Life Research, 2*(6), 451–459.

Centers for Disease Control and Prevention (CDC). (2018). *Health-related quality of life (HRQOL)*. Retrieved from https://www.cdc.gov/hrqol/

Congost-Maestre, N. (2010). El lenguaje de las Ciencias de la Salud: Los cuestionarios de salud y calidad de vida y su traducción del inglés al español. Tesis doctoral. [The language of health sciences: Health and quality of life questionnaires and their translation from English to Spanish. Doctoral thesis.] Universidad de Alicante: España. Retrieved from https://rua.ua.es/dspace/bitstream/10045/17562/1/Tesis_congost.pdf

Coulthard, R. J. (2013). Rethinking back-translation for the cross-cultural adaptation of health related questionnaires: Expert translators make back-translation unnecessary (Unpublished doctoral dissertation). Florianópolis, Brazil: Universidade Federal de Santa Catarina. Retrieved from https://repositorio.ufsc.br/xmlui/handle/123456789/123163

Deutscher, I. (1973). Asking questions cross-culturally: Some problems of linguistic comparability. In D. P. Warwick & S. Osherson (Eds.), *Comparative research methods* (pp. 163–186). Englewood Cliffs, NJ: Prentice-Hall.

Drummond, M. F., O'Brien, B. J., Stoddart, G. L., & Torrance, G. W. (2001). *Métodos para la evaluación económica de los programas de asistencia sanitaria* [*Methods for the economic evaluation of health care programs*] (2nd ed.). Madrid, Spain: Editorial Díaz de Santos.

Grunwald, D., & Goldfarb, N. M. (2006). Back translation for quality control of informed consent forms. *Journal of Clinical Research Best Practices, 2*(2), 1–6.

Guillemin, F., Bombardier, C., & Beaton, D. (1993). Cross-cultural adaptation of health-related quality of life measures: Literature review and proposed guidelines. *Journal of Clinical Epidemiology, 46*(12), 1417–1432. https://doi.org/10.1016/0895-4356(93)90142-n

Hambleton, R. K. (1996). Adaptación de test para su uso en diferentes idiomas y culturas: fuentes de error, posibles soluciones y directrices prácticas [Adaptation of tests for use in different languages and cultures: Sources of error, possible solutions and practical guidelines]. En J. Muñiz (Ed.), *Psicometría* (pp. 207–238). Madrid, Spain: Universitas.

Harkness, J. A. (2003). Questionnaire translation. In J. A. Harkness, F. Van de Vijver, & P. Ph. Mohler (Eds.), *Cross-cultural survey methods* (pp. 35–56). Hoboken, NJ: Wiley-Interscience.

Harkness, J. (2008). Comparative survey research: Goals and challenges. In E. D. de Leeuw, J. How, & D. Dillman (Eds.), *International handbook of survey methodology* (pp. 56–77). New York, NY: Lawrence Erlbaum Associates.

Harkness, J., Dorer, B., & Mohler, P. P. (2016). *Translation: Shared language harmonization. Guidelines for best practice in cross-cultural surveys.* Retrieved from http://www.ccsg.isr.umich.edu/index.php/chapters/translation-chapter/language-harmonization

Harkness, J., Pennell, B. E., & Schoua-Glusberg, A. (2004). Survey questionnaire translation and assessment. In S. Presser, J. M. Rothgeb, M. P. Couper, J. L. Lessler, E. Martin, J. Martin, & E. Singer (Eds.), *Methods for testing and evaluating survey questionnaires* (pp. 453–473). New York, NY: Wiley.

Kaplan, R. M., Sieber, W. J., & Ganiats, T. G. (1997). The quality of well-being scale: Comparison of the interviewer-administered version with a self-administered questionnaire. *Psychology and Health, 12*(6), 783–791. https://doi.org/10.1080/08870449708406739

Kuliś, D., Arnott, M., Greimel, E. R., Bottomley, A., & Koller, M. (2011). Trends in translation requests and arising issues regarding cultural adaptation. *Expert Review of Pharmacoeconomics & Outcomes Research, 11*(3), 307–314. https://doi.org/10.1586/Erp.11.27

Maneesriwongul, W., & Dixon, J. K. (2004). Instrument translation process: A methods review. *Journal of Advanced Nursing, 48*(2), 175–186. https://doi.org/10.1111/j.1365-2648.2004.03185.x

Navarro, F. A. (2006). *Diccionario crítico de dudas Inglés-Español de medicina* [Critical dictionary of doubts English-Spanish of Medicine] (English and Spanish Edition, 2nd ed.). Madrid, Spain: McGraw Hill, Intera/Medicina.

Nord, C. (1991). *Text analysis in translation: Theory, methodology and didactic application of a model for translation-oriented text analysis* (No. 94). Amsterdam, the Netherlands: Rodopi.

Nord, C. (1997). *Translating as a purposeful activity. Functionalist approaches explained.* London, England: Routledge.

Nord, C. (2009). El funcionalismo en la enseñanza de traducción [Functionalism in the teaching of translation]. *Mutatis Mutandis: Revista Latinoamericana de Traducción, 2*(2), 209–243.

Przepiórkowska, D. (2016). Translation of questionnaires in cross-national social surveys: A niche with its own theoretical framework and methodology. *Między Oryginałem a Przekładem, 31*, 121–135.

Sechrest, L., Fay, T. L., & Zaidi, S. H. (1972). Problems of translation in cross-cultural research. *Journal of Cross-Cultural Psychology, 3*(1), 41–56.

Squires, A. (2009). Methodological challenges in cross-language qualitative research: A research review. *International Journal of Nursing Studies, 46*(2), 277–287. https://doi.org/10.1016/j.ijnurstu.2008.08.006

Swaine-Verdier, A., Doward, L. C., Hagell, P., Thorsen, H., & McKenna, S. P. (2004). Adapting quality of life instruments. *Value in Health, 7*(Suppl 1), S27–30. https://doi.org/10.1111/j.1524-4733.2004.7s107.x

University of California, San Diego. (n.d.). *Quality of Well-Being Scale–Self Administered (QWB-SA).* Retrieved from https://hoap.ucsd.edu/qwb-info/

Valderas, J. M., Ferrer, M., & Alonso, J. (2005). Instrumentos de medida de calidad de vida relacionada con la salud y de otros resultados percibidos por los pacientes [Health-related quality of life instruments and other patient-reported outcomes]. *Medicina Clínica, 125,* 56–60.

van Widenfelt, B. M., Treffers, P. D., De Beurs, E., Siebelink, B. M., & Koudijs, E. (2005). Translation and cross-cultural adaptation of assessment instruments used in psychological research with children and families. *Clinical Child and Family Psychology Review, 8*(2), 135–147.

Wagner, A. K., Gandek, B., Aaronson, N. K., Acquadro, C., Alonso, J., Apolone, G., . . . Ware, J. E., Jr. (1998). Cross-cultural comparisons of the content of SF-36 translations across 10 countries: Results from the IQOLA Project. International Quality of Life Assessment. *Journal of Clinical Epidemiology, 51*(11), 925–932. https://doi.org/10.1016/s0895-4356(98)00083-3

Werner, O., & Campbell, D. T. (1970). *Translating, working through interpreters, and the problem of decentering. A handbook of method in cultural anthropology.* New York, NY: American Museum of National History.

Wild, D., Eremenco, S., Mear, I., Martin, M., Houchin, C., Gawlicki, M., & Von Maltzahn, R. (2009). Multinational trials—Recommendations on the translations required, approaches to using the same language in different countries, and the approaches to support pooling the data: The ISPOR patient-reported outcomes translation and linguistic validation good research practices task force report. *Value in Health, 12*(4), 430–440.

Wild, D., Grove, A., Martin, M., Eremenco, S., McElroy, S., Verjee-Lorenz, A., . . . ISPOR Task Force for Translation Cultural Adaptation. (2005). Principles of good practice for the translation and cultural adaptation process for patient-reported outcomes (PRO) measures: Report of the ISPOR Task Force for Translation and Cultural Adaptation. *Value in Health, 8*(2), 94–104. https://doi.org/10.1111/j.1524-4733.2005.04054.x

Nura Knows You Better: Redesigning Conversations With Artificial Intelligence

Arundati Dandapani

This research brief explores the use of artificial intelligence (AI)–powered chatbots to conduct surveys. Starting with an introduction of what chatbots are, the brief includes a real-life use case; best practices based on the author's professional experience developing a major chatbot survey; research on research; and chatbots' promising applications to survey immigrants, Generation Z, seniors, and respondents in fast-growing, mobile-first economies (regions with high mobile penetration or where the default mode of communication is mobile) such as China, India, Brazil, and parts of Africa.

Chatbots: Who or What Are They?

A chatbot is a computer program that uses AI to communicate via text or audio, simulating the conversation of humans through messaging apps, websites, mobile apps, smart devices, or even the telephone (Morgan, 2017). Chatbots are used regularly in marketing and sales, in customer support, when gathering experience feedback, and in market research. In Figure 11-1, Nura the chatbot greets the human respondent with a "warm wave." The bot's script is in gray textboxes, and the human respondent replies in a blue textbox. Chatbots vary from simple to sophisticated and from screen-only to voice- and sensory-enabled formats. Applications of chatbots include helping seniors who might be unfamiliar with digital interfaces and face medical, physical, or other barriers.

Computer intelligence (as being distinct from human intelligence) was a concept first tested in the 1960s by Alan Turing with the Turing test, spawning the birth of the first "chatterbot" program with 200 lines of code, named Eliza by Turing's colleague Joseph Weizenbaum (Gone, 2016). Today, chatbots herald the age of "conversational commerce" (referring to messaging and shopping together) that is predicted to become entirely screenless or mouseless

Figure 11-1. A chatbot screen (mock-up by the author) where Nura, a chatbot, is enticing the user with its friendly tone to engage in some product research for audio short stories at Generation1.ca

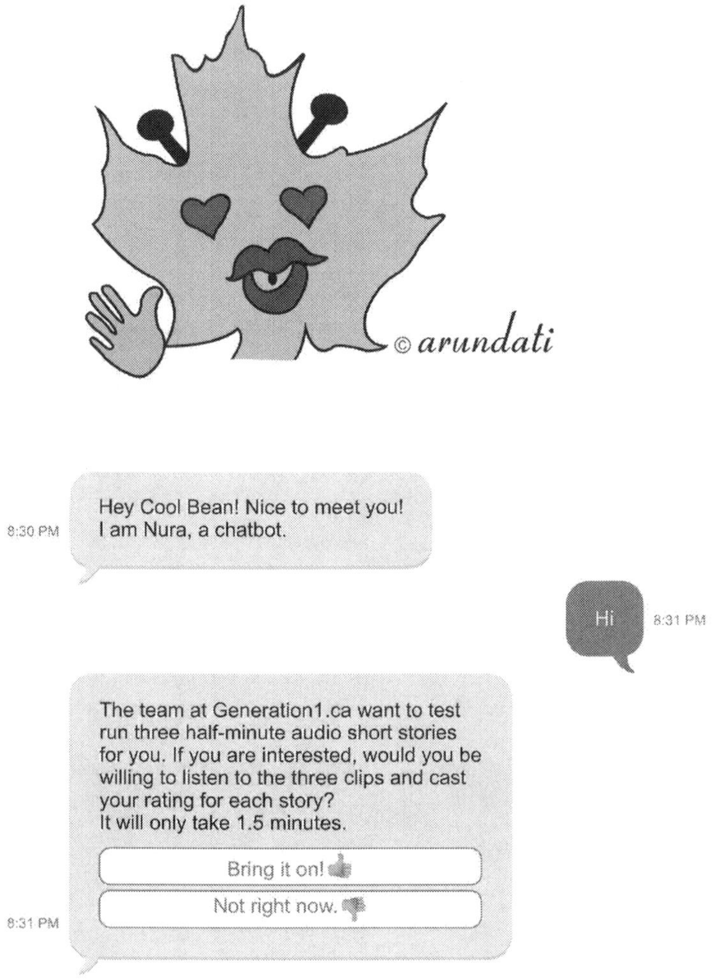

and instead driven by voice commands. One in five searches on the Internet is powered by voice, and tellingly, close to half of all organizations using intelligent chatbots support typing with voice dictation (Brain White Label Chatbots, 2019). Google Home, Amazon Alexa, Siri, and Microsoft's Cortana will all soon be survey vehicles and have been in the news for their varying degrees of success and mishaps with AI-powered chatbots (Brownlee, 2016).

The market size for chatbots today is projected to reach $3,146.4 million by 2023 (Grand View Research, 2017). Chatbots will power 85 percent of all customer service interactions by 2020, according to a Gartner study (Anderson, 2017). Enterprise businesses often use chatbots to improve and expedite customer experience because the customer can connect with a business representative almost instantly on any device with an Internet connection (tablet, smartphone, computer) and receive a real-time response. Well-trained AI chatbots drive conversational commerce and offer personalization to benefit consumers. Chatbots are easy to use and can be launched via web, mobile, or messaging apps.

Conversational interfaces are cross platform and allow humans and computers to interact in a common language to accomplish simple commands or tasks and, in more sophisticated AI, allow for quality data collection through conversational chatbot surveys (Brownlee, 2016). Conversational surveys allow respondents to interact in an informal style to provide longer, more in-depth and engaged feedback through methods like AI-powered chatbots, using social and messaging apps, for richer insights (Powton, 2019). According to conversational survey provider Wizu, chatbot surveys have improved respondent participation for many reasons including the following:

- They elicit deeper insights that are (91 percent) more actionable than traditional surveys.
- Chatbot surveys drive customer loyalty.
- Respondents feel more engaged and provide detailed long-form answers that offer more data points and context into the insights (Hyken, 2018).

Chatbots' popularity is a consequence of the changing dynamic of technology–human dependence. Chatbots offer the instant gratification of conversation, deliver a perception of customer empathy as seen in the Figure 11-1, and can resonate across age cohorts (Reid, 2018). The best executed chatbot surveys are short, host an easy and engaging interface, and lack interviewer bias: the smarter the AI, the more intuitive the interview is. Survey modes have evolved from face-to-face to include telephone, web, mobile, and a variety of chatbot surveys (e.g., from quick-reply chatbots and rule-based chatbot surveys to the smarter AI chatbot surveys). According to Rosie Ayoub (2018), managing director of Norstat UK, in her *NewMR* presentation entitled

"Chatbots: It's not what they say, it's how they say it," tonality and voice of chatbots have a better impact on response rates than neutral open-ended questions. Chatbots thus seem to offer AI-powered connection, comfort and clarity, challenge, and instant rewards that traditional surveys do not. For buyers and suppliers of research, AI adds more exciting elements to traditional qualitative interviews and is cost effective when operating at scale, using fewer human resources. In fact, better AI-powered chatbot surveys could provide firms who blindly opt for automated quant a cheaper and better automated qualitative option (Craig, 2019).

Use Case

An anonymized Canadian university wanted to develop a learning curriculum for one of its academic programs aimed at better integrating new immigrant professionals into the Canadian workforce. To do this, they first needed to know their students' diverse cultural and communication styles. In the past, they asked their students to answer a personality quiz made up of Likert rating scales, but the response rate was not very high and there was evidence of data quality problems due to flatlining and self-report bias, according to the client. The behavioral scientist on the team suggested recording reaction time for each response in the questionnaire to help analyze the results. The resulting chatbot survey used simple English language, emojis, and visuals that illustrated hypothetical situations to help respondents pick choices that best represented their views or feelings. Data would later be analyzed in assigning their diagnostic profile and assessment. Based on the reactions of chatbot survey respondents (who described the experience as "fun!" "exciting," "best survey experience ever"), one could argue it was a lightly gamified survey experience. The chatbot survey was launched first on Facebook messenger followed by a web application programing interface, WhatsApp and WeChat messenger apps, and a mobile short message service. The respondent incentive to participate in this quiz was a personality profile diagnostic assessment of their cultural and communication styles and related recommendations to help them adapt to the Canadian corporate workplace environment. For the pilot test run, the incentive to participate was a "What kind of Canadian are you?" personality profile created by the author in collaboration with the team that engaged and enthralled survey takers. The client bought the methodology and created a proprietary learning management system to host the program (AI-powered bot).[1]

Best Practices in Chatbot Surveys

Based on the author's professional experience developing chatbot surveys and conducting market research with leading brands, especially in tech-first and mobile-first environments, some best practices when using chatbots as surveys include the following:

- Keep them short (e.g., under 10 minutes).
- Adopt data minimalism and request the least amount of data possible (avoid asking for demographic information up front).
- Be adaptive, intuitive, and responsive by using more advanced AI-powered chatbots.
- Do not transpose an online survey to chatbot modality expecting it to work or yield the same or better results.
- Train the chatbot properly to speak in the tone of humans, so that the conversation with the human user has the right balance of conciseness and style to deliver "customer delight" (an experience that far exceeds customer service) and, in the case of surveys, "respondent delight."
- Design questions that are direct, clearly worded, and engaging, with a friendly, helpful tone and voice.
- Create an easy-to-navigate interface without the technical glitches of early-stage AI, such as bots repeatedly replying, "Sorry, I did not understand you."

To illustrate some of these best practices, Figures 11-2 and 11-3 show a "Hotel Stay" survey conversation that used intelligent AI to ask concise questions in an engaging, conversational tone. In Figure 11-2, Wizu the chatbot (depicted with a WIZU icon) made an introduction. Figure 11-3 shows the customer's response in black textboxes. The Wizu chatbot in both figures comes alive as it deals out emojis and adopts a customer-centric tone.

---

1 At the time of this chapter's writing, the learning management system was in beta and was expected to launch some time in 2020.

Figure 11-2. Chatbot Wizu initiates a conversation with a guest about a customer experience hotel stay survey

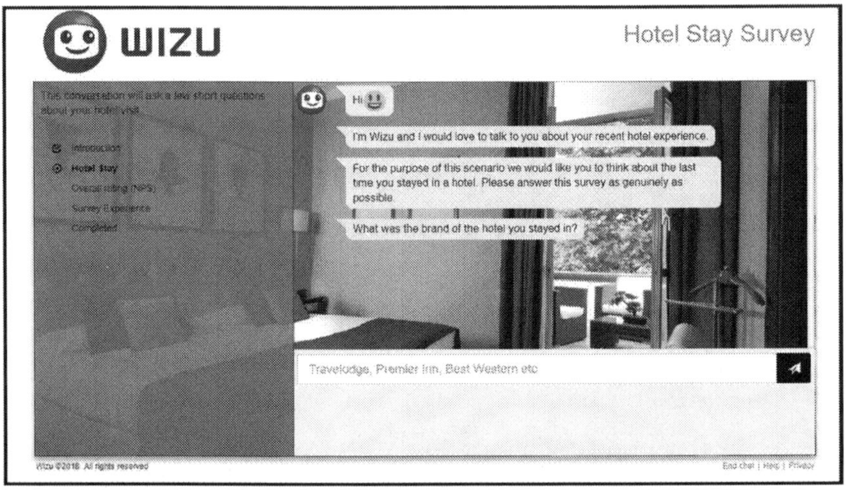

Source: Wizu (2019).

Figure 11-3. When prompted by AI chatbot Wizu, a customer reports on the hotel stay service experience candidly

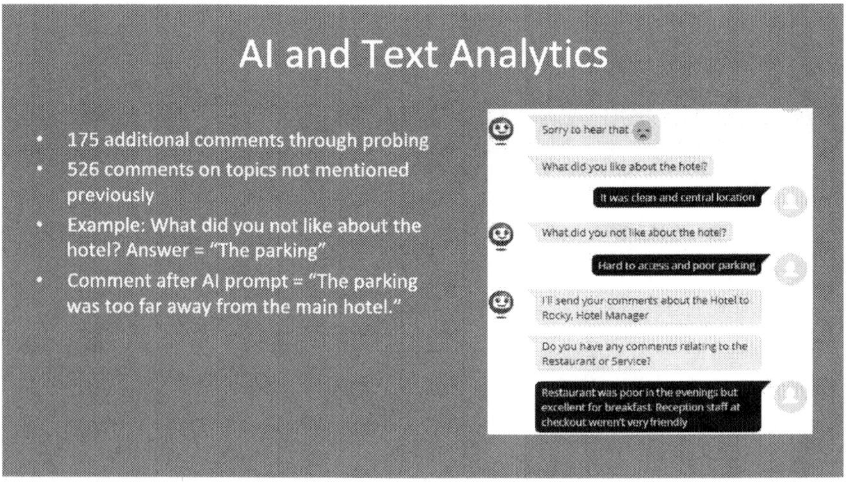

Source: Wizu (2019).

Promising Uses of Chatbot Surveys

There are many promising uses of chatbots including surveying the traditionally hard-to-reach Generation Z, mobile-first populations, and seniors (with audio-based chatbots).

Generation Z Research

Millennials might be the earliest adopters of chatbots, but their successors—the Generation Z cohort—is more technologically savvy, omni-channel, and the hardest to reach cohort due to their immersion in the mobile and social ecosystems (Mazanik & Szymanski, 2019). Chatbot plug-ins are a way of gaining attention, interest, and accurate insights. Known for their simplicity, candor, accessibility, and device-agnostic interface, chatbot surveys that are gamified can reveal some of this population's deepest or most intimate thoughts in real time.

Mobile-First Economies

Respondents in Africa, China, India, and Brazil, for example, are mobile first, meaning their most frequented (often their cheapest) communication channel is the mobile one, making them heavy mobile users (Chatbot Pack, 2019). The platforms these respondents are most familiar with include messaging apps like Skype, WhatsApp, Telegram, Twitter, and Kik. By 2019, eMarketer predicted that more than one-quarter of the world would be using messaging apps, led by China and India, and the best way to leverage consumer context is by meeting consumers in their preferred environments via chatbots (eMarketer, 2016). There are "cultural and structural differences" in mobile-first economies versus mature economies, with the majority of business-to-business software as a service sales, engineering, and product development taking place in the former (Ismail, 2019). Mobile-first consumers' high proficiency with the chatbot interface makes them active participants in the consumer tech and chatbot revolution.

Seniors Research

As societies rapidly age, creating new problems and opportunities globally, advanced AI-powered chatbot technologies and voice agents allow us to glean deeper insights from our seniors, 40 percent of whom experience loneliness globally (Wiggers, 2019). Well-trained AI chatbots, powered by audio commands that record and respond to seniors in accessible formats, offer catharsis, yielding in-depth insights in market, medical, and opinion research.

Scaling Up the Conversations With Smarter AI

Chatbots are paving the way for the future of survey research, making them the go-to approach for mass-scale qualitative research. They appeal as a research method across demographics especially cross-culturally, among the young, in mobile-first economies, and among increasingly audio-commerce-reliant seniors. Jennifer Reid (2018), CEO of Rival Technologies, reports, "The demographics of the people who take chats are not significantly different from those who take traditional surveys." About one in four consumers use a chatbot daily, and about 60 percent of millennials and Generation X adults have interacted with a chatbot (Williams, 2017). Chatbots, as we have seen in the examples in this chapter, can potentially harness deep qualitative insights, leveraging a value- and behavior-driven understanding of customers and their feedback through conversations in market and opinion research.

References

Anderson, J. (2017, February 1). Are chatbots more conversational or controversial? VentureBeat. Retrieved from https://venturebeat.com/2017/02/01/are-chatbots-more-conversational-or-controversial/

Ayoub, R. (2018, May 24). CHATBOTS: It's not what they say, but how they say it. *NewMR*. Retrieved from https://www.slideshare.net/RayPoynter/chatbots-its-not-what-they-say-but-how-they-say-it

Brain White Label Chatbots. (2019, April 18). Chatbot Report 2019: Global trends and analysis. *Chatbots Magazine*. Retrieved from https://chatbotsmagazine.com/chatbot-report-2019-global-trends-and-analysis-a487afec05b

Brownlee, J. (2016, April 4). Conversational interfaces, explained. Fast Company. Retrieved from https://www.fastcompany.com/3058546/conversational-interfaces-explained

Chatbot Pack. (2019, June 20). Chatbots and messaging in Africa. Chatbot Pack. Retrieved from https://www.chatbotpack.com/chatbots-messaging-africa/

Craig, L. (2019, March 4). Using AI to conduct qualitative interviews is faster, less expensive and viable. Green Book Blog. Retrieved from https://greenbookblog.org/2019/03/04/using-ai-to-conduct-qualitative-interviews-is-faster-less-expensive-and-viable/

eMarketer. (2016, November 29). More than a quarter of the world will use mobile messaging apps by 2019. eMarketer Inc. Retrieved from https://www.emarketer.com/Article/More-Than-Quarter-of-World-Will-Use-Mobile-Messaging-Apps-by-2019/1014773

Gone, N. (2016, August 15). A short history of chatbots and artificial intelligence. VentureBeat. Retrieved from https://venturebeat.com/2016/08/15/a-short-history-of-chatbots-and-artificial-intelligence/

Grand View Research. (2017, September 19). Chatbot market size to reach $1.25 billion by 2025 | CAGR: 24.3%: Markets Insider. Retrieved from https://markets.businessinsider.com/news/stocks/chatbot-market-size-to-reach-1-25-billion-by-2025-cagr-24-3-grand-view-research-inc-1002381903

Hyken, S. (2018, December). A comparison of AI conversational surveys and traditional form based surveys. Wizu. Retrieved from https://www.wizu.com/customer-case-studies/conversational-surveys-vs-traditional-surveys/

Ismail, N. (2019). The tech startup scene in India: Growing fast as a mobile first economy. Information Age. Retrieved from https://www.information-age.com/tech-startup-scene-india-mobile-first-123484154/

Mazanik, A., & Szymanski, J. (2019, May 27). Getting a head start on Generation Z: Characteristics & challenges. Generation1.ca. Retrieved from https://generation1.ca/2019/05/27/getting-a-head-start-on-generation-z-characteristics-challenges/

Morgan, B. (2017, March 21). How chatbots will transform customer experience: An infographic. Forbes. Retrieved from https://www.forbes.com/sites/blakemorgan/2017/03/21/how-chatbots-will-transform-customer-experience-an-infographic/#12a395e77fb4

Powton, M. (2019, January 28). Conversational surveys: An introduction. Customer Think. Retrieved from http://customerthink.com/conversational-surveys-an-introduction/

Reid, J. (2018). A research-on-research on the effectiveness of chat surveys. Rival Technologies. Retrieved from https://www.rivaltech.com/chat-survey-research-on-research

Wiggers, K. (2019, July 16). Study: Seniors talk with AI chatbots more when the conversation is deeper. VentureBeat. Retrieved from https://venturebeat.com/2019/07/16/study-seniors-talk-with-ai-chatbots-more-when-the-conversation-is-deeper/

Williams, R. (2017, July 20). Study: Chatbots gain popularity with consumers, especially millennials. Mobile Marketer. Retrieved from https://www.mobilemarketer.com/news/study-chatbots-gain-popularity-with-consumers-especially-millennials/447490/

Wizu (Producer). (2019, June). *Conversational customer surveys.* WIZU. Retrieved from https://www.wizu.com/

Scaling the Smileys: A Multicountry Investigation

Aaron Sedley, Yongwei Yang, and Joseph M. Paxton

Introduction

Contextual user experience (UX) surveys are brief surveys embedded in a website or mobile app (Sedley & Müller, 2016). In these surveys, emojis (e.g., smiley faces, thumbs, stars), with or without text labels, are often used as answer scales. Previous investigations in the United States found that carefully designed smiley faces may distribute fairly evenly along a numerical scale (0–100) for measuring satisfaction (Sedley, Yang, & Hutchinson, 2017). The present study investigated the scaling properties and construct meaning of smiley faces in six countries. We collected open-ended descriptions of smileys to understand construct interpretations across countries. We also assessed numeric meaning of a set of five smiley faces on a 0–100 range by presenting each face independently, as well as in context with other faces with and without endpoint text labels.

Contextual UX Surveys and Smiley Scales

Contextual UX surveys are widely used to measure attitudes and experiences "in context," that is, concurrent with actual product usage. Such contextual measurement is achieved by having the surveys triggered during or immediately after a user–product interaction. Because the survey is shown within an online product or app, it cannot occupy too much user interface (UI) space in its initial state, especially on mobile-sized screens. Failure to do so would render the survey experience overly obtrusive to the users, even to the point of hindering usage of the actual product. Fully labeled text scales often do not fit in this relatively small space. Instead, emoji-based answer scales may be used. Common smiley faces are typical emojis used for this purpose. The smartphone screenshot in Figure 12–1 provides an example.

In addition to saving space in product UIs, smiley face scales may increase survey response rates, due to the visual element being discoverable and differentiated when shown within a product and the one-click survey

Figure 12-1. Smartphone screenshot example of emoji-based answer scales

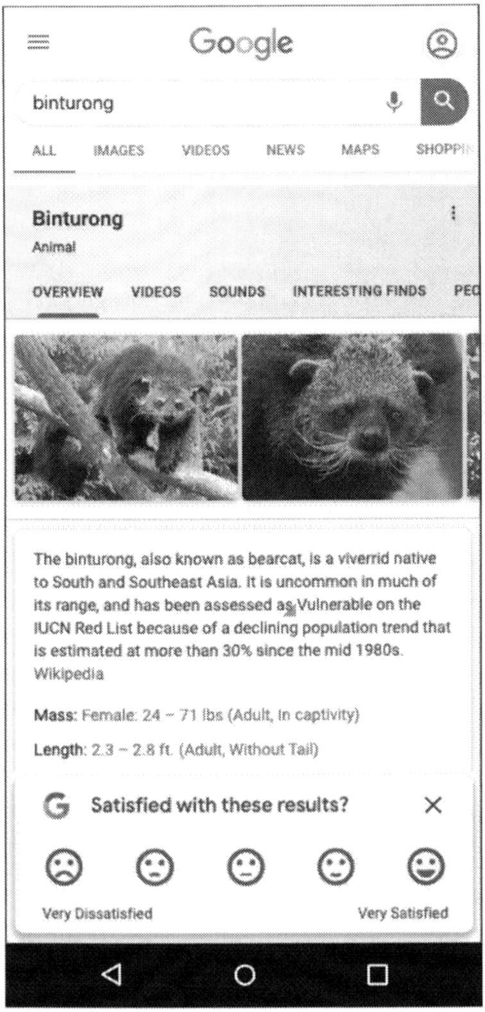

experience the design enables, compared with a two-step flow in which an invitation message precedes the actual question.

A basic smiley scale without labels also requires no translation, which may improve the fidelity and comparability of the responses in cross-cultural settings. Finally, a smiley scale may add an element of personality to the survey experience, making it more attractive and enjoyable for respondents;

however, bias potentially introduced by such a survey UI should also be considered.

Using Smileys for Contextual UX Surveys—Previous Findings in the United States

UX researchers and designers at Google have previously explored various emojis to identify a set of five smiley faces that may be consistently and quickly described by a broad range of users and reasonably differentiated for a 5-point satisfaction scale. During this process, the meanings of variants of smileys were gathered with open-ended construct association research, to ensure a happy or unhappy interpretation, rather than eliciting "dead," "angry," or other meanings. The final set of five faces is shown in Figure 12-2.

Our earlier studies found that a set of carefully selected smiley faces may possess desirable conceptual meaning and be perceived as distributed fairly evenly along a numerical scale (0–100) (Sedley et al., 2017). The interval-like scaling properties were further improved when a smiley was shown in context with the other four smileys rather than individually. The results were encouraging but limited to US respondents. With the global growth of online products and an increasing UX focus on serving users across languages and contexts, it became useful to understand the degree to which the smileys' scaling properties and construct interpretation reliably extended cross-culturally.

Scale-Point Interpretation and Properties

Survey research often uses answer scales constructed by placing a set of terms along a dimension—for example, satisfied to dissatisfied or agree to disagree. Respondents rate their attitudes or perceptions about an object, experience, or topic using these answer scales. Analyzing and interpreting such data requires that the scales behave in desirable ways. At a minimum, the scale points should function in the order as intended. Additionally, the endpoints should stretch to the ends of the intended dimension. If a midpoint is used, it should sit at the center of the dimension. Multiple scale points preferably

Figure 12-2. Smiley faces used for 5-point satisfaction scale

function in an interval manner, where the distances between adjacent scale points are equal throughout the scale. Finally, when comparisons are needed among populations (e.g., age, cultural groups), properties, such as ordinality, endpoint and midpoint locations, and scale-point distance, should be comparable across these populations.

Understanding the meaning and intensity of scale points and the specific words used in them has attracted research dating back several decades (e.g., Bartram & Yelding, 1973; Jones & Thurstone, 1955; Myers & Warner, 1968; Wildt & Mazis, 1978). To understand the meaning of these scale points, one may simply ask respondents to interpret the corresponding words or phrases. To measure their intensity, "direct rating," where respondents assign numeric values to these words or phrases, is often used (Onodera, Smith, Harkness, & Mohler, 2005). Onodera et al. (2005) also used these methods to investigate the meaning and intensity of text scale labels with US, German, and Japanese samples and suggested that bipolar symmetrical scales with a midpoint might be best for cross-national comparisons.

We adopted similar methods to investigate the meaning and scaling properties of smiley faces used in satisfaction ratings. Specifically, we explored the following research questions:

1. What do smiley faces mean conceptually?
2. Do satisfaction scales using smiley faces exhibit desirable properties in terms of ordinality, endpoint locations, midpoint location, and equal distance?
3. Do endpoint verbal labels improve these scaling properties?

Our study extended the research on scale-point meanings and properties to visual stimuli. Moreover, we tested the scale points in the context of the full answer scale, as opposed to only individually. Last but not least, we explored the performance of smiley face scales across six distinct cultural and language settings: the United States (English), Germany (German), Spain (Spanish), Brazil (Portuguese), India (English), and Japan (Japanese).

Methods

Sample Source

Data were collected via the Google Surveys platform (Sostek & Slatkin, 2018). Respondents reached by this platform were Internet users accessing online content.

Survey Question Design

Our study tested the five smiley faces shown in Figure 12-2. Each face was tested under four conditions:

- *separate*, where only one face was presented;
- *in-scale*, where a face was highlighted within the five-face set laid horizontally from unhappiest (left) to happiest (right);
- *in-scale with "very" end labels*, similar to the *in-scale* condition with text labels "very dissatisfied" and "very satisfied" at the two ends; and
- *in-scale with "extremely" end labels*, similar to the *in-scale* condition with text labels "extremely dissatisfied" and "extremely satisfied" at the two ends.

Each respondent received one question only, asking them to either type in the meaning of a single face or assign a numeric value between 0 and 100 to the face. In the former scenario, respondents saw either the "unhappiest" or the "happiest" face, as illustrated by the smartphone screenshots in Figure 12–3. In the latter scenario, the question prompt anchored the two ends of the numeric scale as

Figure 12-3. Smartphone screenshots of meaning interpretation questions

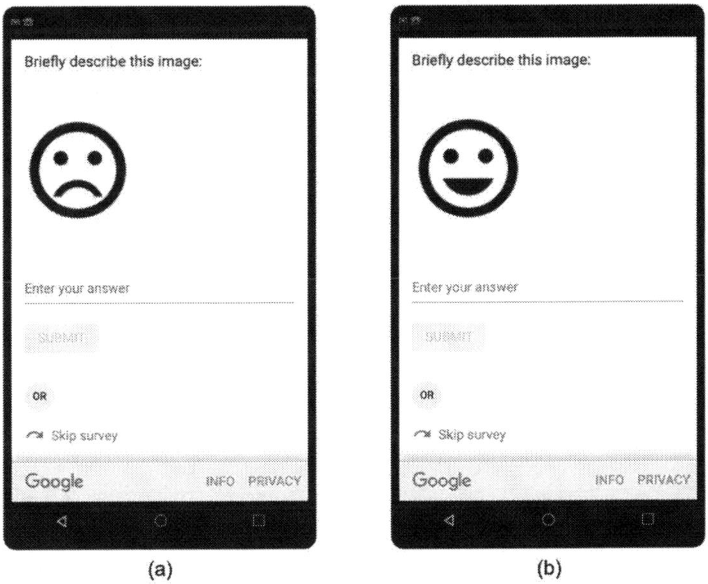

"completely dissatisfied" and "completely satisfied," respectively. Smartphone screenshots in Figure 12–4 illustrate the respondent experience of this scenario with the *separate*, *in-scale*, and *in-scale with "very" end labels* conditions. Full question texts, endpoint labels, and their translations in Japanese, German, Spanish, and Portuguese (Brazil) can be provided upon request.

Procedures

Because respondents were asked one question only, the Google Surveys platform served a large number of surveys. Twelve 1-question surveys, two per country, were conducted to capture respondents' unaided descriptions of the smiley faces (Figure 12–3). One hundred and twenty 1-question surveys, five per country by condition combination (6 × 4), were conducted for numeric meaning of the faces (Figure 12–4).

The target sample size was 400 for each of the 12 smiley, open-ended description surveys. Target sample size for the numeric meaning surveys was 1,500. The Google Surveys platform automatically stops collecting data for a survey when the target sample size is reached. Data were collected between May and August 2019.

Respondents on the Google Surveys platform may provide suboptimal responses for various reasons. The Google Surveys platform also does not

Figure 12-4. Smartphone screenshots of numeric value questions, by condition

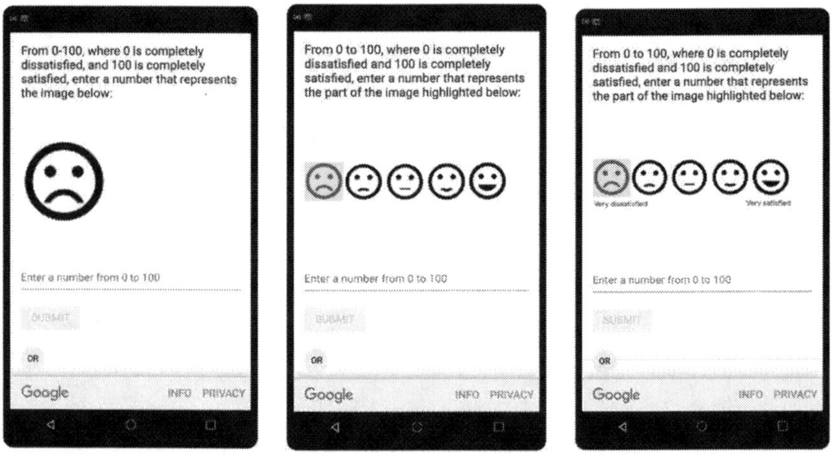

(a) separate | (b) in-scale | (c) in-scale with "very" end-labels restrict the type of responses to an open-ended question—responses can be text or numbers of any values. Thus, for data from the numeric rating questions, we performed a series of data cleaning steps.

First, we reviewed the responses for special characters and converted them to numbers where needed. This is because respondents can input answers that, while essentially numeric, are not in Arabic numerals (e.g., 五十 in Japanese means "50") or are in multibyte format (e.g., ３５). Second, we removed the remaining non-number responses as well as those numeric responses outside the 0–100 range. Next, we reviewed the remaining responses for nonsensical values. For example, "89" is probably nonsensical as a numeric rating of the unhappiest face, whereas "6" or "4" may be nonsensical for the happiest face. To clean out such nonsensical responses, we performed a 20 percent trimming after exploring various criteria. For the directional faces (happy or unhappy), we removed 20 percent of the responses at the opposite end (e.g., 20 percent of responses in the right tail of the distribution for an unhappy face). For the neutral face, we removed 10 percent of the responses from each tail of the distribution.

The final sample sizes were 400 or slightly higher for the text interpretation surveys and ranged from 970 to 1,199 for the numeric rating surveys after data cleaning. Exact sample sizes for each survey, as well as data collection time frames, can be provided upon request.

Results

Construct Meaning

The word clouds in Figures 12–5 and 12–6 illustrate the most common associations for the happiest and unhappiest faces, respectively. (Non-English responses were first translated into English using Google Translate.) The two faces reflected the happy–sad construct consistently across the six countries. Although respondents did not naturally associate "satisfaction" or "dissatisfaction" with these faces in a survey question context, the positive–negative affective bipolarity was aligned with the measurement intent.

Scaling Properties

Figure 12–7 shows the median values of each face in each country and condition. Based on the numeric values respondents assigned, in almost all cases the smiley faces exhibited the desired ordinality—from unhappiest to happiest—and the neutral face always sat in the middle. Putting the faces in

Figure 12-5. Words and phrases associated with the happiest face ☺

context—along with other faces and in a meaningful order—improved their properties as scale points. Most noticeably, in the *in-scale* condition, the endpoints were more stretched to the extremes, and the faces were more evenly distributed, compared with the *separate* condition. Adding endpoint

Figure 12-6. Words and phrases associated with the unhappiest face ☹

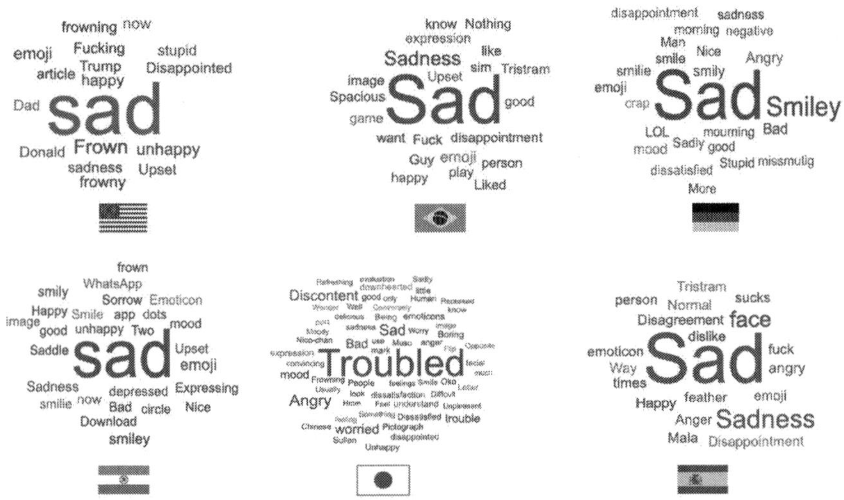

Figure 12-7. Median numeric values assigned to faces

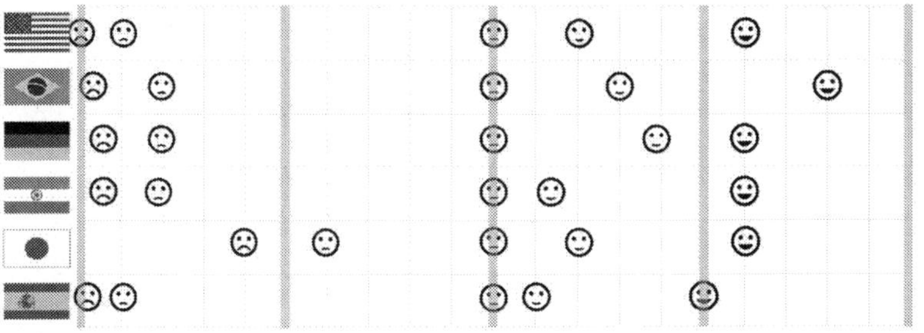

(a) separate

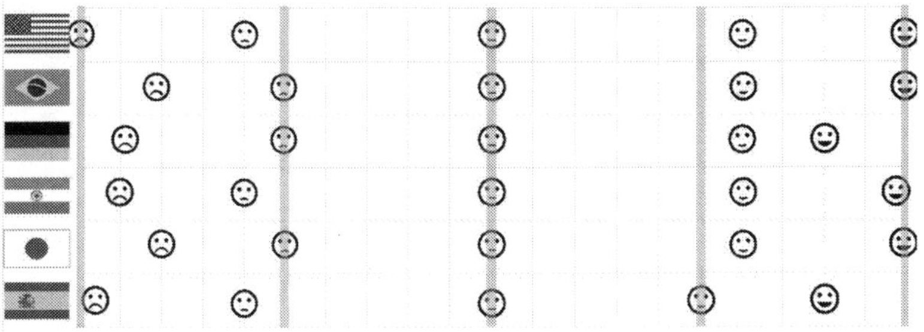

(b) in-scale

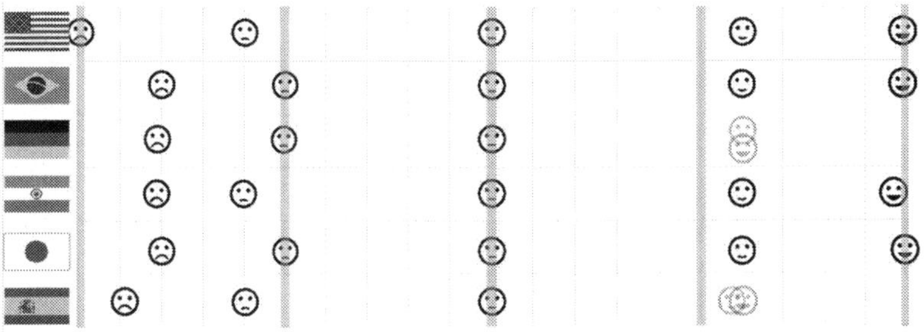

(c) in-scale with "very" end labels

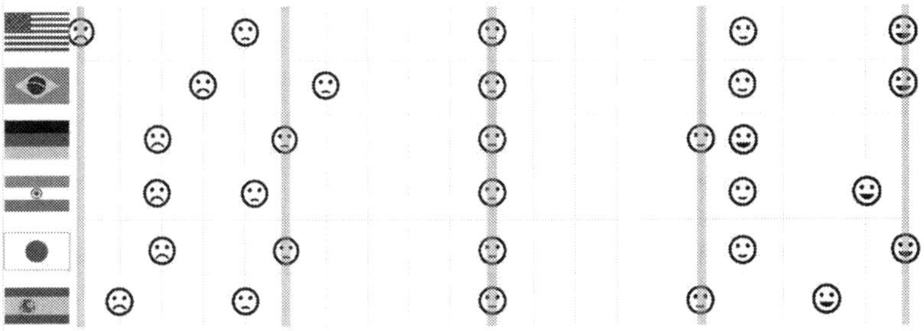

(d) in-scale with "extremely" end labels

Note: Vertical lines, from left to right, correspond to the values 0, 25, 50, 75, and 100.

Table 12-1. Deviation from ideal interval size

Condition	United States	Brazil	Germany	India	Japan	Spain
Average signed deviation from ideal interval size						
separate	−5	−3	−6	−6	−10	−7
in-scale	0	−2	−4	−2	−3	−3
in-scale with "very" end labels	0	−3	−7	−3	−3	−7
in-scale with "extremely" end labels	0	−4	−7	−4	−3	−4
Average absolute deviation from ideal interval size						
separate	15	11	13	14	10	16
in-scale	5	5	7	7	5	6
in-scale with "very" end labels	5	5	10	8	5	11
in-scale with "extremely" end labels	5	6	7	8	5	6

text labels, however, did not appear to improve the scale properties, especially in terms of endpoint locations and interval equivalence.

Table 12–1 further illustrates the findings with regard to the interval equivalence. Here we assumed that, on a 0–100 numeric scale, a 5-point answer scale's ideal interval size would be 25 (i.e., the adjacent scale points are all 25 points apart). Next, we computed the observed interval sizes using the median numeric values found for each face in each country and condition. We then computed the deviations of the observed interval sizes from the ideal of 25 in two ways, as signed or absolute differences. A zero deviation means the interval size matched the ideal. Finally, for each country and condition combination, we computed the average deviations across the four intervals. Table 12–1 presents these average deviation values. Putting faces in a scale-like context made them behave more as interval scales, whereas adding text end-labels did not bring further improvement.

Discussion

Findings from this study, regarding the construct association and scaling properties of the smiley faces, support the use of emoji-based scales for surveys across diverse countries. This is particularly encouraging for contextual UX survey applications given space constraints and response rate implications. Considering the practical difficulties and quality challenges introduced by survey scale translation, using emoji-based scales may ease the design and implementation for multicountry surveys. Finally, from a user-centric perspective, a smiley scale may be both cognitively simpler to process and a better experience for the respondent compared with text-only scales.

However, our findings may not generalize to some scale constructs, especially those that do not possess a clear positive–negative valence that also comports with the natural happy–unhappy interpretation. The smiley faces for the endpoints may need to be further investigated in some countries (e.g., Japan, Germany), as the faces included in our study might not be interpreted with the desired extremity. Furthermore, although the text labels we used did not improve scaling properties in our study, it would still be worthwhile to test the efficacy of other text label anchors.

In a follow-up study, we are replicating the current study with groups of respondents on the Google Surveys platform who tend to be more engaged during the survey response process. Preliminary findings show that, with these respondents, the smiley face scales perform even better. Such findings highlight the importance of reducing satisficing and other less optimal response tendencies.

Our study is a first step toward understanding the validity and utility of using emoji-based answer scales. Future studies may examine various indicators of response experience and quality, such as response rate and relevant respondent engagement metrics. Last, the efficacy of emoji-based answer scales should be put to test in various real-world research contexts, including criterion-related ones, and evaluated by construct-related validity evidence.

References

Bartram, P., & Yelding, D. (1973). The development of an empirical method of selecting phrases used in verbal rating scales: A report on a recent experiment. *Journal of Marketing Research Society, 15*, 151–156.

Jones, L. V., & Thurstone, L. L. (1955). The psychophysics of semantics: An experimental investigation. *Journal of Applied Psychology, 39*, 31–36.

Myers, J. H., & Warner, W. G. (1968). Semantic properties of selected evaluation adjectives. *Journal of Marketing Research, 5*(4), 409–412. https://doi.org/10.1177/002224376800500408

Onodera, N., Smith, T., Harkness, J., & Mohler, P. P. (2005). Methods for assessing and calibrating response scales across countries and language. *Comparative Sociology, 4*(3–4), 365–415. https://doi.org/10.1163/156913305775010106

Sedley, A., & Müller, H. (2016, May). User experience considerations for contextual product surveys on smartphones. Paper presented at 71st annual conference of the American Association for Public Opinion Research, Austin, TX. Retrieved from https://ai.google/research/pubs/pub46422/

Sedley, A., Yang, Y., & Hutchinson, H. (2017, May). To smiley, or not to smiley? Considerations and experimentation to optimize data quality and user experience for contextual product satisfaction measurement? Paper presented at the 72nd annual conference of the American Association for Public Opinion Research, New Orleans, LA. Retrieved from https://ai.google/research/pubs/pub46421

Sostek, K., & Slatkin, B. (2018, June). How Google Surveys works. Retrieved October 11, 2019, from https://services.google.com/fh/files/misc/white_paper_how_google_surveys_works.pdf

Wildt, A. R., & Mazis, M. B. (1978). Determinants of scale response: Label versus position. *Journal of Marketing Research, 15*(2), 261–267. https://doi.org/10.2307/3151256

Afterword: Future Directions in Multinational, Multiregional, and Multicultural (3MC) Survey Research

Julie de Jong, Kristen Cibelli Hibben, and Jennifer Kelley
University of Michigan

Dorothée Behr
GESIS – Leibniz Institute for the Social Sciences

Language is central to the human experience, and its diversity and range of forms and expressions has produced a wealth of cultural output over the course of history. However, with this linguistic diversity come many challenges of communicating across cultural and linguistic groups. As noted by the editors in the preface of this volume, language is the medium through which the entire survey life cycle is carried out. The role of language and issues of language are particularly salient for multinational, multiregional, or multicultural (3MC) comparative surveys that are designed to collect data and compare findings from two or more populations (Johnson, Pennell, Stoop, & Dorer, 2019).

By their nature, 3MC surveys nearly always involve collecting data in more than one language, and the number of languages involved can be extensive. In this volume, Lau, Eckman, Kreysa, and Piper offer such an example, with case studies highlighting the experience of three linguistically diverse countries on the African continent in implementing the Afrobarometer survey. As most large societies have cultural and linguistic minorities, with considerable diversity among these groups and their relative sizes throughout the world (Harkness, Stange, Cibelli, Mohler, & Pennell, 2014), it is impossible to overstate the centrality of language and issues of language to achieving comparable results in cross-national and within-country cross-cultural survey research.

Much of the existing literature related to issues of language in the context of 3MC surveys has focused on translation and subsequent testing (e.g., Harkness, Van de Vijver, & Mohler, 2003; Harkness, Braun, et al., 2010; Park & Goerman, 2019; Goerman, Meyers, Sha, Park, & Schoua-Glusberg, 2019; Zavala-Rojas, Saris, & Gallhofer, 2019). The production of comparable translations is an essential step in the process of collecting comparable survey data, with its own complexities that are often underestimated (for discussion, see the forthcoming report of the American Association for Public Opinion Research (AAPOR) and the World Association for Public Opinion Research (WAPOR) Task Force on Comparative Survey Quality). However, language and culture are deeply intertwined throughout each step of the survey process; several stages of the survey life cycle are particularly vulnerable to measurement error resulting from comparability issues, and issues of language at other stages of the survey life cycle have begun to receive more attention. For example, a chapter in a recent volume on advances in 3MC survey methods addresses the issue of survey languages and how the choice of interview language is handled (Andreekova, 2019), and another addresses the language of administration in surveys of bilingual, bicultural respondents (Peytcheva, 2019). The chapters in the current volume reflect further advancement in this area and highlight the critical need to consider a range of issues pertaining to language at various aspects and stages of 3MC survey design and implementation.

In the following, we relate each of the chapters to the main aspect or stage of the survey life cycle addressed, note the key findings or take-away points, suggest next steps or new approaches from the authors, and offer additional possibilities for expanding the research agenda and innovation in methods. We conclude with a discussion of developments vis-à-vis language in the field of 3MC survey research.

Theory

Work by psychologists and survey methodologists on the cognitive and communication processes underlying survey response contributed essential theoretical groundwork for the field of survey methodology (see, for example, Schwarz, 1999; Sirken, Schechter, Schwarz, Tanur, & Tourangeau, 1999; Sudman, Bradburn, & Schwarz, 1996; Tourangeau, Rips, & Rasinski, 2000). Later efforts integrated cross-cultural concerns by examining cultural differences in how information is processed and its implications for survey response (Schwarz, Oyserman, & Peytcheva, 2010; Uskul, Oyserman, & Schwarz, 2010). However, missing in these discussions is specific mention of the role that language may play in influencing cognition and relevant aspects of the survey response. In Chapter 1, Peytcheva fills this gap by presenting a theoretical framework that maps cognitive mechanisms related to language, such as cultural frame switching and language-dependent recall, to the survey response process, concluding that these mechanisms "may simultaneously play a role at each step" of the response process. She notes several practical recommendations, including the need for better understanding of the different response strategies at play, which are dependent on the cultural identity primed by the language of interview, as well as further investigation to test some of the associated theories. Becoming ever more common, survey research in multicultural and multilingual societies stands to benefit greatly from this line of research.

More broadly, further development of theory is crucial to the future of 3MC surveys, as discussed in a recent volume on 3MC survey methods (Johnson et al., 2019) and the forthcoming AAPOR/WAPOR Task Force Report on Comparative Survey Quality. Work is needed to develop and test a generalizable model or framework of how cultural variations in cognition, social norms, and language may interact with external variables such as characteristics of the interviewer, the interview setting, the sponsoring and implementing organizations, and the language of the interview to affect survey response and error processes. Theory developed by Schwarz et al. (2010) and Uskul et al. (2010) integrating culture in survey response models and by Peytcheva (this volume) addressing cognitive mechanisms related to language in survey response are important first steps. Yet we are still in the early stages. Fundamental theoretical debate continues about how culture should be conceptualized, the dimensions of culture, and the extent to which culture can be viewed as an explanatory variable or variables (Wyer, 2013). For more detailed discussion, see Pennell and Cibelli Hibben (2016) and the forthcoming report of the AAPOR/WAPOR Task Force on Comparative Survey Quality.

The relationship between culture, language, and thought also remains an important topic (Imai, Kanero, & Masuda, 2016). Researchers in cultural psychology, cognitive psychology, linguistics, and related disciplines grapple with similar big picture questions, but communication and collaboration across disciplines is rare. Only recently, for example, have cultural psychology and cognitive psychology begun to see more collaboration in work and sharing of ideas on the relationships between culture, language, and thought (Imai et al., 2016). Similar further collaboration between survey methodologists, cultural psychologists, and researchers in related fields is required to create interdisciplinary theoretical frameworks for the survey response process and other stages and areas of the survey life cycle to strengthen the theoretical underpinnings, science, and in turn, practice of 3MC surveys.

Study Design

The challenge in 3MC surveys is to determine the optimal balance between local implementation of a design within each country or culture that will also optimize comparison across countries or cultures, while assessing the limitations posed by available resources, budget, and research capacity of individual study countries (for further discussion, see Pennell, Cibelli Hibben, Lyberg, Mohler, & Worku, 2017; and Pennell & Cibelli Hibben, 2016). One such decision concerns the number of languages in which a survey is offered and the resulting implications on the extent to which the data are representative of the population. The definition of the target population and the associated issue of language in a 3MC study can affect multiple potential sources of both measurement and representation errors within the total survey error (TSE) framework and comparability (for a general discussion of TSE, see Groves et al., 2009; for TSE in the context of 3MC, see Pennell et al., 2017; and Smith, 2011, 2018). Some countries may exclude language groups at the sampling stage, thereby introducing noncoverage error. Others may exclude these populations at the data collection stage, thereby introducing nonresponse error (Lepkowski, 2005). Differences in how members of language groups are handled can result in sample designs with highly divergent coverage properties.

In Chapter 6, Heck-Grossek and Dardha analyze data from European Social Survey (ESS) contact information sheets in several countries to examine potential differences in dwelling and area characteristics between sampled units with and without a language barrier, determining that, overall, households with at least one person who has a language barrier are more likely to live in lower socioeconomic conditions than those with no language barrier. The results demonstrate that exclusions due to language barriers could be a potential source of bias for some ESS estimates. The authors suggest expansion of future analysis to other ESS data and additional collection of auxiliary data on excluded units to assess inclusion feasibility. Future research design may also include a nonresponse bias study, whereby interviewers return to a sample of excluded households and administer an abbreviated version of the full questionnaire. The shortened questionnaire would focus on measures on which nonresponding households could be expected to differ from responding households, with the instrument translated into the most common languages spoken by those with language barriers. In practice, Heck-Grossek and Dardha's work demonstrates the importance of considering potential adverse effects of language barriers depending on the particular survey topic and outcomes of interest.

Questionnaire Design and Translation

The understanding of how language and culture affect the response process has led to the introduction of new methodologies to evaluate commonly used translations. In Chapter 4, Lee, Hu, Liu, and Kelley explore the impact of translation on conceptual understanding of response scales, demonstrating how such experimental data can be used for evaluating translation through quantitative methods rather than the more oft-used qualitative approach. Moreover, their research shows (in line with Chapter 1) that the interview language of bilinguals impacts survey data. Side-stepping, to some extent, the issue of translation altogether, Sedley, Yang, and Paxton (Chapter 12) offer another approach to the challenge noted by Lee et al. through the use of pictorial scales with emojis as anchoring points rather than written language. While there has been limited research on similar approaches in monolingual studies (Cernat & Liu, 2019; Emde & Fuchs, 2012; Stange, Barry, Smyth, & Olson, 2018), results have been mixed. However, this approach has the potential to minimize measurement error introduced during the translation process in 3MC surveys. Additional experimental research on construct validity in a comparative setting, and particularly among respondents with varying degrees of literacy, would be beneficial in understanding the full utility of this pictorial approach and what disadvantages might arise vis-á-vis translated response categories.

The use of appropriate translation procedures and adequately skilled translation teams is crucial for producing high-quality and comparable translations. State-of-the art translation procedures (e.g., Harkness, 2003; Pan & de la Puente, 2005) include team-based methods focusing on the translation itself, thereby excluding back translation. Using back translation, nevertheless, is a prevalent translation approach. Both Lor and Gao (Chapter 9) and Congost-Maestre and Lor (Chapter 10) provide critiques of this approach. The former demonstrate how back translation is an ineffective method for evaluating the translation of qualitative interview questions, while the latter share similar evidence from an assessment of a widely used health survey. The authors argue that a better understanding of the impact of different translations on the resulting data will lead to improved translation processes and ultimately higher data quality. These chapters add to a growing consensus that back translation provides limited or misleading insights (Behr, 2017; Bolaños-Medina & González-Ruiz, 2012; Colina, Marrone, Ingram, & Sánchez, 2017; Douglas & Craig, 2007; Harkness, 2003; Harkness, Pennell, & Schoua-Glusberg, 2004; see also the forthcoming report of the AAPOR/WAPOR Task Force on Comparative Survey Quality). Nonetheless, calls have been made for further research to investigate empirically different translation and translation assessment procedures (e.g., various TRAPD implementations or the use of back translations in certain situations) and to assess the extent to which these procedures can contribute to translation quality and comparability (e.g., through quality rating or empirical tests and by applying a sociolinguistics framework). Further assessment of the translations of widely used survey instruments, particularly in the area of health research, is critical to improving data quality.

Pretesting

In the effort to increase comparability across populations, pretesting plays an essential role by allowing identification and potential reduction of measurement error in 3MC surveys. In Chapter 7, Aizpurua reviews a number of pretesting methods commonly used in 3MC surveys and distinguishes among methods that strive to account for heterogeneity of language, while also noting the lack of agreement regarding best practices for pretesting design and implementation. Establishing minimum standards for pretesting in 3MC surveys and investigating the relative effectiveness of question evaluation methods or combinations thereof in detecting problems in the 3MC context are much needed. Further, research-specific approaches that combine quantitative and qualitative pretesting methods and investigate the possibilities of transitioning from qualitative identification of problems to quantification of prevalence are also needed in 3MC research.

In Chapter 8, Sha, Park, Pan, and Kim consider the role that language plays in the specific pretesting method of the focus group. By conducting both quantitative and qualitative analyses to illustrate focus group participants' verbal behaviors, they uncovered observable patterns of interaction across different language groups that may, in turn, affect the efficacy of the focus group as a means of pretesting in a 3MC context. The authors provide practical recommendations for how these differences can be mitigated to increase the effectiveness of focus groups. Furthermore, they argue that understanding the resultant impact on quality with particular language or cultural groups is essential. As noted previously, it would also be beneficial to compare the effectiveness of focus groups with other forms of pretesting in the 3MC context.

Respondent/Interviewer Interactions

Language barriers have the potential to affect interviewer/respondent interaction and rapport. In addition, they also impact how (or whether) the interviewer is able to complete their key tasks such as contacting the household, selecting the respondent, motivating the respondent to participate, and accurately recording the respondent's answers, among others.

In Chapter 2, Kapousouz, Johnson, and Holbrook examine interviewer- and respondent-level variables that can predict whether respondents ask for clarification on deliberately problematic questions in a cross-cultural study, as well as differences that may exist depending on whether the primary or secondary language is used and the level of acculturation to American culture. The authors intend to conduct future exploratory analyses examining cultural similarities and differences in the survey response process. In Chapter 5, Lau, Eckman, Sevilla-Kreysa, and Piper investigate the choice of interview language in relation to the respondent's and the interviewer's first language. Future research should examine other ways in which language can impact the respondent's and interviewer's behavior during both the interview and the contact process and any implications for error. Finally, research should focus on development of interviewer training and protocols to standardize how interviewers navigate language challenges and language choice in interviews in 3MC surveys.

Dandapani offers a possible alternative solution to language challenges in her review of the chatbot survey in Chapter 11. A chatbot survey can be seen as harnessing a new type of language and communication style and can provide a consistent and documented interaction with the respondent. However, while there has been limited research in monolingual surveys on other technologies that try to remove the effect of the interviewer (Conrad & Schober, 2008; Conrad et al., 2008, 2015; Lind, Schober, Conrad, & Reichert, 2013), little is known about whether such technology can be successfully implemented in other cultures and whether there will be any systematic introduction of measurement error, particularly in 3MC surveys.

Nonresponse and Data Quality

Language can lead to differences in use of survey mode when multiple data collection modes are offered, potentially leading to bias in the statistics of interest and lower data quality. In Chapter 3, Smalley explores the effects of the household language on mode and finds significant difference in mode choice by language group. This finding supports the argument of de Leeuw, Suzer-Gurtekin, and Hox (2019) that 3MC mixed-mode surveys where multiple languages are offered are likely to increase measurement error due to the additive complexity when multiple modes and languages are combined. One could also argue that it is not only languages that should be taken into account when selecting mode, but other culturally relevant factors (e.g., literacy rates, culturally sensitive topics) that could differentially impact measurement error depending on the type of mode selected and survey languages offered.

Future Directions

Many strategic regional and global decisions on important societal issues, including health, poverty, economics, education, and family planning, are based on 3MC data. Yet ample evidence suggests that the comparability of such data is not optimized and in some cases is even significantly jeopardized, in part due to challenges presented by linguistic and cultural heterogeneity. Fortunately, important work is currently underway to address these issues, as there is growing recognition of the urgent need to expand the research agenda regarding issues of language throughout the survey life cycle.

The Comparative Survey Design and Implementation (CSDI) initiative arose nearly two decades ago in a coordinated effort to establish an annual workshop on comparative survey. CSDI has met annually since 2003 and has fueled the advancement of ideas such as TRAPD as a leading approach to translation (Harkness, 2003; Harkness et al., 2004; Harkness, Villar, & Edwards, 2010; Mohler, Dorer, De Jong, & Hu, 2016). Other initiatives generated by the CSDI executive committee include two large international conferences on survey methods in 3MC contexts, with a resulting monograph in 2010 (Harkness, Braun, et al., 2010) that won the 2013 AAPOR book award and another monograph in 2019 (Johnson et al., 2019). CSDI members also produced a free, comprehensive online resource, the Cross-Cultural Survey

Guidelines (http://ccsg.isr.umich.edu/) and a series of short online courses on international survey research (https://ccb.isr.umich.edu/) hosted by the Survey Research Center at the University of Michigan.

The momentum created by CSDI also led 3MC research to be recognized as an important topic by major national and international organizations. Both the National Center for Education Statistics and the Organisation for Economic Co-operation and Development have organized seminars in the past two years revolving around the challenges of 3MC surveys. Moreover, in its annual meeting, AAPOR now has a session stream labeled 3MC and a cross-cultural and multilingual affinity group and has jointly initiated a task force on 3MC survey quality with WAPOR. On a regional level, a European initiative called Synergies for Europe's Research Infrastructures in the Social Sciences (SERISS) was formed to bring together European 3MC survey networks, with funding from the European Union's Horizon 2020 research program. The objective of SERISS was to address key challenges facing cross-national data collection in Europe by focusing on practical issues rather than theory building. Meanwhile, work has begun on the successor to SERISS—The Social Sciences and Humanities Open Cloud (SSHOC), also funded by the European Union. Issues surrounding the role of language have featured across all of these resources and initiatives.

There is ample evidence that 3MC surveys are increasing in number, geographic spread, and topic coverage (Cibelli Hibben, Pennell, Hughes, Lin, & Kelley, 2019; Smith, 2010; Smith & Fu, 2014). The potential impact of the data collected in 3MC surveys is perhaps more significant than ever (Johnson et al., 2019). Large-scale surveys and harmonized data studies provide cross-national data and official statistics for key public domains, including education testing, health, labor statistics, population demographics, and economic indicators (Lyberg, Japec, & Tangur, 2019; Smith, 2010). The comparability of data collected in 3MC surveys is essential for advancing social science research, isolating the role of contextual factors in explaining complex human behaviors and attitude formation, and establishing "ranking" of the participating sites (e.g., countries) so that local needs are identified and local interventions are implemented. As globalization further diversifies populations, researchers' needs for tools to address the challenges arising from culture and language when studying these issues will only intensify.

References

Andreekova, A. (2019). How to choose interview language in different countries. In T. P. Johnson, B.-E. Pennell, I. A. L. Stoop, & B. Dorer (Eds.), *Advances in comparative survey methods: Multinational, multiregional and multicultural contexts (3MC)* (pp. 295–324). Hoboken, NJ: John Wiley & Sons.

Behr, D. (2017). Assessing the use of back translation: The shortcomings of back translation as a quality testing method. *International Journal of Social Research Methodology, 20*(6), 573–584.

Bolaños-Medina, A., & González-Ruiz, V. (2012). Deconstructing the translation of psychological tests. *Meta: Journal Des Traducteurs/Meta: Translators' Journal, 57*(3), 715–739.

Cernat, A., & Liu, M. (2019). Radio buttons in web surveys: Searching for alternatives. *International Journal of Market Research, 61*(3), 266–286.

Cibelli Hibben, K. L., Pennell, B.-E., Hughes, S. M., Lin, Y., & Kelley, J. (2019). Data collection in cross-national and international surveys: Regional case studies. In T. P. Johnson, B.-E. Pennell, I. A. L. Stoop, & B. Dorer (Eds.), *Advances in comparative survey methods: Multinational, multiregional and multicultural contexts (3MC)* (pp. 521–532). Hoboken, NJ: John Wiley & Sons.

Colina, S., Marrone, N., Ingram, M., & Sánchez, D. (2017). Translation quality assessment in health research: A functionalist alternative to back-translation. *Evaluation & the Health Professions, 40*(3), 267–293.

Conrad, F. G., & Schober, M. F. (Eds.), (2008). *Envisioning the survey interview of the future*. Hoboken, NJ: John Wiley & Sons.

Conrad, F. G., Schober, M. F., Jans, M., Orlowski, R., Nielsen, D., & Levenstein, R. (2008, May). *Features of animacy in virtual interviewers.* Presented at the American Association for Public Opinion Research Annual Conference, New Orleans, LA.

Conrad, F. G., Schober, M. F., Jans, M., Orlowski, R. A., Nielsen, D., & Levenstein, R. (2015). Comprehension and engagement in survey interviews with virtual agents. *Frontiers in Psychology, 6*, 1578.

de Leeuw, E. D., Suzer-Gurtekin, T. Z., & Hox, J. J. (2019). The design and implementation of mixed-mode surveys. In T. P. Johnson, B.-E. Pennell, I. A. L. Stoop, & B. Dorer (Eds.), *Advances in comparative survey methods: Multinational, multiregional and multicultural contexts (3MC)* (pp. 387–408). Hoboken, NJ: John Wiley & Sons.

Douglas, S. P., & Craig, C. S. (2007). Collaborative and iterative translation: An alternative approach to back translation. *Journal of International Marketing, 15*(1), 30–43.

Emde, M., & Fuchs, M. (2012). Exploring animated faces scales in web surveys: Drawbacks and prospects. *Survey Practice, 5*(1), 1–6.

Goerman, P. L., Meyers, M., Sha, M., Park, H., & Schoua-Glusberg, A. S. (2019). Working toward comparable meaning of different language versions of survey instruments: Do monolingual and bilingual cognitive testing respondents help us uncover the same issues? In T. P. Johnson, B.-E. Pennell, I. A. L. Stoop, & B. Dorer (Eds.), *Advances in comparative survey methods: Multinational, multiregional and multicultural contexts (3MC)* (pp. 251–269). Hoboken, NJ: John Wiley & Sons.

Groves, R. M., Fowler, F. J., Couper, M. P., Lepkowski, J. M., Singer, E., & Tourangeau, R. (2009). *Survey methodology.* Hoboken, NJ: John Wiley & Sons.

Harkness, J. A. (2003). Questionnaire translation. In J. A. Harkness, F. J. R. Van de Vijver, & P. Ph. Mohler (Eds.), *Cross-cultural survey methods* (pp. 35–54). Hoboken, NJ: Wiley-Interscience.

Harkness, J. A., Braun, M., Edwards, B., Johnson, T. P., Lyberg, L. E., Mohler, P. Ph., ... Smith, T. W. (Eds.). (2010). *Survey methods in multinational, multiregional, and multicultural contexts.* Hoboken, NJ: John Wiley & Sons.

Harkness, J. A., Pennell, B.-E., & Schoua-Glusberg, A. (2004). Survey questionnaire translation and assessment. In S. Presser, J. M. Rothgeb, M. P. Couper, J. T. Lessler, E. Martin, J. Martin, & E. Singer (Eds.), *Methods for testing and evaluating survey questionnaires* (pp. 453–473). Hoboken, NJ: John Wiley & Sons.

Harkness, J. A., Stange, M., Cibelli, K. L., Mohler, P. Ph., & Pennell, B.-E. (2014). Surveying cultural and linguistic minorities. In R. Tourangeau, B. Edwards, T. P. Johnson, K. Wolter, & N. Bates (Eds.), *Hard-to-survey populations.* Cambridge, UK: Cambridge University Press.

Harkness, J., Van de Vijver, F. J. R., & Mohler, P. Ph. (Eds.). (2003). *Cross-cultural survey methods*. Hoboken, NJ: Wiley-Interscience.

Harkness, J. A., Villar, A., & Edwards, B. (2010). Translation, adaptation, and design. In J. A. Harkness, M. Braun, B. Edwards, T. P. Johnson, L. E. Lyberg, P. Ph. Mohler, B.-E. Pennell, & T. W. Smith (Eds.), *Survey methods in multinational, multiregional, and multicultural contexts* (pp. 115–140). Hoboken, NJ: John Wiley & Sons.

Imai, M., Kanero, J., & Masuda, T. (2016). The relation between language, culture, and thought. *Current Opinion in Psychology, 8*, 70–77.

Johnson, T. P., Pennell, B.-E., Stoop, I. A. L., & Dorer, B. (Eds.). (2019). *Advances in comparative survey methods: Multinational, multiregional and multicultural contexts (3MC)*. Hoboken, NJ: John Wiley & Sons.

Lepkowski, J. M. (2005). Non-observation error in household surveys in developing countries. In *Series F No. 96. Household sample surveys in developing and transition countries* (pp. 149–169). New York, NY: United Nations.

Lind, L. H., Schober, M., Conrad, F. G., & Reichert, H. (2013). Why do survey respondents disclose more when computers ask the questions? *Public Opinion Quarterly, 77*(4), 888–935.

Lyberg, L., Japec, L., & Tangur, C. (2019). Prevailing issues and the future of comparative surveys. In T. P. Johnson, B.-E. Pennell, I. A. L. Stoop, & B. Dorer (Eds.), *Advances in comparative survey methods: Multinational, multiregional and multicultural contexts (3MC)* (pp. 1055–1077). Hoboken, NJ: John Wiley & Sons.

Mohler, P. Ph., Dorer, B., De Jong, J., & Hu, M. (2016). *Translation: Overview* (Guidelines for best practice in cross-cultural surveys). Survey Research Center, Institute for Social Research, University of Michigan. Retrieved from http://www.ccsg.isr.umich.edu/

Pan, Y., & de la Puente, M. (2005). *Census Bureau guidelines for the translation of data collection instruments and supporting materials: Documentation on how the guideline was developed*. Washington, DC: US Bureau of the Census, Statistical Research Division.

Park, H., & Goerman, P. L. (2019). Setting up the cognitive interview task for non-English speaking participants in the U.S. In T. P. Johnson, B.-E. Pennell, I. A. L. Stoop, & B. Dorer (Eds.), *Advances in comparative survey methods: Multinational, multiregional and multicultural contexts (3MC)* (pp. 227–249). Hoboken, NJ: John Wiley & Sons.

Pennell, B.-E., & Cibelli Hibben, K. L. (2016). Surveying in multicultural and multinational contexts. In C. Wolf, D. Joye, T. W. Smith, & Y. Fu (Eds.), *Handbook of survey methodology* (pp. 157–177). London, UK: SAGE.

Pennell, B.-E., Cibelli Hibben, K. L., Lyberg, L., Mohler, P. Ph., & Worku, G. (2017). A total survey error perspective on surveys in multinational, multiregional, and multicultural contexts. In P. Biemer, E. De Leeuw, S. Eckman, B. Edwards, F. Kreuter, L. Lyberg, C. Tucker, & B. T. West (Eds.), *Total survey error in practice*. New York, NY: John Wiley & Sons.

Peytcheva, E. (2019). Can the language of survey administration influence respondents' answers? In T. P. Johnson, B.-E. Pennell, I. A. L. Stoop, & B. Dorer (Eds.), *Advances in comparative survey methods: Multinational, multiregional and multicultural contexts (3MC)* (pp. 325–340). Hoboken, NJ: John Wiley & Sons.

Schwarz, N. (1999). Self-reports: How the questions shape the answers. *American Psychologist, 54*, 93–105.

Schwarz, N., Oyserman, D., & Peytcheva, E. (2010). Cognition, communication, and culture: Implications for the survey response process. In J. A. Harkness, M. Braun, B. Edwards, T. P. Johnson, L. Lyberg, P. Ph. Mohler, B.-E. Pennell, & T. W. Smith (Eds.), *Survey methods in multinational, multiregional, and multicultural contexts* (pp. 175–190). Hoboken, NJ: John Wiley & Sons.

Sirken, M., Schechter, S., Schwarz, N., Tanur, J., & Tourangeau, R. (Eds.), (1999). *Cognition and survey research*. New York, NY: John Wiley & Sons.

Smith, T. W. (2010). The globalization of survey search. In J. A. Harkness, M. Braun, B. Edwards, T. P. Johnson, L. Lyberg, P.-Ph. Mohler, B.-E. Pennell, & T. W. Smith (Eds.), *Survey methods in multinational, multiregional, and multicultural contexts* (pp. 477–484). Hoboken, NJ: Wiley.

Smith, T. W. (2011). Refining the total survey error perspective. *International Journal of Public Opinion Research, 23*(4), 464–484.

Smith, T. W. (2018). Improving multinational, multiregional, and multicultural (3MC) comparability using the total survey error (TSE) paradigm. In T. P. Johnson, B.-E. Pennell, I. A. L. Stoop, & B. Dorer (Eds.), *Advances in comparative survey methods: Multinational, multiregional, and multicultural contexts (3MC)* (pp. 13–43). Hoboken, NJ: John Wiley & Sons.

Smith, T. W., & Fu, Y.-C. (2014). *The globalization of surveys* (Cross-National Report No. 34). The General Social Survey. Chicago, IL: National Opinion Research Center.

Stange, M., Barry, A., Smyth, J., & Olson, K. (2018). Effects of smiley face scales on visual processing of satisfaction questions in web surveys. *Social Science Computer Review, 36*(6), 756–766.

Sudman, S., Bradburn, N. M., & Schwarz, N. (1996). *Thinking about answers: The application of cognitive processes to survey methodology.* San Francisco, CA: Jossey-Bass.

Tourangeau, R., Rips, L. J., & Rasinski, K. A. (2000). *The psychology of survey response.* Cambridge, UK: Cambridge University Press.

Uskul, A. K., Oyserman, D., & Schwarz, N. (2010). Cultural emphasis on honor, modesty, or self-enhancement: Implications for the survey-response process. In J. A. Harkness, M. Braun, B. Edwards, T. P. Johnson, L. Lyberg, P. Ph. Mohler, B.-E. Pennell, & T. W. Smith (Eds.), *Survey methods in multinational, multiregional, and multicultural contexts* (pp. 191–201). Hoboken, NJ: John Wiley & Sons.

Wyer, R. S. (2013). Culture and information processing: A conceptual integration. In R. S. Wyer, C. Chiu, & Y. Hong (Eds.), *Understanding culture: Theory, research, and application.* New York, NY: Psychology Press.

Zavala-Rojas, D., Saris, W. E., & Gallhofer, I. (2019). Preventing differences in translated survey items using the Survey Quality Predictor. In T. P. Johnson, B.-E. Pennell, I. A. L. Stoop, & B. Dorer (Eds.), *Advances in comparative survey methods: Multinational, multiregional and multicultural contexts (3MC)* (pp. 357–384). Hoboken, NJ: John Wiley & Sons.

About the Authors

We are researchers, practitioners, students, and managers, including those in commercial and noncommercial survey organizations, as well as funders of research studies.

Book Editors

Mandy Sha, MA, PMP, www.mandysha.com
Mandy directs research studies and increases the scientific body of knowledge through publications, international speaking engagements, and professional service. She is coauthor of 2019 book *The Sociolinguistics of Survey Translation*. @MMandySha

Tim Gabel, MBA, RTI International
Tim is Executive Vice President, for Social, Statistical, and Environmental Sciences for RTI International. He provides strategic oversight and guidance to a team of almost 3,000 world-wide staff in pursuit of RTI's Mission to Improve the Human Condition by Turning Knowledge Into Practice. As one of the executive sponsors for RTI's Diversity and Inclusion efforts, Tim is passionate about bringing out the best in everyone through collaboration, innovation, and teamwork.

Chapter 1. The Effect of Language of Survey Administration on the Response Formation Process

Emilia Peytcheva, PhD, RTI International
Emilia is a survey methodologist with more than 16 years of experience. Among her research interests is measurement error-inducing factors in cross-cultural surveys.

Chapter 2. Seeking Clarifications for Problematic Questions: Effects of Interview Language and Respondent Acculturation

Evgenia Kapousouz, MA, MSc, University of Illinois at Chicago
Evgenia is a PhD student in the Department of Public Administration with a concentration in survey methodology at the University of Illinois at Chicago.

Timothy P. Johnson, PhD, Independent Researcher
Timothy is retired Professor of Public Administration and Director of the Survey Research Laboratory at the University of Illinois at Chicago.

Allyson L. Holbrook, PhD, University of Illinois at Chicago
Allyson is Professor of Public Administration and Psychology at the University of Illinois at Chicago.

Chapter 3. A Longitudinal Perspective on the Effects of Household Language on Data Quality in the American Community Survey

Heather Kitada Smalley, PhD, Willamette University
Heather is an applied statistician and an expert in data visualization using R and data science education. Her research in public opinion and survey statistics has focused on developing and improving methodology for bias estimation and correction.

Chapter 4. Quantitative Evaluation of Response Scale Translation Through a Randomized Experiment of Interview Language With Bilingual English- and Spanish-Speaking Latino Respondents

Sunghee Lee, PhD, University of Michigan
Sunghee is an expert in data collection with population subgroups that are rare, hard to sample, and/or hard to reach.

Mengyao Hu, PhD, University of Michigan
Mengyao is an expert in the field of survey methodology with a focus on measurement errors in cross-cultural survey research.

Mingnan Liu, PhD, University of Michigan
Mingnan's research focuses on the use of technology in surveys and international and cross-cultural survey research.

Jennifer Kelley, PhD, University of Michigan
Jennifer is a survey methodologist and project manager for University of Michigan's Survey Research Center International Unit, specializing in questionnaire design, interviewer training, and quality control.

Chapter 5. Language Differences Between Interviewers and Respondents in African Surveys

Charles Q. Lau, PhD, RTI International
Charles is a survey methodologist who specializes in improving the quality of face-to-face survey data in low- and middle-income countries.

Stephanie Eckman, PhD, RTI International
Stephanie is a Fellow at RTI, where she conducts research into survey data quality. She has designed surveys and taught survey methods around the world.

Luis Sevilla Kreysa, PhD, RTI International
Luis is a survey scientist at RTI who directs large-scale surveys in low- and middle-income countries.

Benjamin Piper, PhD, RTI International
Ben is the Senior Director for Africa Education at RTI, where he provides technical support to RTI's education programs.

Chapter 6. Void of the Voiceless: An Analysis of Residents With a Language Barrier in Germany, France, and the United Kingdom

Nicholas Heck-Grossek, PhD student, City, University of London
Nicholas is a data scientist with a background in survey methodology and survey fieldwork optimization.

Sonila Dardha, PhD student, City, University of London
Sonila is a survey methodologist and practitioner researching and coordinating comparative and cross-cultural surveys.

Chapter 7. Pretesting Methods in Cross-Cultural Research

Eva Aizpurua, PhD, Trinity College Dublin
Eva is a Research Fellow for the European-wide PRILA Project. Her main research interests include questionnaire design and pretesting with a focus on multinational and multilingual surveys.

Chapter 8. Cross-Cultural Comparison of Focus Groups as a Research Method

Mandy Sha (see Editors)

Yuling Pan, PhD, Independent Researcher

Yuling is a leading researcher in the field of sociolinguistics and multilingual survey research. She has more than 30 years of experience in language and cultural research, and 16 years of experience in survey translation and questionnaire pretesting.

Hyunjoo Park, MS, HP Research Korea
Hyunjoo is a social scientist with 20 years of experience conducting international marketing and social science research in Korea and the United States.

Jennifer Kim, PhD, US Census Bureau
Jennifer directs Language and Translation Services, Content and Forms Design, Puerto Rico and Island Areas Operations for the 2020 US Census.

Chapter 9. Hmong and Chinese Qualitative Research Interview Questions: Assumptions and Implications of Applying the Survey Back Translation Method

Maichou Lor, PhD, RN, University of Wisconsin-Madison
Maichou's research focuses on improving patient–provider communication through developing and evaluating information visualization tools and addressing translation and interpretation issues.

Chenchen Gao, PhD, RN, Wenzhou Medical University China
Chenchen's research focuses on health management of chronic disease in older adults, using technology to improve self-management of the elderly with chronic disease.

Chapter 10. Sociocultural Issues in Adapting Spanish Health Survey Translation: The Case of the Quality of Well-Being Scale (QWB-SA)

Nereida Congost-Maestre, PhD, Alicante University Spain
Nereida's research interests include the translation of health questionnaires and the teaching of specialized languages.

Maichou Lor (see Chapter 9)

Chapter 11. Nura Knows You Better: Redesigning Conversations With Artificial Intelligence

Arundati Dandapani, MLITT, CAIP, CMRP, Generation1.ca
Based in Toronto, Arundati helps clients deliver actionable insights on their communications, research, and marketing objectives. In 2019, she was honored as an insight leader on the inaugural GRIT Future List.

Chapter 12. Scaling the Smileys: A Multicountry Investigation

Aaron Sedley, Google, Inc.
Aaron has 16 years of experience planning and implementing research at Google. He is a user experience researcher, focused on measuring and analyzing users' attitudes via surveys.

Yongwei Yang, PhD, Google, Inc.
Yongwei is a survey research scientist who helps clients and colleagues use sound measurement tools, implement evidence-based interventions, and evaluate the resulting business impact.

Joseph M. Paxton, PhD, Google, Inc.
Joseph is a quantitative user experience researcher with expertise in experimental psychology.

Index

Page numbers followed by t and f indicate tables and figures. Numbers followed by n indicate footnotes.

B

C

Made in the USA
Columbia, SC
21 May 2020

97919009R00159